The Other Henry James

New Americanists   *A Series Edited by Donald E. Pease*

The Other Henry James

John Carlos Rowe ✑

Duke University Press   *Durham and London*   1998

For Kristin, Kevin, Mark, Sean, and Katherine

© 1998 Duke University Press
All rights reserved
Printed in the United States of America on acid-free paper ∞
Typeset in Adobe Garamond by Keystone Typesetting, Inc.
Library of Congress Cataloging-in-Publication Data appear
on the last printed page of this book.

The climax of this extraordinary experience—
which stands alone for me as a dream-adventure
founded in the deepest, quickest, clearest act of
cogitation and comparison, act indeed of life-
saving energy, as well as in unutterable fear—was
the sudden pursuit, through an open door, along a
huge high saloon, of a just dimly-descried figure
that retreated in terror before my rush and dash (a
glare of inspired reaction from irresistible but
shameful dread,) out of the room I had a moment
before been desperately, and all the more abjectly,
defending by the push of my shoulder against hard
pressure on lock and bar from the other side.

—Henry James, *A Small Boy and Others* (1913)

Contents ‿

Preface   ix

Introduction: Henry James and Critical Theory   1

1   Swept Away: Henry James, Margaret Fuller, and "The Last
of the Valerii"   38

2   A Phantom of the Opera: Christopher Newman's Unconscious
in *The American*   56

3   Acting Lessons: Racial, Sexual, and Aesthetic Politics
in *The Tragic Muse*   75

4   Textual Preference: James's Literary Defenses against Sexuality
in "The Middle Years" and "The Death of the Lion"   101

5   The Portrait of a Small Boy as a Young Girl: Gender Trouble
in *What Maisie Knew*   120

6   Spectral Mechanics: Gender, Sexuality, and Work in
In the Cage   155

Conclusion: Henry James and the Art of Teaching   181

Notes   199

Index   233

Preface ॐ

In June 1993, I participated in the Henry James Sesquicentennial Conferences in New York.[1] Along with many others, I was impressed with the vitality and diversity of new scholarly approaches to James's life and works. Although some people in New York spoke of the "revival" of interest in Henry James, I think this exciting new work marks yet another of the several transformations Henry James has undergone in this century. As a novelist, he has been held up as the master of realism, modernism, and postmodernism in quick succession. As a theorist, he has been claimed by New Critics, phenomenological and reader-response critics, structuralists, and deconstructive critics. Cultural critics have identified his limitations, but often in ways that have testified to his generally progressive ideals and the subtlety of his understanding of how social power works.

We have not needed, then, to "revive" Henry James for the 1990s, because we continue to construct him in ways that reflect our changing intellectual methods and literary concerns. Such an argument is likely to lend support to those who have argued recently for a return to so-called classic works and authors, and I do not object to paying respect to important works and authors as long as such regard includes our contemporary scene. If James is valued because his hopes and worries still speak to us, then let us celebrate his masterful adaptability, even changeable qualities, rather than his testament to some dubious universal truth. By beginning with his own anxieties concerning sexuality, conventional gender roles, authorship, and nationalism at the turn of the last century and interpreting them in relation to our own concerns with these same issues at the end of this century, the most exciting new work on James has done just this. The case is decidedly not that nothing has changed, but that the changes we have passed through are readable historically from James and his contemporaries to us.

Positive change begins with our recognition of certain impasses—repetitions and thus repressions—in our previously settled ways of thinking; this has certainly been the case in our transformation of the pompous figure of James as master of the novel—captured perfectly in John Singer Sargent's famous 1912 portrait of James at age seventy—into the vulnerable, sexually anxious, and lonely writer struggling with the new modern art and new age he had helped make possible. The latter James, decidedly more human and accessible, as Fred Kaplan has rendered him in *Henry James: The Imagination of Genius* (1992), is aptly portrayed in Alvin Langdon Coburn's photographs of the author in June 1906, at Rye, taken just as James was deciding that Coburn would be "the solution to the problem of illustrations" for the New York Edition.[2] Coburn's studies of James at Rye clearly express vulnerability, self-doubt, and worry even as they still offer us the dominance of head and eye, of intellect and vision, that virtually holds James up.

How liberating it is to discover how much James needed other people, and how desperately lonely he could be when visitors failed to appear, canceled, or left early! Lifting the repression concerning James's life, especially his passionate friendships with Hendrik Andersen and Howard Sturgis, changes not just our own attitudes toward his sexuality but also our attitudes toward his work. In one sense, this means the degree to which James's later works can now be reread as rich with homoerotic suggestiveness, helping us overcome critical categories that once refused the wit and fun, as well as the literary disguises, of the diverse sexual performances in *The Tragic Muse,* "The Middle Years," "The Death of the Lion," *What Maisie Knew, The Turn of the Screw, In the Cage,* "The Beast in the Jungle," "The Jolly Corner," and a host of others now being rediscovered by scholars and critics.

Somewhat less obviously, this new understanding of what I can only term James's *sociability*—a quality essential to his writings all along, of course— affects how we understand the vaunted craft of his fiction. The ambitious Henry James vigorously committed to his successful literary career must now be understood in conjunction with the other James, who challenged ideas of literary authority and mastery in ways that would help our teachers announce the "death of the Author," grant new respect to readers, and reduce the myth of literary authority to the rhetorical features of an "author-function." As I argue in the final chapter of this book, this Henry James is not only more accessible to contemporary readers but also far more *teachable.* As a teacher of James's writings, I am unwilling to defend the pleasures of reading his texts without being able to justify such pleasure. Jamesian style is rarely the consequence of purely aesthetic effects; he writes well because he has so much to say about the societies in which he participated. The complexity of the Jamesian sentence says less to me about James's genius as a writer than it does about the vast intricacies of the social systems he was at such pains to represent and interpret.

This "other" Henry James helps us understand the difficult and intercon-
nected qualities of our modern and now postmodern societies, so dependent
on their means of communication, and he strikes me as immediately relevant
not only to sophisticated academic debates about the social values of literature but also to the everyday lives of high school students struggling to cope
with media overload and what a popular song calls "communication breakdown." I refer to this other Henry James with particular awareness of this
title's ironic allusion to a tradition of criticizing Henry James for his limitations as a bourgeois writer who idealized the ruling class and neglected the
working class. Just six paragraphs into his monumental effort to dethrone
Henry James as the master of the modern novel, Maxwell Geismar describes
"the Henry James of this study" as "very different from the figure which has
been established in the artistic consciousness of the United States in the mid-
twentieth century. We might call him the 'other Henry James.' "[3] Geismar
meant, of course, the Henry James he tried to represent in his strangely
comprehensive study as the writer who "was not a major writer at all," but
instead "a major *entertainer* (something quite different) of a rare and exotic
sort, a cross, if you like, between the master magician which James used to
describe himself, and the kind of literary monster which he really was."[4]
Geismar's portrayal of Henry James as a legitimist of the leisure class, "artificial and fanciful" in his "immensely elevated" artistic techniques, was intended to expose the monstrosity of what in our day has come to be known as
the aesthetic ideology of modernism. Clearly, my own study of the "other
Henry James" challenges this still pervasive view of James as aesthetic and
social elitist, but the echo of Geismar's phrase in my title serves more than just
an ironic function. Attempting to cover the entire canon of James's art,
Geismar wanted to prove conclusively his point, but he also wanted to demonstrate the importance of his interpretation of Henry James for our general
assessment in the 1960s of late Victorian and early modern art and literature.
Geismar attacks the James "industry" in large part because he recognizes its
contemporary influence on our ideas of culture and practices of education.
Henry James and the Jacobites thus criticizes Henry James and modern art in
general and in so doing testifies to their contemporary importance, even if
Geismar concludes that such modernism can be extremely damaging to its
acolytes. Henry James the aesthete and an avowedly depoliticized modernism
are still very much part of our ideas of "literate culture," and they continue to
be taught, often in profoundly uncritical ways, to further generations of

students. Geismar's criticisms of Henry James the master, and the modernism with which he is so deeply identified, often misread James's own challenges to the dominant ideologies of Great Britain and the United States, but Geismar's general skepticism regarding celebrated literary genius and elite literary movements informs this study as well, however much my "other Henry James" differs from the "literary monster" Geismar portrays.

Relevant as Henry James remains today, I do not want to overemphasize his clairvoyance regarding our contemporary circumstances. Just because James was a conflicted writer who struggled with changing attitudes toward gender, sexuality, class, and ethnicity in his own times, he holds interest for us in part because of these conflicts. His demonization of lesbians for the sake of representing homosexual desire and his repeated treatment of feminine "sacrifice" for the sake of criticizing patriarchal practices are problems in his work as well as warnings to liberal intellectuals today. Equally troublesome, but for that very reason of great interest to scholars, are James's ambivalent representations of Jews and peoples of color, immigrants to the United States, and the role of other cultures in the future of both the United States and Great Britain. James's commitment to English-language standards (and thus advocacy of monolingualism) for both nations and the example of his own elaborate late style are evidence of a cultural elitism in James's thought and writings that I address in this book.

In the following chapters, I do not represent this "other" Henry James in the definitive, comprehensive fashion that is sometimes assumed to be the purpose of the critical monograph. The literary works I have chosen to interpret are not meant to constitute some alternative Jamesian canon, but instead to cast new light on all of James's writings. In this regard, I turn again to familiar classics in the Jamesian canon, such as *The American* and *What Maisie Knew*, but I read these works in ways that challenge their conventional roles in that canon. By the same token, I hope to encourage renewed critical interest in major works, such as *The Tragic Muse, In the Cage,* and *A Small Boy and Others* (the first of his three-volume autobiography), whose central concerns with changing gender roles, sexual preferences, and class and racial identities have made them relatively marginal to the interpretive tradition of Henry James the master. On the other hand, I make no claim to elevate in critical regard such neglected writings as "The Last of the Valerii," "The Middle Years," "The Death of the Lion," or even *William Wetmore Story and His Friends.* These works hold our interest by telling us about James's histor-

ically specific attitudes toward women, gays and lesbians, and his transcendentalist precursors; in strictly aesthetic terms, they are certainly minor writings in James's career.

In short, this is not an encyclopedic study of some "new" Henry James, just
as it is not a systematic effort to transvalue a more traditional, aesthetically
formal Henry James. The latter James will benefit, I think, from interaction
with this other Henry James, but the conversation is meant to be friendly,
even at its most argumentative pitch. I have been inspired to write this book
in large part by the many scholars, young and old, who are transforming our
understanding of Henry James and thus making him more relevant to our
contemporary debates. My own contribution claims to be, as perhaps most
critical books should, little more than one step in the direction of such new
thinking about Henry James. In short, I want this book to be read as a modest
provocation to scholars and teachers who still find Henry James interesting,
in hopes that these chapters will help them explain this enduring interest as
more than simply "genius."

Such recontextualizations are necessary preludes to the final task of representing Henry James differently than we have usually seen him—once again,
in the 1912 portrait by Sargent that James himself had judged "awesome." The
Jameses we discover in his place are anxious, conflicted, marginal, sometimes
ashamed of themselves, utterly at odds, it would seem, with the royal "we"
that James assumed in his last deathbed dictations, slipping in and out of
Napoleonic delusions.[5] These new Henry Jameses are instead full of life and
interest, not only in their times, but for our own, which as we begin to understand it continues to wind its way back to its early modern origins as it unfurls
into our new century. We recognize belatedly that this is the path of the
Jamesian sentence, whose serpentine coils still grip us and yet more than ever
offer the possibility of a grateful embrace.

When I began writing about Henry James nearly thirty years ago, my
greatest fear was that I would become a "Jamesian." In the late 1960s, as the
Vietnam War raged in Southeast Asia and at home in the United States, I
imagined the Jamesian to cultivate a distinguished retirement from life and
sober dedication to Art that seemed vaguely repugnant and even slightly
immoral to me. Henry James was simply one literary example in my doctoral
dissertation, and I was determined not to be caught in the fine silken web of
his alluring prose. Like so many of the illusions of youth, however, the
stereotype I had fabricated of the Jamesian has proven in time to be generally

false. I count myself particularly fortunate in my professional career to have been for much of it a Jamesian, in part for the marvelous company I have been able to keep.

It would take me far too long at this end of this preface to list the many scholars and critics who have in their own ways and at various times been great Jamesians, but of the sort that differs wildly from my youthful caricature. These friends and colleagues have exemplified what is most generous in James's thinking and writing—his openness to new ideas, his curiosity about people and ideas initially thought to be foreign, and his enthusiasm and support for other writers, however diverse their talents. Daniel Mark Fogel, founding editor of *The Henry James Review,* simply wouldn't let me stop being a Jamesian; he was always urging me to write something new and in a new way, then promptly publishing my work. Susan Griffin, the new editor of *The Henry James Review,* has followed Dan's example and encouraged me to keep on writing about Henry James, even as the millennium approaches. Paul Armstrong, Charles Caramello, Stuart Culver, Wai-Chee Dimock, Dennis Foster and Nina Schwartz, Al Habegger, Eric Haralson, Richard and Elaine Hocks, Carren Kaston, Kevin McNamara, David McWhirter, David Minter, Ross Posnock, Russ Reising, Julie Rivkin, Mark Seltzer, Cheryl Torsney, Bill Veeder, Pierre Walker, and Ken Warren have inspired me by their own work and encouraged me to keep on writing about Henry James. Al Habegger took the time while busy finishing his biography of Emily Dickinson to read carefully and comment in detail on an earlier version of chapter 5. Pierre Walker shared with me his new research on the Jameses' stay in Boulogne from 1857 to 1858, work that made a significant difference in my interpretation in chapter 5 of James's account of those months in *A Small Boy and Others.* There are undoubtedly others I have forgotten, Jamesians all, with whom I am very grateful to have been associated at the many conferences, professional meetings, campus visits, and Internet exchanges by which we have sustained our friendships and shared our love of Henry James.

Several of the following chapters were first presented as papers at scholarly conferences. I am grateful to my hosts and audiences for their invitations and valuable discussion of these ideas at the Modern Language Association Convention, the International Conference on the Fantastic, and the Henry James Sesquicentennial Conferences. I also wish to thank the following presses for permission to publish substantially revised versions of work that first appeared as articles in their journals or chapters in their books: Stanford Univer sity Press for permission to use part of my foreword to *Henry James's New York Edition: The Construction of Authorship,* edited by David McWhirter; the Greenwood Press for portions of the introduction that first appeared in *A Companion to Henry James Studies,* edited by Daniel Mark Fogel; and the Johns Hopkins University Press for permission to use portions of chapter 1 that first appeared in *Readers in History: Nineteenth-Century American Literature and the Contexts of Response,* edited by James L. Machor, and the portions of chapter 2 and the conclusion that first appeared in *The Henry James Review.*

✑ Introduction: Henry James and Critical Theory

> Theory never aims simply at an increase of knowledge as such.
> Its goal is man's emancipation from slavery.
> —Max Horkheimer, postscript to
> "Traditional and Critical Theory" (1937)

In *The Theoretical Dimensions of Henry James,* I argued that Henry James has been the subject of so many different theoretical and scholarly approaches in large part because he is himself a writer concerned centrally with the philosophical, social, and linguistic problems of interest to theorists.[1] Using a wide variety of different theoretical approaches is necessary in reading James's oeuvre because he was always an experimental writer, interested in new ideas that encompassed far more than merely aesthetic questions. In his own times, such an attitude was termed "philosophical," even more precisely *pragmatic* in the philosophical sense of that word in the early modern period. As scholars such as Richard Hocks have shown us, Henry James was not simply influenced by the pragmatism of his brother, William James; Henry James is by his own rights a major figure in that philosophical school.[2]

In his adaptation of his thinking, as well as literary style and form, to the rapidly changing circumstances of the late nineteenth and early twentieth centuries, his emphasis on the inextricable relation of consciousness and experience, and his understanding of moral value as a consequence of social acts (rather than idealist principles), Henry James adds to the American pragmatist tradition that is often traced from Emerson to Richard Rorty.[3] James's literary pragmatism is distinguished by a consistent openness to ideas—one might say to an understanding of thinking itself as an open system—that challenge existing habits and behaviors, thereby making something "happen" in the public sphere. Indeed, nothing so interests James as a disturbance in the otherwise smooth surface of social life, especially when that society encompasses the ruling class.

In *The Theoretical Dimensions of Henry James,* I relied on James's pragmatic flexibility with regard to new ideas and social situations to investigate some of

the most important theoretical questions of the 1970s and early 1980s. I read
literary and cultural influence studies, feminist criticism, literature and psychoanalysis, Marxist critiques of modernism, phenomenology and aesthetics,
and reader-response criticism in terms of various texts by James that exemplified the problems and possibilities in these contemporary approaches.
My methodological framework was deconstructive, as I made clear in my
introduction and conclusion, and each of the critical approaches studied was
interpreted in terms of both its chief claims and its fundamental limitations.
My operative assumption was that Henry James's writings could be used as
deconstructive pretexts for the critical understanding of these important theoretical approaches. My emphasis on intellectual conflict and contradiction,
then, rested on the theories I examined, and James's texts were assumed to
meet the demands of deconstructive rigor. The reader was thus left to draw
the reasonable conclusion that James's writings anticipated postmodern theory, especially as it has critically appropriated key aspects of those theories
that have had the greatest influence on deconstruction.

I did not investigate in *The Theoretical Dimensions of Henry James* the ways
Henry James's own thinking and creative practices changed throughout his
career in response to the new ideas and social issues that would most profoundly affect social reality. Of course, I understood that the "deconstructive
Henry James" was primarily a strategic illusion—true in many respects, but
hardly as systematically applicable to his large and diverse oeuvre as my thesis
in that book had suggested. What I did not understand in 1984 was the degree
to which feminism, gay studies and queer theory, and cultural studies would
reveal the interesting conflicts in James's life and literary career in ways that
exceed considerably the limited scope of my previous genealogy of postmodern theory. Although these more recent approaches to James (and literature
and culture in general, of course) have often drawn on the insights of deconstruction, they have in their own rights critically appropriated deconstruction to expand postmodern theories to include gender, sexual preference, race, and ethnicity as crucial aspects of the discursive construction of
social reality.

In short, reading today "the theoretical dimensions of Henry James" requires careful attention to the social categories of gender, sexuality, race, and
ethnicity that were relatively marginal to the interpretation of Henry James
until the mid-1980s. Pioneering work since then, such as Alfred Habegger's
 Henry James and the "Woman Business" and Eve Sedgwick's *Epistemology of the*

Closet, have helped us understand how deeply conflicted James was about the social changes occurring in the early modern period even as he struggled to address those changes as they affected both his literary work and his personal identity.[4] Critical theory today is far more concerned with the social conse-quences of discursive acts than it was in the late 1970s and early 1980s, and this turn has been complemented by the rise of cultural studies as a critical movement.[5] Once understood as a term designating various epistemologies, with special attention to the aesthetic and literary roles in knowing, critical theory designates today a much wider range of methods and practices con-cerned with the construction, maintenance, and transformation of social reality. In this regard, cultural critics have drawn far more directly from the Frankfurt school's modern definitions of critical theory than from the mean-ings formulated by Anglo-American literary theorists.

It is in this more contemporary sense of what might be termed precisely "critical social theory," especially as it has been derived from the Frankfurt and Birmingham schools, that I propose to write once again on the subject of the theoretical dimensions of Henry James. My current approach will thus have to address from the outset the degree to which Henry James anticipates or serves merely as a historical example of the critical social theory that informs the best work in cultural studies, especially the work concerned primarily with the roles of gender, sexuality, race, and ethnicity in the con-struction of social institutions and values. In this introduction, then, I will try to locate Henry James in terms of the more important influences on the development of critical theory as a social, rather than primarily aesthetic or literary, theory. And if there is a dimension to James's writings that may be interpreted as fundamentally concerned with the criticism and change of social reality, then we ought to examine the extent to which this critical dimension challenged those modern Euramerican attitudes toward gender, sexuality, race, and ethnicity that have been so profoundly criticized by con-temporary cultural critics. In this introduction, I ask the question, "What kind of critical theorist was Henry James?" In this book as a whole, I ask the larger question, "How does critical social theory read Henry James?"

By turning my critical attention in this book away from the traditional literary and aesthetic questions so central to many studies of Henry James, I have found that some of the best examples in his writings are texts that have often been the least read by, or the most baffling to, more aesthetically inclined critics. Thus my title for this book, "The Other Henry James," refers not only to a Henry James whose theoretical implications exceeded the limits of my previous book but also to those "other" writings that have remained neglected by, or simply baffling to, several generations of interested readers. Nothing better illustrates this "otherness" than the texts that recent gay studies and queer theories have made so dramatically interesting once they are read outside conventional categories such as "the international theme," "stories of artists," "ghost stories," and "the major phase." As an experiment in modernist style or a protoexistentialist melodrama, "The Beast in the Jungle," for example, is a dry little text that turns John Marcher's fate—the man to whom "nothing" was ever to have happened—into an ironic meta-commentary on the story itself. As an allegory of homosexual panic, repressed homoerotic desire, or general anxieties about same-sex preference in a profoundly homophobic society, "The Beast in the Jungle" is a tense drama with much to tell us both about our habitual phobias and about the difficulties of self-expression in highly conventional societies. As a long novel about the aesthetic ideals of painting and theater and their trivialization by modern society, *The Tragic Muse* seems unnecessarily drawn out and excessively crowded with irrelevant characters, such as Gabriel Nash. When read as a struggle between the homosocial cultural conventions of London politics and the flexible gender roles of aesthetic culture, however, the novel becomes far more readable.

Some of these works also become, I think, better literature than they have previously been considered. As a windy colony in the "stories of artists and writers," *The Tragic Muse* is full of clichés and conventional characters; as a protogay novel, struggling between an emancipated world of the arts and the respectability of the London ruling class, the novel belongs to that aesthetic avant-garde pejoratively labeled "the Decadents" in its own time. Read as a work preceding by a year and complementing the themes of Oscar Wilde's *The Picture of Dorian Grey,* James's *The Tragic Muse* addresses new and complex interpersonal and social relations, even if it fails as clearly as Wilde's text does to transvalue the prevailing homophobia and homosociality of late Victorian society. As a philosophical investigation into how we know and when we know, *What Maisie Knew* is an interesting but abstract story that tells us little about actual childhood development; as a narrative that complements James's subsequent account of his own childhood in *A Small Boy and Others,* the novel makes important claims about actual childhood experience and its relation to more general problems of epistemology. When the racial, gender, sexual, and class instabilities in *What Maisie Knew* are added to the child's typical confusion about social and verbal realities, James's dramatic action takes on special relevance for our postmodern condition. As a novella about a poor working-class woman's fascination with the lives of the rich and famous, *In the Cage* seems a mere soap opera next to the high tragedy of its contemporary, *The Turn of the Screw*. But when the class, gender, and sexual issues in *In the Cage* are interpreted in their mutual relations, then its comedy becomes the ludic antidote to the otherwise apocalyptic conclusion of *The Turn of the Screw*.

It would be foolish, of course, to argue that the shift in attention from aesthetic to social theory in the study of Henry James should result in some systematic elevation of minor works over major works. Much of the interest in this book in "other," less familiar works by Henry James rests in the internal conflicts in James's own mind over just the problems of gender, sexuality, race, and ethnicity otherwise resolved in the major works. Neither the early story "The Last of the Valerii" nor the early novel *The American* measures up to James's considerably more confident treatment of the "modern woman" in *The Portrait of a Lady*. For the very reason of such conflicts and hesitations in these earlier works, just what James was trying to address in more sophisticated literary works becomes more readily visible. There is, then, no effort in this book to construct any sort of "new" canon of Jamesian masterpieces. The selections of works are motivated more by what will help foreground James's own struggles with changing social attitudes toward gender, sexuality, ethnicity, and race. If by making some of these works more readable I have also made them more valuable as literature, then this is a happy side effect of my principal aim to elucidate James's effort to come to terms with the social consequences of his aesthetic theories and with the need to change those theories in terms of a rapidly changing modern society.

I also want to include in the argument for "the other Henry James" the problem of teaching Henry James in traditional and nontraditional educational contexts. One of my contentions in this book is that the Henry James interpreted in various formalist traditions (literary modernism, Anglo-American New Criticism, phenomenology, and some version of structuralism and deconstruction) has been compatible with ideas of "aesthetic education" inherited from the romantic idealists. We have infrequently questioned these assumptions about the role of literature in liberal education—the spiritual "example" it sets, its transcendence of historical circumstance, its privileged discourse—and have consequently helped marginalize important authors, such as Henry James, in modern pedagogical contexts where other criteria for literary education prevail. I am referring to the changes that have occurred already in high school, community college, and some four-year college curricula in literature. The cultural diversification of literary study, its interdisciplinary connections with social sciences and history, and the globalization of literature as a field are all changes that have occurred at many high schools, community colleges, and four-year colleges where student demographics, other regional factors, and related changes in theories of literary knowledge and value have influenced curricular changes.

I conclude this book with considerations of how important the study of Henry James can be in these new curricula, but only if we begin to interpret another Henry James from the great modern and formalist "master" of the Anglo-American novel. The recent revival of interest in major authors, such as Shakespeare and James, represents two competitive claims for the continuing relevance of the Anglo-American cultural heritage, effectively reinitiating the periodic debate in culture between the "ancients" and the "moderns." Vigorous defenders of the sanctity of the Western cultural tradition, such as William Bennett and Lynne Cheney, view cultural studies, queer theories, and critical theory (at least in its socially critical dimensions) to be direct threats to the proper transmission of the "best that has been thought and written." From this perspective, new dramatic and cinematic productions of Shakespeare and contemporary films based on James's novels affirm the "great tradition" in the face of powerful and even dangerous challenges to the cultural "values" these canonical authors represent.

From the other perspective, including the perspective of *The Other Henry James,* however, late-twentieth-century adaptations of Shakespeare and cinematic interpretations of James's fiction often speak directly to the changes that have occurred in the understanding of these writers in their times and for our own. Historical reinterpretations and adaptations of major authors are traditionally signs of their canonical status; therefore traditionalists may claim Shakespeare and James as classic authors no matter how they circulate in different contemporary cultures. Yet such claims to enduring classic or canonical status, often invoked to provide evidence of an author's or work's transcendent value, should not be accepted before we examine carefully just how such classic authors and works are *taught* at the several levels of education where they are said to play such influential roles in the formation of cultural values.

My conclusion is also meant to call attention to the general importance of testing our scholarly and critical claims in terms of their applicability to curricular design and pedagogy. In this way, I challenge traditional literary scholarship by calling it to pedagogical account and appealing to every scholar and critic to justify thereby his or her work in terms of its relevance and use in the formal courses and alternative classes—the museum, stage, movie theater, television, academic conference, the reading chair at home—where literary education occurs. I hope to suggest in this manner yet another meaning for the "other Henry James" in the figure who "queers" or destabilizes artificial distinctions among scholarship, literature, education, and theory.

Interpreting Henry James as a critical social theorist and thus a forerunner of cultural criticism and queer theories seems a quixotic task, given his central role, along with T. S. Eliot and other literary moderns, in the history of Anglo-American New Criticism. For Frankfurt school theorists such as Adorno, Horkheimer, Marcuse, and Benjamin, Bertolt Brecht would be a far better example than James or Eliot of the literary author as critical theorist. For these same theorists and the heirs of their Marxist traditions of cultural criticism, any claim for the importance of James and Eliot in the development of twentieth-century critical theories would be simply another indication of how often that term is confused with literary theory or aesthetics. Yet this confusion of critical and literary theory is part of the academic history of critical theory. Henry James and T. S. Eliot were indisputably important modern critics; each played an important role in defining the terms of subsequent schools of academic criticism, most of them admittedly *literary* schools and movements. Eliot, more clearly than James, established the framework for Anglo-American New Criticism. James's essays on impressionism (literary and visual), naturalism, the theory of the novel, and a wide range of authors were less specifically adapted to a particular school of criticism, although they have been used with great authority by the New Critics.

James and Eliot did not write only literary criticism, although their other nonfiction works are often classified with the former, if only in obedience to the publisher's convention of treating a literary author's nonfiction in this category. Eliot's *Notes toward the Definition of Culture* (1948) and James's *The American Scene* (1907) are clearly works of cultural criticism that critically interpret European and American societies, respectively, in terms of a utopian conception of how society ought to be organized. These are arguably works of critical theory.[6] In the case of James, we might add other examples, including his twenty dispatches for the *New York Tribune* from 1875 to 1876, collected as *Parisian Sketches* (1957) by Leon Edel and Ilse Dusoir Lind, and perhaps *William Wetmore Story and His Friends,* if we read that curious volume as James's anthropology of American expatriates in Europe. Bits and pieces of the other travel writings might be included, as well as selected essays and reviews. A similar claim could be made for the critical function of James's three volumes of autobiography as a social and cultural critique comparable to Henry Adams's effort in his *Education.*[7] Even so, the list of explicitly "literary" or "socially critical" works in James's canon would still be modest, given the great volume of James's other writings.[8] In a similar sense, Eliot's own claims to status as critical theorist would be slim indeed if based only on specific expository prose concerned with social and cultural theory. The vast majority of Eliot's prose deals with literary and philosophical topics.

The argument for either of these great modern writers as a critical theorist ought, then, to be based not on his specific contributions to literary criticism, comments on the state of contemporary English and American societies, but instead on the entire oeuvre of each writer. In short, the poetry and drama of Eliot and the vast body of James's fiction should be considered resources for defining either of these moderns as a critical theorist, and it is precisely this goal I set for myself in this introduction. This approach is, as I hope to show, in keeping with the Frankfurt school theorists' original conceptions of critical theory as a discursive practice and mode of social action; critical theory is not a mere "genre" of literary writing, but rather a kind of intellectual attention or focus that may express itself in a variety of different genres. Any more limited definition of critical theory is likely to limit unnecessarily its possibilities as both academic discourse and social practice.

At stake in such an argument is James's role in the development of Marxist and various post-Marxian theories, including in the latter category deconstruction, feminism, New Historicism, and cultural studies. Each of these kinds of critical theory is in one way or another a social theory before it is a literary, aesthetic, or philosophical theory. I shall not attempt to survey these theories and their relative judgments of James's role in modern art and culture; instead, I shall make reference along the way to such theories as I try to

work out James's fit to critical theory as it has been defined by the Frankfurt
school and has influenced the political aims of post-Marxian and postmodern
theories. In using James in this fashion, I am also interested in the possible
relation among these diverse, often heterogeneous, versions of critical theory.
My contention is that insofar as James can be understood as a critical theorist,
the James so constructed will help us understand what such theories might
have in common. Even before beginning this work, however, I want to write
clearly that James's very *unfitness* for a Marxist definition of critical theory
must also be part of our interest. Despite his great sensitivity to the subtleties
of ideological manipulation and control, James was no Marxist. However we
may justify the attention he pays to a newly empowered bourgeoisie and a
fading aristocracy, generally on the grounds that these are the classes through
which we understand the powers of ideology, I cannot absolve James from his
relative neglect of that "grey immensity" of the European and American
"underclass." Yet to label James simply a bourgeois writer, implying thereby
that he legitimated capitalist cultural values, is to miss entirely James's critical
dimension—one that has a prophecy for our own age that is still unrecognized. In short, I shall argue that James meets many of the criteria for the
critical social theorist defined by the Frankfurt school and subsequent Marxist intellectual approaches, even as he stubbornly resists classification within
the various orthodoxies such groups represent.

For traditional Marxists, James typifies bourgeois mystification. James's
valorization of aesthetic experience, his relentless abstraction, his studious
refusal of concrete details, and his fictional concentration on middle-class
manners seem to identify him unmistakably as just another author intent on
justifying the bourgeoisie's rights to rule.[9] This general Marxist interpretation
of James is behind Fredric Jameson's more sophisticated criticism: "Jamesian
point of view, which comes into being as a protest and defense against
reification, ends up furnishing a powerful ideological instrument in the perpetuation of an increasingly subjectivized and psychologized world, a world
whose social vision is one of a thoroughgoing relativity of monads in coexis-
tence. . . . This is the context in which the remarkable transformation of
Henry James from a minor nineteenth-century man of letters into the greatest American novelist of the 1950s may best be appreciated."[10] Jameson means
that James is merely one among many who contributed to the legitimation of
bourgeois values, simply another figure caught up in what David Lloyd has

termed the "aesthetic ideology" framed by romantic idealism and developed in nineteenth-century "intellectual history" from Hegel to Matthew Arnold and carried on by such modern disciples as T. S. Eliot and Henry James.[11]

At the other end of the spectrum, there is the deconstructive James, enormously popular in the late 1970s and throughout the 1980s, and quite clearly a central modern literary figure in the so-called American version of deconstruction. The label "American" may be unjust, since it refers more specifically to the work of the "Yale school," best represented in the work of Geoffrey Hartman, J. Hillis Miller, Paul de Man, and Harold Bloom.[12] Among the chief figures in the Yale school, only Miller has interpreted James in any sustained manner, but Henry James as modernist heir of romanticism is certainly implicit in the formulation of deconstruction as developed by de Man, Hartman, and Miller, as well as the poetics of influence developed by Bloom.[13] More important, of course, has been the adaptation of the theories of Hartman, Miller, de Man, and Bloom to the interpretation of the strategic, even systematic, verbal ambiguity of Henry James. That Henry James understood his mind-numbing prose, especially in the writings of the Major Phase, to represent the essential undecidability of language, is one of the distinguishing characteristics of American deconstruction's reading of him.[14] This, of course, is what distinguishes so-called American deconstruction from Continental poststructuralism: the former aestheticizes deconstruction by celebrating writers who are themselves "protodeconstructive" theorists; the latter has little interest in literary authors, except as useful examples, and sticks to the fundamental insight of deconstruction that every author must be read as a critical fiction in need of deconstruction (including the deconstructive critic's own bid for authority). Even in that case, however, the deconstruction of "Henry James" is an interesting issue for deconstructive critics who do not follow the literary lead of the Yale school, since "Henry James" has been subject to such a wide variety of influential literary critical constructions. Because those constructions have been in many cases fundamental to our thinking about modern art and even modern culture, the deconstruction of Henry James becomes a topic of far more than merely local literary interest.

Feminist interpretations of Henry James cannot be as easily generalized as I have those of Marxist and deconstructive theorists. On the one hand, James has often appeared to be one of the few masculine moderns to be eminently concerned with the problems facing modern women. Insofar as the majority of his novels and tales are organized around the difficulties confronting intelligent young women in predominantly patriarchal societies on both sides of the Atlantic, he seems a likely ally for feminist politics and an apt subject for feminist literary criticism. It is worth noting that several of the most important contemporary feminist theorists paid careful and often sympathetic attention to James's fiction early in their careers. Jane Tompkins's introduction to, and edition of, *Twentieth-Century Interpretations of "Turn of the Screw"* appeared in 1970, and it is a far cry from her compelling critique of nineteenth-century canonical American literature in *Sensational Designs: The Cultural Work of American Fiction, 1790–1860* (1985).[15] James is appropriately treated in *Sensational Designs* as the heir of the elitist and decidedly patriarchal literary traditions of Hawthorne and the transcendentalists, but he is also given credit for taking seriously "domestic space," in the manner of women writers such as Susan Warner and Jane Austen.[16] Susanne Kappeler's intricate post-Freudian psychoanalytical reading of James in *Writing and Reading in Henry James* (1980) can be read as a sort of preface to her later *The Pornography of Representation* (1986).[17] And the elements of Juliet Mitchell's important contributions to feminist psychoanalysis are sketched in her 1972 essay "*What Maisie Knew:* Portrait of the Artist as a Young Girl," in which the development of Maisie's psychic and moral insight follows the model of James's own artistic process.[18]

On the other hand, James's narratives lead these intelligent young women relentlessly toward sacrifice, exile, or death (often all three at the same time, in the cases of Daisy Miller and Milly Theale), in keeping with the dominant cultural rhetoric of feminine abjection, victimization, and madness analyzed so well by Sandra Gilbert and Susan Gubar in *The Madwoman in the Attic*.[19] Those who "succeed" do so only in the most problematic ways, often by accepting the patriarchal terms of their societies and learning to "play the game." Politically committed women, such as Oliver Chancellor in *The Bostonians,* or women who have their own careers, such as Henrietta Stackpole in *Portrait of a Lady,* are relentlessly mocked by James for having "missed" something deeper and more profound about the *real* bases for social interaction. It is not just *The Bostonians* that troubles feminists who judge James to be the ultimate version of patriarchal aestheticism, but the subtler ways in which James sets his feminine characters up for the finest triumphs only at the very last to steal their fire.[20]

The "failure" of James's feminine protagonists is almost always the occasion for James's own bid for power, his insistence that as author he has succeeded where these fragments of his imagination have failed. Thus Isabel Archer is only "true" to herself in those moments of intense reflection when she comes "closest" to James himself. And serious women writers such as Margaret Fuller or George Sand are judged by James to have failed because they did not write enough, well enough, or wrote too much.[21] Despite William Veeder's convincing arguments regarding James's uses of nineteenth-century popular fiction, especially written by women, James confirms his critical reputation for literary elitism by repeatedly trivializing the work of popular women writers.[22] Alfred Habegger has demonstrated how ambivalent James was on the "Woman Question," both in its specific political and more general cultural and social dimensions. Just what is at stake for those feminists most critical of Henry James is the degree to which he used his feminine characters and apparent feminist sympathies for the sake of his own bid for literary power and mastery. In this regard, of course, James is all the more insidious just insofar as his conservative values are disguised in liberal rhetoric.[23]

For New Historicists, too, James is an equivocal figure, on the one hand simply victimized like all others by his times, but on the other hand capable of comprehending at least partially the boundaries of the ideological prison in which he lived and worked. In some cases, such knowledge makes James more responsible for ideological complicity than he is in traditional Marxist judgments. This is the sort of case made by Mark Seltzer in *Henry James and the Art of Power* (1984).[24] In this same regard, James is a crucial figure for New Historicists because he wrote in such a critically transitional historical period. Rather than simply effecting the literary transition from the prevailing literary realism of the later Victorian period to the literary impressionism of the early modern novel, James worked in concert with other artists and scholars to textualize social reality. Like Oscar Wilde's Vivian in "The Decay of Lying" (1889), James argues that "life imitates art far more than art imitates life," or in his own words, "It is art that *makes* life, makes importance, for our consideration and application."[25]

This apparently charming iconoclasm, this bid for mere *literary* authority, especially in an age in which the arts appeared to be increasingly irrelevant, has a more insidious dimension, insofar as it helps pave the way for postindustrial societies, in which the laws of economic production are determined more by immaterial than material commodities. In our own economy, information, services, entertainment, and fashion are no longer secondary effects, by-products, of industrial production, but the central activities of more than two-thirds of the workforce. Thus James's and Wilde's fictions may be said to anticipate the paradigms of the marketeer, the models of the computer programmer and artificial intelligence expert, and even the development plans of the contractor or Pentagon officer. Behind the New Historicist's concern with the powers of representation in whatever historical period is just this contemporary question of how we are controlled and constrained by elaborate, surprisingly artistic modes of social signification. In that regard, of course, James must be considered a crucial figure, either for his anticipation of a coming age dedicated to semiotic controls or for his modest contributions to our adaptation to such a reality principle.

The argument that the unconscious of a literary author's work finds its visible manifestation in institutional practices and procedures, like the Elizabethan stage and court for Stephen Greenblatt or the institutions of criticism in our own modernity, seems to me to be an essential part of New Historicism.[26] By the same token, such a position argues against any effort to theorize an author such as Henry James as a "critical theorist." After all, critical theory involves active ideological analysis that is predicated on a theory of utopia, of social transformation in light of the failings of contemporary reality, which are most often the consequences of institutional constraints. Such a definition is in keeping with the Frankfurt school's prevailing Marxist understanding of the uses of intellectual activity for the purposes of social emancipation. For New Historicists, this definition leaves most *literary* authors trapped within the discursive limits of their own historical—that is, ideological—moments and assigns the work of cultural criticism to the ultimate avant-garde composed of political scholars.

We are thus dealing with a spectrum of judgments of Henry James that range from the sympathetic to thoroughly critical, leaving "Henry James" in his old, familiar position of radical ambiguity, variously available for interpretation and contemporary use. Such a view might well be considered the encompassing perspective that might relegitimate the name of "Henry James" as the modern most suitable for the title "theorist," literary or critical. However we evaluate James's literary contributions, he remains an important figure in our most powerful methods of interpretation and aesthetic evaluation, virtually inescapable as the "master" of the modern novel. In a sense, that was the issue, if not the conclusion, of my own *The Theoretical Dimensions of Henry James,* and in that regard, I was simply following the lead of post-

Freudian psychoanalytical critics such as Shoshana Felman, who finds in James the sort of rhetoric suited to elicit interpretation while escaping the reader's authoritative control.[27] This, I think, also reflects a continuing deconstructive interest in James, elements of which can be found in Frank Kermode's definition of the "modern classic," which seems so appropriate to James's literary oeuvre and its twentieth-century influence.[28]

I have claimed that some of these differences might be negotiated by reconsidering James as critical theorist in his own right, rather than as *constructed* by various critical theories. In this regard, I turn to a work that is at once the most appropriate for understanding what we mean by "critical theory" and the least likely to make the case for Henry James: Max Horkheimer's 1937 essay "Traditional and Critical Theory."[29] It is the locus classicus of critical theory as a specific discipline, especially in its formulation by the Frankfurt school. There is simply no chance that the reader will take Horkheimer's critical theory for literary or aesthetic theory; indeed, the essay is written against such idealist adaptations of what must be understood as a unique blend of social theory and political action, of ideological analysis and a utopian project. In fact, Horkheimer published his postscript to the essay in another 1937 issue of the journal he edited (from 1932 to 1941), *Zeitschrift für Sozialforschung*, which included Herbert Marcuse's "Philosophie und Kritische Theorie," as if to challenge his colleague's greater sympathy with the philosophical foundations of critical theory. For Horkheimer, critical thinking must replace philosophy, and social practice replace intellectual history.

For Horkheimer, "traditional theory" encompasses bourgeois individualism, rationalism, and nationalism: "Bourgeois thought is so constituted that in reflection on the subject which exercises such thought a logical necessity forces it to recognize an ego which imagines itself to be autonomous. Bourgeois thought is essentially abstract, and its principle is an individuality which inflatedly believes itself to be the ground of the world or even to be the world without qualification, an individuality separated off from events."[30] In many regards, this definition suits James's authorial practice quite precisely. If the "autonomous subject" of romantic idealism was no longer socially available in James's own era, then writers such as James sought to reconstruct the subject in and through the autonomous world of art. This is the formalist James, so dear to the New Critics, committed "eternally but to draw, by a geometry of his own, the circle within which [relations] shall happily *appear*" to cohere.[31] The fractured, alienated self may well be James's topic in most of his novels and tales, but it may be redeemed by an authorial act that gives the appearance of coherence and integrity. When Strether advises Little Bilham in Gloriani's garden in *The Ambassadors,* he is responding to the modern individual's fear of social determinism. "Live all you can; it's a mistake not to" is glossed by Strether: "The affair of life . . . [is] at the best a tin mould, either fluted and embossed, with ornamental excrescences, or else smooth and dreadfully plain, in which, a helpless jelly, one's consciousness is poured. . . . Still, one has the illusion of freedom."[32]

Horkheimer goes on to include under "traditional theory" the "direct contrary" of such radical and finally "bourgeois" individualism: "The attitude which holds the individual to be the unproblematic expression of an already constituted society; an example would be a nationalist ideology. Here the rhetorical 'we' is taken seriously; speech is accepted as the organ of the community. In the internally rent society of our day, such thinking, except in social questions, sees nonexistent unanimities and is illusory."[33] For James, the cosmopolitan writer, forerunner of the high-modern American expatriates in Europe, such a view appears inimical unless we begin to take seriously the Americanness of Henry James in relation to his international pretensions. Indeed, the American identity that James condemns from *The American* to *The Golden Bowl* focuses on the provincial, isolationist American identity that we associate with Christopher Newman's and Adam Verver's naïveté, sometimes charmingly mystified as their innocence. We know, of course, that such innocence is no longer a virtue in adult life, and James makes it abundantly clear that in adults innocence must be taken for ignorance, if not downright evil.

But against such naïfs, James pits the knowledgeable Americans, who learn how to adapt European values to American interests. They include Christina Light, victimized in *Roderick Hudson,* only to learn how to exploit more finely as the Princess Casamassima, Basil Ransome in *The Bostonians,* and Maggie Verver in *The Golden Bowl,* among a long list of others, in which James includes his own name. For his own cosmopolitanism is as profoundly involved with America's emerging social and political power as the melodramas these characters arrange. Given America's imperial ambitions in the early modern period—including John Hay's Open Door policy in the Far East, our annexation of the Philippines, our negotiated control of Central America and the Caribbean in conjunction with the various treaties covering the Panama Canal, and our role in the First World War—James's cosmopolitanism must be read in terms of America's geopolitical ambitions in the same period.³⁴ There is a special suitability, I think, to what otherwise must appear as a rather tenuous analogy, since America developed a new brand of imperial domination, distinctly different from the costlier and even less efficient colonial policies of the nineteenth-century European imperial powers. Unlike England, France, and Germany, America did not seek to control its territories materially, except in such cases as the Canal Zone and the Philippines. Instead, America sought "spheres of influence," in which foreign policy was based on "winning hearts and minds" to the American way and, of course, the American self.

James's cultivated Europeans are generally impoverished, increasingly desperate scions of the old aristocratic orders; his new Europeans include bourgeois characters as vulgar as their American equivalents. Only his new Americans have a chance at adapting to a new age in which national identity, hereditary titles, and material wealth will be replaced by cosmopolitanism, intelligence and imagination, and the sort of spiritual wealth that his predecessor, Walt Whitman, associated with the power of the self to emulate and even incorporate others. This is the traditional site of Jamesian compassion and humanity, as well as their insidious subtexts, psychological control and domination—the subjective equivalents of American imperialism. Thus far James suits only the traditional theory of Horkheimer's essay, and the prospect for Henry James as critical theorist appears gloomy indeed.

Horkheimer's definition of critical thinking and its theory is predictably Marxist, focused as it is on the responsibilities of the individual to his or her identification with some collectivity and to his or her commitment to the production of social reality: "Critical thinking is the function neither of the isolated individual nor of a sum-total of individuals. Its subject is rather a definite individual in his real relation to other individuals and groups, in his conflict with a particular class, and, finally, in the resultant web of relationships with the social totality and with nature. The subject is no mathematical point like the ego of bourgeois philosophy; his activity is the construction of the social present."³⁵ Horkheimer's last point seems conspicuously directed at writers such as Henry James, whose literary production has been so adaptable to philosophical reflection. Dorothea Krook's *The Ordeal of Consciousness in Henry James*, Richard Hocks's *Henry James and Pragmatistic Thought*, Paul Armstrong's *The Phenomenology of Henry James*, and Sharon Cameron's *Thinking in Henry James* are only a few notable examples of the many scholarly books that explore the fundamentally philosophical nature of James's writing.[36] Even Horkheimer's reference to "the subject" as "no mathematical point like the ego of bourgeois philosophy" seems directed at the Henry James who could insist on the "abstractness" of the philosophical subject, its status as the mere "ado of consciousness" in that hopelessly abstract (and deliberately awkward) phrase he used to describe Isabel Archer's subjectivity in his preface to *The Portrait of a Lady* in the New York edition.

As Horkheimer points out in his postscript to "Traditional and Critical Theory," the two philosophical models for the essay are Descartes and Marx: "Theory in the traditional sense established by Descartes and everywhere practiced in the pursuit of the specialized sciences organizes experience in the light of questions which arise out of life in present-day society."[37] Horkheimer is referring to the rationalist tradition represented by Cartesian thought, its logic—systematic doubt—and the intellectual history it initiated—an intellectual history intent on proving the unprovable: the essential rationality of mind and its a priori status with respect to experience and even the empirical data given to us by the natural world. Horkheimer's Marxian conception of critical theory is thus quite understandably critical of rationality, technology, and the authority of the sciences: "The critical theory of society, on the other hand, has for its object men as the producers of their own historical way of life in its totality. The real situations which are the starting-point of science are not regarded simply as data to be verified and to be predicated according to the laws of probability. Every datum depends not on nature alone but also on the power man has over it. Objects, the kind of perception, the questions asked, and the meaning of the answers all bear witness to human activity and the degree of man's power."[38] To be sure, this view hardly dismisses technology, insofar as "human activity" and the "degree of man's power" may well find science and technology to be primary tools. Even so, it is as human tools that science and technology are to be understood, rather than as the paradigms for "consciousness-in-itself," that "absolute ego," in whose evolving "spirit" man might achieve victory "over the dumb, unconscious, irrational side" of his nature.[39]

Quite to the contrary, Horkheimer understands these tools to be properly put to use in "work in society, and the class-related form of this work puts its mark on all human patterns of reaction, including theory. The intervention of reason in the processes whereby knowledge and its object are constituted, or the subordination of these processes to conscious control, does not take place therefore in a purely intellectual world, but coincides with the struggle for certain real ways of life."[40] Now, the least likely category in which to explore James's status as a critical theorist would seem to be his contribution to any class consciousness beyond bourgeois class consciousness—his "Consciousness" of consciousnesses, as it were—with which his work is traditionally associated by Marxists. If there is any "class conflict" in James, it appears to involve the struggle of the bourgeoisie to define itself against the lingering claims of the landed gentry, and in this work, the myth of "classless" America seems to serve James quite well. Often enough the bourgeoisie merely imitates what it understands to be the signs of aristocratic privilege and distinction. Christopher Newman buying up bad copies of European paintings, Adam Verver "stocking" his American museum with the fragments of European art history, Gilbert Osmond laboring at his own copies of antiquities, Ned Rosier collecting them, and the narrator of *The Aspern Papers* snooping about for unpublished manuscripts are examples of James's own critique of the "culture industry." Such dilettantism, if not commodity fetishism, is the antithesis of what Horkheimer means by "the struggle for certain real ways of life"; nothing could be more illusory or more the property of a "purely intellectual world."

But such collectors and fetishists are easy enough for James to caricature; even Newman in *The American,* early as that novel is, serves primarily as an occasion for exploring the subtler ways in which the bourgeoisie legitimates its authority. "Manners" hardly covers the repertoire of discursive tricks through which the crude powers of this ruling class are disguised. James understood better than any of his contemporaries how profoundly bourgeois capital resides in its command of representation, rather than money or land. Both Nick Dormer in *The Tragic Muse* and Maisie Farange in *What Maisie Knew* will reflect at length on the troublesome connotations of the word and act of "representation." For Nick, the term crosses the boundaries of art, politics, and psychology; for Maisie, it confuses the categories of law, the family, and ethics. It is in this regard that James's ideological criticism still seems contemporary and justifies in part the elaborate abstractions of his prose style, even as such an insight calls for a critique of its own medium, of the novelist's techniques and values as parts of the problem so analyzed.

For Horkheimer, such a defense would make sense only when supported on the evidence of James's identification with proletarian interests and his contributions to the formation of such a class consciousness. To be sure, the traditionally defined proletariat lingers only on the margins of James's fictional worlds, as long as we understand the "working class" in traditional terms. Although works such as *What Maisie Knew, Turn of the Screw,* and *In the Cage* centrally involve working-class characters, I agree with recent cultural critics that such a narrow definition of the proletariat ignores the labor of others whose work is also likely to be exploited, in part because such work has no properly established "exchange value." In this group, I include James's women and children, the two groups in James's writings most prominently victimized by bourgeois authority. In this context, James also recognized how fundamentally women experience their dispossession through the everyday use of language and how their access to language is always conditioned by patriarchal rhetoric, even when used by other women. But James's fiction also calls attention to the unacknowledged labor of women in birth, child rearing, and education. Contemporary feminists have pointed out that one of the fundamental omissions from traditional Marxist theory is the work of women, both in the workforce and in the domestic world.[41]

Less explicitly central to James's critique of bourgeois authority, but nonetheless crucial to any "class consciousness" identifiable in his writings, would be gays and lesbians. As recent scholars have begun to show us, James's fiction is full of characters and situations that challenge conventional gender roles and sexual identities, but both characters and dramatic situations tend to be disguised by James, often sublimated into "aesthetic" problems or "existential" situations. Certainly, such literary disguise is not unusual for writers in an era when homosexuality was legally defined and thus demonized; we should never forget how dangerous it was to one's reputation and civil liberties to be identified as a homosexual in late-nineteenth-century England and America. Despite the various disguises by which James introduces gay and lesbian characters and situations into his fiction, as well as his own conflicts regarding the social significance of lesbian and gay sexual preferences, there can be little question that gays and lesbians constitute another group in his writings victimized by bourgeois values.

If we are to look for a "class consciousness" in Henry James, then, perhaps we should look first to women, lesbian and straight, children, and gays as contributors to such a class consciousness. It is my contention in this book that once the victimization of these groups is understood as an essential part of James's social critique of bourgeois values, an accompanying recognition of the "working class" also becomes visible in James's fiction. We may also discover along the way that the apparent "neglect" of the proletariat in James's writings is to a certain extent a function of our own critical habits and preferences for certain novels and stories over others, much as scholars in gay studies have shown us that homosexual characters and situations often belong to texts we do not know how to read and thus remain outside our conventional critical view. This does not mean, of course, that simply by shifting our critical perspective we will suddenly bring into view a "Marxist" Henry James thoroughly compatible with a traditional analysis of class conflict between the industrial proletariat and the bourgeoisie. James was deeply conflicted throughout his career with respect to the appropriate social roles of the very groups he represents as victimized by an unjust, narrow-minded, and decidedly patriarchal social order. A great intellectual and literary distance separates such abject women characters as Claire de Cintré, Verena Tarrant, and May Bartram from such powerful and assertive characters as Isabel Archer, Miriam Rooth, and Maggie Verver. In a similar fashion, he struggles with the proper social roles to be played by lesbians and gays in a changing social order. Such conflicts in James's fiction are the subject of this book, but taken together, they demonstrate James's interest in expanding the more limited categories of nineteenth-century class to include groups increasingly central to the organization of social power.

So much of James's fiction is given over to the bourgeois work of courtship and marriage that we tend to forget the central roles children play in his fiction. In its obsession with its own forms, rituals, and powers, bourgeois society ignores its children. The Principino in *The Golden Bowl* is just what his name suggests: a mere bibelot, another collectible for the Ververs. Maisie Farange, of course, dramatizes the confusions and alienation experienced by children attempting to adjust to family relations and parental roles that seem to change overnight. In *The Turn of the Screw,* such alienation turns fantastic for Miles and Flora, whether we accept the truth of what the governess reports or simply her madness. In either case, these children, orphaned by their parents and emotionally abandoned by their uncle, are left to grow up in a world that seems hostile to their interests. We forget that Verena Tarrant in *The Bostonians* is, after all, little more than a child when her father first pushes her before a revivalist audience; to the very end, she has grown little, except in her capacity to mime, as the young Maisie does, the rhetoric of what she can only guess controls adult behavior and values. There are many other examples of children given center stage by James, yet marginalized by their parents and other adults. I select these familiar fictional children in part because they so self-evidently *work* and work *hard* either for their parents' and guardians' material profit or simply for the sake of a little attention and affection. The trivialization of the work of children goes hand in hand with the patriarchal disregard for the labor of women, in both reproduction and the work of child rearing, in addition to the more demonstrable forms of work performed by women in Victorian society. Indeed, in addition to the labor of the factory, the sweatshop, and cottage industry, we should add the work of governesses, servants, and cultivated companions, despite the subtleties of traditional class divisions that separate such drudging and unrewarded labors from those of the working class.[42]

Like bourgeois women, James's middle-class children are more than just alienated; they are imprisoned, psychologically damaged, physically abused, and in some cases quite literally killed by the pressures or neglect of their parents. In this regard, Pansy Osmond is one of the most familiar examples, shut away in an Italian convent for her "edification," when in fact she is hidden as the visible sign of her father's affair with Madame Merle. Isabel goes back to Osmond as much for Pansy's sake as for any commitment to middle-class marriage, but saving Pansy is much harder work than James knows how to articulate; it can be left only as a prospect for Isabel at the very end of the novel. Pansy's prison extends well beyond the convent, and in this regard, she anticipates the pathetic fate of Tina Bourdereau, locked up with her "great-aunt" (or illegitimate mother) in their ruined Venetian palazzo, only to be offered to that "publishing scoundrel" as a guarantee that Juliana might reach beyond the grave to keep this niece/daughter in bondage to Juliana's fantastic secret. Like Tina, Pansy has value as an exchangeable commodity, whether such value is determined by Gilbert Osmond, Lord Warburton, or even the pathetic Ned Rosier.[43] Amid the rhetorical and social complications of *What Maisie Knew*, readers often overlook the ways Maisie is *physically* abused. Stroked, squeezed, pinched, and pushed, Maisie compares herself with her doll, Lisette, or a badminton shuttlecock. James deliberately confuses the rhetorical, psychological, and physical aspects of such child abuse in the novel to suggest their complementarity, as in the following passage: "It brought again the sweet sense of success that, ages before, [Maisie] had had at a crisis when, on the stairs, returning from her father's, she had met a fierce question of her mother's with an imbecility as deep and had in consequence been dashed by Mrs. Farange almost to the bottom."[44]

Whether Tina develops finally, in open rebellion against the lies of Juliana and the treachery of the narrator, hardly matters when we consider her wasted life. The fires that consume Aspern's papers—"There were so many," she taunts the narrator in one of those rare moments that satisfy James's reader with justice achieved—have already consumed Tina, no matter how beautiful she appears at the very last to the zealous editor. In a similar fashion, the horror of the governess in *The Turn of the Screw* is the hint that Douglas offers that she, too, has never grown up and is yet another abandoned child, whose failure to develop is one of the causes of the terror at Bly. The equivalence of women and children in this bourgeois economy is an effect not of James's paternalism but of the virtual hostility his social world expresses to the social and personal growth of women and children.

Children in James's writings generally represent cases of arrested development, of the failure of maturation and acculturation, to the point that we are inclined to forget them, unwilling to engage the ugly truth they reveal. The extremity of this parental abuse of children is murder, and it is murder that we must judge the outcome of the Ambients' struggle over the "morality" of little Dolcino in "The Author of Beltraffio," as it is murder with which both the governess and uncle must be charged in the death of Miles in *The Turn of the Screw.* In another of those tragic and perverse stories, "The Pupil," Morgan Moreen dies of a "broken" or "weakened" (it matters little which) heart when his parents agree to give him to his tutor, Mr. Pemberton. Morgan understands as well as the others that he is Mr. Pemberton's delayed "payment," in one of James's marvelously perverse ironies—that the "reward" for Pemberton's care and education of this extraordinary boy is the boy himself. It is, of course, just what Morgan has seemed to want all along, as Mrs. Pemberton wails: "But I thought he *wanted* to go to you!"[45] Even the most casual reader, Pemberton included, knows that what the child most wants is the care and attention of his parents. Maisie's early childhood similarly revolves around her sense of identity as an item of exchange, like the sovereigns the American countess gives her for cab fare or the money Maisie's mother, Ida, starts to give her in Folkestone, only to withdraw the bill when Maisie fails to please—that is, to *pay*—her.

Such children understand their young years to involve work, often very hard work, which they are willing to perform, if only it will bring them a proper return. Yet, like the tutor, Mr. Pemberton, these children are never paid for their labors. Aware of the boy's pain and confusion living with parents whose lives are dedicated to leisure and luxury that they cannot afford, Mr. Pemberton proposes, if somewhat in jest: "We ought to go off and live somewhere together." The bond that unites the tutor and his charge is just their sense that their respective labors are not respected, that they are mere victims of a confidence game they both understand with perfect clarity but somehow are powerless to escape. When Pemberton elaborates, "I'd get some work that would keep us both afloat," Morgan replies promptly: "So would I. Why shouldn't *I* work? I ain't such a beastly little muff as *that* comes to."[46] And yet it is a "beastly little muff," or "bungler," that best represents Morgan's image of himself, or at least what his parents have led him to believe of himself. In his choice of words, however, in the decisively American idiom Morgan chooses—"muff" as "bungler" comes from a baseball term still current today—Morgan rebels ever so slightly in the cultivated Italy where the vulgar term is uttered.

What child labor laws might be enacted to protect children such as Maisie and Morgan, dispossessed and possessed by the fantastic adult world around them? James's representation of these bourgeois children is perhaps his most profound indictment of the bourgeoisie's lack of a proper historical consciousness, its failure to develop those means through which it might transform and renew itself. And yet we hardly notice how the children in Henry James's fiction are as orphaned, abandoned, and abused as the fictional children of Mark Twain. Isabel Archer in *The Portrait of a Lady,* Milly Theale in *The Wings of the Dove,* and even Chad Newsome in *The Ambassadors* are young adults who have experienced in their own ways just such dispossession and have been scarred for life. It is a neglect or repression that we cannot attribute to James but may well be a consequence of our own reading habits as bourgeois readers, intent as we are on separating the serious business of adult relations from the trivial work our children must perform every day.

I have suggested that these children are workers as alienated from their labor of acculturation as the children of sweatshops and factories. They only remind us again of how profoundly James's bourgeois women are dispossessed, cast in roles either as confining as that Bronzino painting Milly views at Matcham—"dead, dead, dead"—or as perversely conventional as Maggie's triumphant role as the prince's wife and her father's daughter at the end of *The Golden Bowl.* When Milly Theale leaves the offices of Sir Luke Strett in *The Wings of the Dove,* she plunges into the "grey immensity" of London that "had somehow become her element."[47] Her long walk through working-class

London has been analyzed before as one of the rare moments in James's writings in which high society must confront the underclass world on which it builds its palaces. To be sure, it is a little sentimental, even an indulgent insight for the doomed Milly to recognize in the exhausted lives of those around her a metaphor for her own fate.

There is nonetheless a serious dimension to her recognition that her own mortality links her not just with common humanity but with precisely those for whom the daily question is one of survival, of the "practical question of life."[48] Her mental gestures are significant, even as they connect her with her fictional predecessor, Hester Prynne: "It was as if she had to pluck off her breast, to throw away, some friendly ornament, a familiar flower, a little old jewel, that was part of her daily dress; and to take up and shoulder as a substitute some queer defensive weapon, a musket, a spear, a battle-axe—conducive possibly in a higher degree to a striking appearance, but demanding all the effort of the military posture."[49]

James repeats the military metaphor in his account of Milly's march through the London slums. At first, it is merely a sign of her fortitude, her strength of will in the face of her own doom, but soon enough it becomes her identification with the working classes: "She found herself moving at times in regions visibly not haunted by odd-looking girls from New York, duskily draped, sable-plumed, all but incongruously shod and gazing about them with extravagance; she might, from the curiosity she clearly excited in the by-ways, in side-streets peopled with grimy children and costermongers' carts, which she hoped were slums, literally have had her musket on her shoulder, have announced herself as freshly on the war-path."[50] Seeing herself imaginatively (another "odd-looking" New York girl) in the whores of London, who are represented here as mournful ghosts ("duskily draped, sable-plumed") in recognition of their living deaths and Milly's impending doom, she is driven to military solidarity with these outcasts. Even in her extremity, however, her rebellion is finally trivial. Coming out on the familiar lawns of Regents Park, "she looked for a bench that was empty, eschewing a still emptier chair that she saw hard by and for which she would have paid, with superiority, a fee."[51]

Perhaps Olive Chancellor's and Tina Aspern's rebellions are more significant, but both are similarly doomed to just such glimmers of solidarity with the oppressed. It is the "nameless fear" that the governess senses in Miles and Flora and that binds her to them, too tightly to be sure, but nonetheless in a sympathy that initially indicates how much their exploitation partakes of that belonging to the more demonstrable working class. The governess fears those ghosts of Peter Quint and Miss Jessel in the same sense that she struggles with Mrs. Grose for authority: all are servants, despite the different authority they are respectively granted by their master. Their work does not belong to them, and even Miss Jessel's pregnancy carries with it a "horror" of illegitimacy and immorality that steal even that work from her. It is fitting that her pregnancy should remain merely a rumor, never confirmed by James's text.

These sympathies for the exploited labor of bourgeois women and children may seem indulgent in their own right if we take into account the sorts of exploitation experienced daily by industrial workers in nineteenth-century Europe and America. But James's point is that the most insidious exploitation works through the psychological and verbal practices that make a "musket, spear, or battle-axe" appear just what they are for Milly's imagination: anachronistic weapons with which to combat a subtler enemy. Maud Lowder at her account books reminds James of Britannia, armed not so much with martial weapons as with quills for the ledgers. And the uncle in *The Turn of the Screw* decorates his apartment with "trophies of the hunt," but one conducted clearly by way of the verbal blandishments and billets-doux that in part seal his contract with the governess. Maisie learns soon enough that she must use words in all their connotative and duplicitous complexity to protect herself against the violent sophistry of parents such as Beale Farange, Ida, Mrs. Beale, and even Sir Claude. The bourgeois pen is mightier than the sword, and it is James's rather accurate prophecy that the power of late capitalism will find itself best in the rhetorical legerdemain we too often treat reductively as the manners of high society.

It is little coincidence that the few proletarians to assume central roles in James's fiction are occupied in daily tasks intimately connected with this emergent rhetorical power, the discourse of the bourgeoisie. Hyacinth Robinson in *The Princess Casamassima* is a bookbinder, and the telegraph operator in *In the Cage* is another circuit in the communications system of the ruling class. The sources of capital may be repressed, if only to disguise the sheer vulgarity of that nameless commodity on which the Newsomes' fortune is based in *The Ambassadors*. Yet as Newman's own entrepreneurial history makes clear in *The American,* the power of the bourgeoisie has little to do with actual production, with commodities per se. Leather washtubs or railroads, oil or the stock market, Newman knows the trick of making money.

More often than not, such a trick is rhetorical, a sleight of hand by which the labor of another may become your own. In this regard, the incriminating letter Newman thinks of publishing to expose the supposed treachery of the Bellegardes is less the plot device of some old romance than it is a marker in the new economy's high-stakes game of discursive power.

In the case of James's imaginative, intelligent young women, such trickery aims at their very vitality. It is the productivity of such women, both intellectually and physically understood, that the ruling class seeks to possess. *The Sacred Fount* is not just metaphorically a narrative of vampirism; it quite graphically describes how the ruling class works to take possession of others. Understood exclusively in terms of the limited opportunities available to Isabel Archer, Milly Theale, and even the mystified Maggie Verver, such exploitation and alienation hardly compare with that of the vast and largely unrecognized underclass in James's fiction. Yet when we add to this company James's fictional children, and the extent to which his most promising young adults still bear the scars of such childhoods, there is a rather numerous fictional company capable of the sort of class consciousness that Horkheimer demands for critical theory.

We must add to these women and children the men and women whose sexual and psychological preferences for members of the same sex drive them either to lives of secret desperation or to elaborate sublimations of their real desires. Even without strict biographical evidence to support James's homosexuality, on the evidence of his autobiographical writings and his fiction, we should add Henry James himself to such company. In these writings, James expresses his understanding of the difficulties facing men and women whose sexual preferences and psychological behaviors differ from the strict social and sexual mores of late Victorian and nineteenth-century American cultures. To be sure, James's understanding is unevenly expressed throughout his long career, and his sympathies for male aesthetes and homosexuals often depend on his mockery of female "culture vultures" and overt lesbians. Without ignoring these problems in James's fiction, we can nevertheless acknowledge James's effort to represent the interests of men and women who live and love "the other way round," to borrow from the title of Dora Forbes's (nom de plume of the male author) popular novel in "The Death of the Lion."[52]

On one level, James is defensive in his representation of same-sex relations, preferring to subordinate any explicit sexuality to textual and aesthetic issues. In this regard, James often acts out the homosexual panic Eve Sedgwick finds structurally integral to masculine writing in the Victorian period and a necessary corollary of its basic homosociality.[53] On the other hand, James includes in his fiction, especially from the 1890s to the end of his career, a diverse group of male characters who suit Sedgwick's definition of "coming out of the closet," of accepting rather than repressing "homosexual possibility," "whether as *a homosexual man* or as a man with a less exclusively defined sexuality that nevertheless admits the possibility of desires for other men."[54] In her sense, "coming out of the closet" refers not simply to the declaration of homosexual identity but to the acceptance of such homosexuality as part of a diverse and healthy society—a society liberated from the repressive constraints of Victorian patriarchy.

The long list of male characters in James's fiction who express in one way or another their desires for this more liberated social utopia is evidence of James's own aesthetic and autobiographical desire to theorize specific alternatives to nineteenth-century gender binaries. Ned Rosier and Ralph Touchett in *The Portrait of a Lady,* Hyacinth Robinson in *The Princess Casamassima,* Gabriel Nash and Nick Dormer in *The Tragic Muse,* Doctor Hugh and Dencombe in "The Middle Years," Neil Paraday and the narrator in "The Death of the Lion," the narrator of *The Aspern Papers,* John Marcher in "The Beast in the Jungle," and Lambert Strether and Little Bilham in *The Ambassadors* are only a few of the many male characters in James's fiction who reject the dominant modes of male affirmation, display an especially aesthetic sensibility, have "difficulties" of various sorts marrying the women with whom they often share many qualities, and often lead explicitly "secret" lives that repudiate what is expected of them as socially responsible men.

Such characters sometimes make connections with other male characters who are designedly revolutionary or iconoclastic, as in Hyacinth's association with the anarchists of "The Sun and the Moon" in *The Princess Casamassima* or Nick Dormer's dependence on Gabriel Nash's advice in choosing a career as a painter and abandoning his political career and parliamentary seat in *The Tragic Muse.* James often distinguishes such male friendships from the more obviously homosocial relations of male bonding that describe Newman's friendship with Valentin de Bellegarde in *The American* and Rowland Mallett's relationship with Roderick Hudson, both of which rely on paternal hierarchies. Nevertheless, the implicit social criticism of certain relations between men in James's fiction rarely achieves the equivalent of an economic class consciousness that might genuinely threaten bourgeois respectability. I shall argue in the following chapters that James's attitudes toward homosexuality changed during his career and that the writings of the 1890s display a much greater openness with respect to male homosexuality as a viable alternative to Victorian sexual norms, but James's prevailing attitude toward homosexuality, especially as one basis for social protest and reform, seems to be conflicted. As Joseph Bristow has put it: "It is not at all unusual to find James at once revealing and concealing his homophile interests."[55] Such rhetorical ambivalence is not readily adaptable to political activism, which is perhaps why James's homophile interests so often find expression by way of a less threatening and depoliticized aestheticism.

Yet we should not conclude too easily that James identifies the limitations of same-sex relations, especially between men, either to defend against his own homosexual desires or to endorse conventions about homosexual "powerlessness" that are still prevalent today. Kaja Silverman's distinction between the biographical Henry James—"the author 'outside' the text"—and the author function produced by his texts—"the author 'inside' the text"—reinforces the conception of Henry James, the "master," struggling to contain within his literary productions a psychic unconscious that is profoundly anxious, fundamentally marginalized, haunted by homosexual desires, and incapable of escaping the repetitive cycles of unresolved Oedipal conflict.[56] Silverman's revisionary Freudian interpretation of James's "inside" or "phantasmic" author as situated between the positive heterosexual and "negative or homosexual versions of the Oedipus complex" is illuminating, but it inevitably reproduces some of Freud's worst misinterpretations of homosexual identity as powerless, abject, and narcissistic.[57] The frequent "failure" of same-sex relations in James's fiction, including those between women (such as Olive and Verena in *The Bostonians*), is often attributed by James in thoroughly conscious ways (that is, as the "outside," biographical author) to the prejudices and conventions of Victorian sexual and social ideology. Unfortunately, there is little evidence in James's fiction of *political* self-consciousness on the part of male partners like those mentioned in the previous paragraph, although Gabriel Nash and Nick Dormer do use their aestheticism to rebel against social conventionality. Nevertheless, such fictional couples are not inevitably to be understood as powerless, abject, sexually and psychically confused, or hopelessly narcissistic, even if all of these traits are represented by some of these and many other heterosexual characters in James's fiction.

Silverman interprets "sodomitical identification" with the father as crucial to homosexual subject formation in James's fiction, thus rendering homosexual intercourse as "wounding" and the experience of "domination."[58] But the slippage in James's fiction between homosocial and homosexual relations—categories that have been rigidly distinguished in late-twentieth-century discourse—may also be read as James's conscious effort to accommodate a fuller range of sexual behaviors and modes of erotic and social expression than were permitted by the Victorian ideology he consistently criticizes. There is a great deal of tenderness between men, "feminine" sensitivity (as it is delimited by the Victorians) shown by male characters toward women, and "passionate" interest of women in other women that extends from the overtly erotic to the aesthetic and intellectual. Silverman concludes:

> Despite the ostensible gender of the biographical Henry James, the author "inside" his texts is never unequivocally male; situated at a complex intersection of the negative and positive Oedipus complexes, that author is definitively foreclosed from the scene of passion except through identifications which challenge the binarisms of sexual difference. He aspires to knowledge only under the sign of masochism, and is unable to grasp castration as a condition exclusive to woman. Finally, his recourse to vision is more generative of trauma than of power. The author "inside" James's stories and novels bears so little resemblance to what is popularly thought of as the "Master" that I can only think of that Jacobite specter as a compensatory construction of the author "outside" the text.[59]

Again, much of Silverman's analysis is insightful and relevant to James's changing attitudes toward his own sexuality and his literary production throughout a long career that parallels English and American processes of modernization. The *other* Henry James suggested in Silverman's analysis appears to be the binary opposite of the "master" constructed by devoted Jacobites. I shall argue for *another* Henry James, who is not just subject to "masochism" and to the vision resulting from psychic "trauma," but who also achieves a psychic alterity that can take erotic pleasure and intellectual satisfaction from subject positions no longer tied to strict gender and sexual binaries. Such Jamesian scenarios help us imagine powers of care, sympathy, and love beyond those conventionally linked in the Foucauldian equation of

"power" with "knowledge."[60] Well before Freud's gender hierarchies and
sexual binaries were deconstructed by subsequent traditions of psychoanalytic and cultural interpretation (notably feminism, queer theory, and gay
studies), James's fiction is already working out the consequences of more
flexible social, psychological, and sexual relations, even if the explicit *politics*
of these new human relations remain decidedly, if understandably, unclear in
James's thought.

One interesting consequence of reinterpreting women, children, and gays
in James's fiction is the concomitant surfacing of issues of race, ethnicity, and
nationalism. Often considered a writer who simply avoided the debates concerning African American rights during Reconstruction or the growing anti-
Semitism in late Victorian England, James becomes readable as a writer with
much more to say about religious and ethnic minorities when read with close
attention to relations among class, gender, and sexuality. Race and ethnicity
often become in James's fiction other means by which women, children, and
gays are marginalized. Thus Miriam Rooth's presumed Jewish ancestry both
exoticizes and marginalizes her in proper English society, whereas the American Countess's description as "brown" or "almost black" in *What Maisie Knew*
suggests how color now informs social identity in an English society whose
boundaries have been threatened by the very imperialist policies that have
buoyed up the ruling class.

Indeed, any class consciousness I have tried to forge from the victimized
and marginalized characters in James's fiction must appear contrived insofar
as it is shaped primarily from within the bourgeoisie. It is clear enough that
James feared the "masses," especially the immigrants to America, for whom
he could at once express sympathy for their socioeconomic oppression and
contempt for their lack of development and cultivation. *The American Scene*
gives ample evidence of James's fears of immigrant cultures.[61] It would be
wrong to force my adaptation of Horkheimer's Marxist definition of critical
theory to suit James's ambivalence regarding the rapid demographic and
cultural changes in modern America. Yet for all his conservative commitments to such dangerous clichés as national integrity, the special tone of a
culture or civilization, there is a social utopianism in James that meets the
requirements of Horkheimer's critical theory, precisely because such utopia is
predicated on the common interests discovered through shared labor. That
utopian dimension rests squarely in our capacities to control our means of

communication and thus to *produce* our own representations. In this regard, James anticipates the central questions facing us in our postmodern condition, in which the powers of social speech seem further every day from the control of the ordinary citizen.

James's utopianism is nowhere better expressed than in his commencement address to the graduating class at Bryn Mawr College on June 8, 1905, "The Question of Our Speech." From Marxist, feminist, and cultural studies perspectives, it is a troubling, if not nasty, little talk, filled with James's fears of what immigration will do to the "American idiom" and his appeals to his women auditors for whom "voice" and "tone" are matters of special importance. Add to all of this James's unspoken assumption that the vox Americana must be monolingual and cannot be thought of as other than "American English," and you have the elements of a very strong case against James as "critical theorist," certainly in the twentieth-century context that I have been developing that term. From the perspective of cultural studies, James is simply too utterly imbued with the inherited values of Western civilization to entertain any alternative to it. Along with this civilization come those "torch-bearers," those "articulate individuals" among whom he counts himself in the example of his speech.[62] Against such a standard of "articulation," James pits "the common schools and the 'daily paper,' " traditional enemies of the high-cultural ideals that he and many of his modernist followers would develop so elaborately, especially in the face of dramatic changes in the class structures of Europe and America at the turn of the century (*QS*, 44).

I cannot leave aside these problems in James's appeal to his bourgeois auditors to "purify" the language and emulate the "tone" that distinguishes French and Italian and their correlative cultures and arts. Yet even amid these fears and prejudices, James recognizes that the common aim of those dispossessed must be to achieve some control over the means of their communication. Insofar as James celebrates the social and political powers of language, he treats verbal communication as the chief basis for forming what a proper critical theorist would term "class consciousness." To be sure, for James it remains "national" consciousness, the vox Americana, full of all the mystifications of a nationalism repugnant to Horkheimer and the Frankfurt school, as well as many so-called Americanists in our contemporary period. Even so, James's nationalism begins with the recognition of a shared alienation from the means of social articulation and thus discursive power:

All the while we sleep the vast contingents of aliens whom we make welcome, and whose main contention, as I say, is that from the moment of their arrival, they have just as much property in our speech as we have, and just as good a right to do what they choose with it—the grand right of the American being to do just what he chooses "over here" with anything and everything: all the while we sleep the innumerable aliens are sitting up (*they* don't sleep!) to work their will on their new inheritance and prove to us that they are without any finer feeling or more conservative instinct of consideration for it, more hovering, caressing curiosity about it, than they may have on the subject of so many yards of freely figured oilcloth, from the shop, that they are preparing to lay down, for convenience, on the kitchen floor or kitchen staircase. (*QS*, 44–45)

Certainly James recoils from his own excessively material metaphor for language, with its insistence on the sheer instrumentality of language, which for these "innumerable aliens" remains simply "convenient" and "wonderfully resisting 'wear' . . . an excellent bargain: durable, tough, cheap" (*QS*, 45–46). The metaphor is overdetermined with an anti-Semitism that surfaces more explicitly elsewhere in "The Question of Our Speech" and cannot be ignored. Bought as it is "cheaply" in a "shop" for practical use in the kitchen, the immigrants' version of the vox Americana threatens to reinforce their essential privacy, their confinement to the provincialism of the tenement and their exploitation by those more "articulate." Even such a generous interpretation suggests that James endorses a "melting pot" thesis through which the immigrants' access to American society depends on a certain acculturation to proper American English.[63]

Yet the "influences of example and authority" are not so easily identified by James as they might be by Horkheimer's traditional theorists appealing to the conservators of European culture: "I grant you here that I am at a loss to name you particular and unmistakable, edifying and illuminating groups or classes, from which this support is to be derived; since nothing, unfortunately, more stares us in the face than the frequent failure of such comfort in those quarters where we might, if many things were different, most look for it" (*QS*, 48). James prefers instead to insist on simply "a consciousness, an acute consciousness" of "formed and finished utterance, wherever, among all the discords and deficiencies, that music steals upon your ear" (*QS*, 50).

James's reluctance to specify the "class" or "group" from which we might expect the models for cultivated speech stems from his democratic sentiments, tainted with the prejudices of his age and his own cultivated experience. His idea that the refinement of speech may come from any class or group is distinctly American and clearly distinguishable from the class specificity of British nationalism he satirizes in *The Tragic Muse*. Troublesome as this ideal must be in his articulation, it still carries a certain conviction that the ultimate social capital is communication and the capacity for, and access to, those means of representation from which his victimized characters are so often banned:

> It is prosperity, of a sort, that a hundred million people, a few years hence, will be unanimously, loudly—above all loudly, I think!—speaking it, and that, moreover, many of these millions will have been artfully wooed and weaned from the Dutch, from the Spanish, from the German, from the Italian, from the Norse, from the Finnish, from the Yiddish even, strange to say, and (stranger still to say) even from the English, for the sweet sake, or the sublime consciousness, as we may perhaps put it, of speaking, of talking, for the first time in their lives, *really* at their ease. (*QS,* 42)

The "consciousness" of "proper speech" that he advises his auditors to "cultivate" is thus not necessarily English, but much rather a social discourse that makes this diverse population capable of communicating. There is a hint of just this utopianism in *The Tragic Muse,* in which the foreigner Miriam Rooth succeeds in playing Shakespearean heroines—and thus legitimating British nationalism—better than properly English actresses. James's irony in that novel, of course, is that Miriam is perfectly English in origin; only her Jewish ancestry and her cosmopolitan experience cause others to judge her "foreign." James has in mind the development of "American English" that will eventually take the place of "English" and thus incorporate those elements of immigrants' speech that may be made to serve the purposes of verbal "discrimination and selection," of judgment and precise evaluation. Just who are to be the arbiters of what should be retained and what suppressed in this development of the vox Americana is left deliberately vague, but we can read clearly enough his implication. That he himself might be counted one of the judges of such linguistic propriety, even as he liberally embraces the ideal of a language capable of responding "from its core, to the constant appeal of time, perpetually demanding new tricks, new experiments, new amusements," goes without saying (*QS,* 46).

But what remains compelling about James's formulation of a social utopia predicated on popular access to the most sophisticated modes of communication is the possibility of reconceiving class consciousness in these general terms: that is, the shared interests of those members of a society effectively dispossessed of these very means of social communication. This is precisely the situation of James's bourgeois women and children, of his gay characters and those identified variously as "different," who are victimized just insofar as they are required to speak a language that expresses only their powerlessness or dispossession. Milly Theale's recognition of her mortality is less a consequence of her visit to Sir Luke Strett than it is the result of her experiences in the social world of London. She has no voice, and it is entirely fitting that the "voice" she finally chooses can be articulated only by others, in her absence. If such is the case, then her identification with the underclass of London is more political than sentimental, and James's politely biased address to these Bryn Mawr graduates may suggest a subtler bond they share with the immigrants arriving in America. In a similar sense, James's male characters who suffer their secrets of artistic or homosexual passion are also victims of social orders in both England and America that do not permit the expression of masculine aestheticism or same-sex eroticism. They, too, share the immigrants' destiny in trying to figure out the dominant discourse in order to change it, so that their social problem is also an aesthetic and linguistic one. When Nick Dormer must choose between Gabriel Nash as his artistic muse and Julia Dallow as his political muse, he chooses the former and then must struggle to find the proper medium in which to represent this choice. In some of his writings, James understands aestheticism to be a means of disguising homosexual desire, but in others, such as *The Tragic Muse,* he understands the problems of homosexual identity and aesthetic questions of social representation to be integrally related.

There is nonetheless a great distance separating such symbolic identification of bourgeois women or gay men with the working class from the ideal of diverse peoples "speaking . . . *really* at their ease," in which both "ease" and "reality" are assumed to have some equivalence insofar as they are *produced* by such peoples. The hint in James that the true economic production of a society is its capacity to communicate among its many cultural and ethnic differences seems confirmed in his repeated references to the "economy" and "property" of language in "The Question of Our Speech." Even so, James remains a victim of his own contemporary and class-specific situation, insofar as he insists on what he terms a "conscious" speech that is "imitative": "Conscious, imitative speech—isn't that more dreadful than anything else?" James poses rhetorically his auditors' objections to what must be understood idiomatically as the stilted and elaborate speech of his European aristocratic models. "It's not 'dreadful,' I reply, any more than it's ideal: the matter depends on the stage of development it represents. It's an awkwardness, in your situation, that your own stage is an early one, and that you have found, round about you—outside of these favoring shades—too little help. Therefore your consciousness will now represent the phase of awakening, and that will last what it must" (*QS*, 51). Unable to make the leap to the formation of either class or, even more narrowly, *national* consciousness based on its own means of representation, James reverts at the last to the cultural traditions that so often serve to prop up the artist's bid for authority. "The Question of Our Speech" is James's version of Eliot's "Tradition and the Individual Talent," which more than any other essay by the moderns shaped our twentieth-century justifications of the modernist avant-garde.[64]

This much of James's endorsement of human language remains perfectly defensive, specific to the patriarchal and bourgeois ideology of his age. Yet insofar as his fiction focuses on those who find such traditional access to language, social or personal, to exclude precisely them in their own social particularity and in the real conditions of their labor, James contradicts his own conservative impulses. Recognizing that the work of socialization, especially for those judged "foreign" or "different," the work of child rearing, and the child's own work of acculturation have something in common with the more material work of the proletariat, he discovers the elementary terms for such an expansive class consciousness in our access to, and competency in, that elusive ideal of "conscious speech."

In this regard, James anticipates those post-Marxians who understand the powers of the ruling class to reside less in its control of the material world of wealth and capital than in the property of language and the powers of representation.[65] Insofar as his fiction attempts to work out the ethical terms by which we might judge and interpret the speech of others in the interests of a more democratic language, he was a critical theorist in the best sense. There is a hint of just this political dimension to James's theory of language in J. Hillis Miller's conclusions regarding the ways James's style calls attention to the necessity by which any speech act invokes the common laws of language—laws of interpretation and judgment that must be said always to exceed any particular text. For Miller, the "unreadability" of the text, literary or otherwise, must be understood in precisely its relation to the invocation of such a "law":

> The text in this specific sense is unreadable. It does not transmit its own law or make its own law legible in it. Its law cannot be read within it but remains in reserve. . . . The critic or reader is tempted to make this one text the ground of a universal legislation for all mankind as readers, though the text neither offers nor claims any authority for that move. The text is not the law nor even the utterance of the law but an example of the productive force of the law. We respect or ought to respect not the example but the law of which it is an example, the ethical law as such.[66]

The "law" to which Miller refers is the productive necessity of language, which works only insofar as it encompasses a more "goodly company," circulates without exhaustion or consumption, and thus remains ever historical. It is one of the ways in which Marx and Engels's promise of men and women experiencing their own "real, sensuous activity" as producers of their social worlds might be approached. And in the lie this law of linguistic performance gives to Cartesian rationalism, to "idealists" of all sorts, this speech offers a finer justice than Reason.

Some such law is what governs the utopian social order of a "classless society" dreamed in the Marxist imaginary, and it has affinities with James's own flawed respect for the social prospects of a language genuinely produced and cultivated by "the people." As James worked throughout his long career to respond to modern changes in class, gender, sexual, racial, and national identities, his democratic ideals became more inclusive, criticisms of the elitism of his later style notwithstanding. Insofar as we have formalized James's writings as literary experiments in language or dismissed those writings as unproblematic contributions to bourgeois ideology, we have dismally failed to understand what James meant by the redeemed society that an easier speech might bring. In the following chapters, I look at aspects of, and examples from, James's fiction that allow the reader to imagine an other Henry James, more attentive to questions of class, race, gender, and sexual preference relevant to the changing social order of his time. This other Henry

James is no longer the master of the modern novel, the willful inheritor of the great tradition of English and American letters, but often a baffled and conflicted man struggling with the complex realities of his age. For these very reasons, he is a more accessible, readable, and finally joyful Henry James than the cold, formally distant novelist of bourgeois manners so celebrated by literary critics of the 1940s and 1950s.

1 ঞ Swept Away: Henry James, Margaret Fuller, and "The Last of the Valerii"

> How did you ever dare write a portrait of a lady? Fancy any woman's attempting a portrait of a gentleman! Wouldn't there be a storm of ridicule! . . . For my own part, in my small writings, I never dare put down what men are thinking, but confine myself simply to what they do and say. For, long experience has taught me that whatever I suppose them to be thinking at any especial time, that is sure to be exactly what they are *not* thinking. What they *are* thinking, however, nobody but a ghost could know.
>
> —Constance Fenimore Woolson to
> Henry James, February 12, 1882

Having met Margaret Fuller in 1843, Henry James Sr. wrote to Emerson, who had introduced him to her: "The dear noble woman! I shall often think of her with joy—and with hope of fuller conferences and sympathies somewhere."[1] In the 1840s, the elder Henry James and Margaret Fuller shared interests in Swedenborg's social philosophy (rather than his mysticism) and women's rights, including rights to divorce. In view of the elder James's endorsement of Fourier's socialism, James's consistent attacks on private property, and the social imposition of institutional limits on the otherwise "infinite" self, his general philosophy agrees with Margaret Fuller's transcendentalism. Discussing Henry James Sr.'s defense of Fourier's "heterodox" views of marriage, Alfred Habegger concludes that the father's views "belonged to the radical wing of utopian socialism." Nevertheless, Habegger argues that these "radical views" by no means included endorsement of Fuller's feminism or of other nineteenth-century women's rights activists.[2]

Fuller's famous claim in *Woman in the Nineteenth Century* that "there is no wholly masculine man, no purely feminine woman" follows the logic of transcendentalist philosophy.[3] Yet her characteristic rejection of any essential sexual difference had obvious consequences for practical social reforms that transcendentalists such as Emerson and Henry James Sr. were not ready to accept. Emerson's 1855 lecture "Woman" supports women's rights to education, property, and the vote but concludes by urging women to seek more "spiritual" rights by "improving" and "refining" their *men:* "Woman should find in man her guardian."[4] His arguments are perfectly Hegelian, insofar as Hegel insisted on the maintenance of woman's domestic role and man's public role as mediator between family and state.

Like Emerson, the elder James was not a radical for women's rights, even though in the 1840s he advocated "a new and much less restrictive sexual order."[5] Nevertheless, alternatives to monogamy and popular acceptance of divorce did not necessarily mean for him an expansion of women's rights; the elder James's ideas about sexual liberation are bound up with nineteenth-century conventions about women's servitude to men: "Everything is calculated with certain male needs in mind, and women's own dissatisfactions and desires or liberties never once enter into the matter. Woman is man's angel, a totally different kind of being from himself."[6] Attacked both by women's rights activists and by conservatives, Henry James Sr. would gradually abandon his "radical" views of marriage and divorce, and the history of his changing and often contradictory positions expresses well the inherent contradictions in many male transcendentalists' thinking about the changing status of women in nineteenth-century American society.[7] By 1853, when the elder James published "Woman and 'The Woman's Movement,'" his position regarding women's rights had become so profoundly conservative that he "insisted with remarkable emphasis that women were intellectually inferior to men."[8] Fuller's application of transcendentalist ideas to women's rights thus had the consequence of exposing the liberal hypocrisy and intellectual confusion of these male transcendentalists; it is little wonder they felt such ambivalence about her as a person and intellectual.

The elder James, Emerson, and Hawthorne are Henry James Jr.'s most influential and complex fathers. Their ambivalence toward Margaret Fuller's radicalism is repeated by Henry James Jr. in his scattered references to Margaret Fuller from early writings such as "The Last of the Valerii" (1874) and *Hawthorne* (1879) to *William Wetmore Story and His Friends* (1903). But James's repetitions are compounded by the strategic repressions they serve. In the matter of the "Margaret-ghost," as James was to name his anxiety, the repressions would entangle Oedipal rebellion of the son against the father, as well as poetic rebellion of the modern against his romantic and very American precursors, with James's critical reaction to the women's rights movement.

In his review of James Elliot Cabot's *A Memoir of Ralph Waldo Emerson* (London, 1887) in *Macmillan's Magazine* in December 1887 (reprinted in *Partial Portraits*, 1888), James characterizes Emerson's general response to Fuller in the figure of Emerson retreating, "smiling and flattering, on tiptoe, as if he were advancing."[9] James quotes Emerson in his journals: "She ever seems to crave something which I have not, or have not for her," and James concludes that "only between the lines . . . we read that a part of her effect upon him was to bore him" (*American Essays*, 64). Boredom is hardly an emotion we might expect Margaret Fuller to have inspired; her contemporary reputation rested on her sharp intellect, her unabashed egotism, her political convictions, and her brilliant conversation. Yet James is relying on a judgment he had expressed earlier in *Hawthorne* that Margaret Fuller was finally, fatally superficial: "Her function, her reputation, were singular, and not altogether reassuring: she was a talker; she was *the* talker; she was the genius of talk. . . . She has left the same sort of reputation as a great actress. Some of her writing has extreme beauty, almost all of it has a real interest; but her value, her activity, her sway . . . were personal and practical."[10] James's judgment of Fuller's writings in this context is patronizing, although perhaps no more so than his judgment of Hawthorne's work. In another sense, however, Fuller is represented as Hawthorne's complete opposite. Public and gregarious, practical and personal, James's Fuller casts in shadow Hawthorne's privacy, introspective dreaminess, and hopeless detachment from the urgencies of politics and economics.

In the previous lines, James is describing the Fuller who would become Hawthorne's model for Zenobia in *The Blithedale Romance,* just before James quotes Hawthorne's account in *The American Notebooks* of his first meeting with Fuller in the woods on his return from Emerson's house: "It is safe to assume that Hawthorne could not, on the whole, have had a high relish for the very positive personality of this accomplished and argumentative woman, in whose intellect high noon seemed ever to reign, as twilight did in his own. He must have been struck with the glare of her understanding, and, mentally speaking, have scowled and blinked a good deal in conversation with her. . . . We may be sure that in women his taste was conservative" (*Hawthorne*, 78). For each of Henry James's transcendentalist fathers, Fuller is a provocation and a riddle, even as each makes his best defensive effort to acknowledge her wit. Knowing what we do of James's vigorous efforts throughout his life and career to replace these fathers with his own authority, we might expect him to find a kindred spirit in Margaret Fuller, who challenged his father's position on women's rights, "bored" Emerson, and caused Hawthorne to "scowl and blink a good deal."

The issue here is, of course, neither solely antiquarian nor merely psychopoetic but concerns the more pressing question of James's own position on women's rights. The divergent critical views on this subject can be summarized by way of the emphases various critics place on the following characters in James's fiction. On the one hand, we have Daisy Miller, Isabel Archer, Tina Aspern, Mme. de Vionnet, Milly Theale, and Maggie Verver. Each in her own way is committed to some overt or subtle rebellion that calls into question the patriarchal authority of bourgeois society. On the other hand, we have Henrietta Stackpole, Miss Birdseye, Olive Chancellor, Verena Tarrant, and other "progressives" mocked ruthlessly by James. Critics intent on defending James as a champion of women's rights stress the first group of characters and the ways they combat the subtler effects of sexism reproduced in the psychological warfare of interpersonal relations. In this view, James's modern novel of manners focuses on the more complex fiction of bourgeois patriarchy. Other critics use the second series of characters to deconstruct the first, insofar as James's contempt for overt feminists—ranging from career women such as Henrietta to political feminists such as Olive and Verena—suggests his own fears of the New Woman and his preference for the subtler, more manageable domestic rebellion of Isabel Archer and Maggie Verver and its complement, the grand renunciations of Claire de Cintré and Milly Theale.[11] James's "drawing-room" feminists are most often associated with artistic and imaginative powers missing from the second group of characters, who rant and lecture but rarely write or paint. Having acknowledged the interest of Margaret Fuller's writings, James might be expected to identify her with the first group of fictional characters. She wrote one of the politically most influential books of the 1840s, joined the cause of Italian independence, married Count Ossoli, a follower of Mazzini and the Republican cause, and died tragically in a shipwreck off Fire Island on her return to the United States with her *History* of the risorgimento in hand.

Yet James shows no sympathy for Margaret Fuller, who haunts his writings as a ghost of that faded, failed transcendentalism of his father, Emerson, and Hawthorne. Even more clearly than James's Hawthorne, James's Fuller represents just what he feared he himself might become: an adept at intellectual conversation, a cosmopolitan tourist, a naive social reformer and "progressive" (that word James often marked with quotation marks): more Henrietta and Olive than Isabel or Milly. James's judgment of Fuller's limitations as a writer and intellectual are virtual paraphrases of Emerson's remarks in his portion of *Memoirs of Margaret Fuller Ossoli,* which he edited with J. F. Clarke and William Ellery Channing in 1852. Praising the "ease with which she entered into conversation," Emerson also noted: "But in book or journal she found a very imperfect expression of herself, and it was the more vexatious, because she was accustomed to the clearest and the fullest."[12] These anxieties surface with a vengeance in James's most sustained treatment of Margaret Fuller in *William Wetmore Story and His Friends,* that curious biography James wrote for the money and at the urging of the Storys' children and published in 1903. The two-volume work is a curious tangle of the sculptor William Story's romantic Rome from the late 1840s to the Civil War and James's own impressionistic recollections of his youth there in 1869 and the winter of 1873. This is the Italy so indistinguishable for James in 1903 from the general ambience of Hawthorne's *The Marble Faun* (1860), the little artistic circle of the Storys, the Bootts, the painter Tilton, traces of the English romantics in Italy, and a cast of James's characters throughout his career— Daisy, Tina, Amerigo, Rowland Mallet, Christina Light, Prince Casamassima. Carl Maves calls it the "sensuous pessimism" of James's romantic, doomed Italy—his early modern equivalent for the romantics' infatuation with ancient ruins.[13]

The volume I am describing is much more than just the biography of William Story; it is James's personal history of artistic Italy, the demonic other of Robert Browning's Italy, the prelude to Pound's Italian tone in the Malatesta cantos and Eliot's "La figlia che piange." The book's imaginary frontispiece ought to be Guido Reni's *Beatrice Cenci,* that tourist attraction at the Palazzo Barberini, where the Storys lived. Beatrice Cenci haunted the writings of the Anglo-American romantics, and she returns in the strangest way in James's judgment of Margaret Fuller in the first volume of *William Wetmore Story and His Friends.*[14] James has just described the Storys and Fuller viewing the usual tourist sights: "They do the regular old pleasant things in the regular old confident ways; at the Rospigliosi Casino first, to see Guido's 'Aurora,' and then to the Barberini Palace, unconscious as yet of their long installation there, to guess the strange riddle that the Cenci asks over her shoulder."[15]

Shelley had answered the riddle of Beatrice Cenci in a manner that helped turn her into one of the favorite attractions of Victorian tourism and sexism. In Shelley's *The Cenci* (1819), Beatrice's complicity in the murder of her father, Francesco, represents the rebellion of all those oppressed by tyranny. Even so, it is Shelley's cautionary tale, in which he warns the reader against impetuous revenge, insisting in his preface: "Revenge, retaliation, atonement, are pernicious mistakes."[16] With his own youthful political radicalism and the "failure" of the French Revolution in mind, Shelley uses Beatrice Cenci to illustrate the tragic fate of those who abandon patience and forbearance even in the face of cruel tyranny. Insofar as *The Cenci* focuses the issue of tyranny in a father's rape of his daughter, Shelley's argument for "stoic, martyr-like forbearance" on the part of the abused accords well with meliorist responses to women's rights such as Emerson's and the elder James's.[17] For Shelley, Beatrice's innocence and beauty are defiled by both the tyranny of her father and her own desire for revenge. Even as her violation reinforces conventions of the chaste, innocent, childlike woman, so it also inspires her with the power and mystery of sexual transgression. Her rebellion thus enacts for Shelley a repetition of her father's tyranny.

It is just the sort of argument that would appeal to the subsequent Victorian sensibility that prized woman's patient endurance of oppression and often figured feminist rebellion in terms of perverse sexuality or unnaturalness. In the Victorian imagination, Beatrice Cenci typifies the ambivalent representations of woman that Nina Auerbach analyzes so well in *Woman and the Demon*. Writing of the mermaid, Auerbach notes her "broader spiritual resonance [with] her ancestor the serpent woman. Her hybrid nature, her ambiguous status as creature, typify the mysterious, broadly and evocatively demonic powers of womanhood in general."[18]

This "hybrid nature" applies quite well to what James will call a few lines later in *William Wetmore Story* the "Margaret-ghost." Guido Reni's portrait of Beatrice Cenci narratively gives birth to James's fullest impression of Margaret Fuller, whom he had met only in the whispers of his fathers: "We succeed to generations replete with Guido's tearful turbaned parricide, but are ourselves never honestly to taste of her more, inasmuch as, tearful and turbaned as she is, she is proved, perversely *not* a parricide, or at least not the one we were, in tourist's parlance, 'after' " (*Story*, 126–27). In the case of the "tearful turbaned parricide," James is probably thinking of the popularization of Beatrice Cenci as merely an abused innocent. Francesco Domenico Guerrazzi's popular romance *Beatrice Cenci* (1854) sentimentalized her history by transforming her rape by her father into merely the count's unrealized desire. The event that had been the obsessive focus of romantic treatments of the doomed Cenci family was sentimentalized into an unaccomplished, albeit still profoundly evil, incestuous lust.[19] In his *Italian Notebooks*, Hawthorne notes how contemporary copyists tend to sentimentalize the mysteriously ambivalent look of Guido's Beatrice:

> Its peculiar expression eludes a straightforward glance, and can only be caught by side glimpses, or when the eye falls upon it casually as it were, and without thinking to discover anything, as if the picture had a life and consciousness of its own, and were resolved not to betray its secret of grief or guilt, though it wears the full expression of it when it imagines itself unseen. . . . The picture never can be copied. Guido himself could not have done it over again. The copyists get all sorts of expression, gay as well as grievous; some copies have a coquettish air, a half-backward glance, thrown alluring at the spectator, but nobody ever did catch, or ever will the vanishing charm of that sorrow. I hated to leave the picture, and yet was glad when I had taken my last glimpse, because it so perplexed and troubled me not to be able to get hold of its secret.[20]

The Jamesian tourist is *after* the Beatrice Cenci who plotted with her lover to murder her evil father in his sleep to avenge the violation of her innocence, and it is on just this reflection that James turns to the most extended reflection on Margaret Fuller in his writings. Beatrice's parricide here must refer to the threat Fuller posed to James's own Boston fathers, unmanned by her refusal to accept their authority: "The unquestionably haunting Margaret-ghost, looking out from her quiet little upper chamber at her lamentable doom, would perhaps be never so much to be caught by us as on some occasion as this. What comes up is the wonderment of *why* she may, to any such degree, be felt as haunting" (*Story*, 127).

James's curious judgment of Margaret Fuller is full of references to Hawthorne, as if James were working to subsume this powerful predecessor. James's "Margaret-ghost" borrows directly from Hawthorne's imaginary portrait of Beatrice Cenci, leaving her cell in the Castello Sant' Angelo for execution: "How ghost-like she must have looked when she came forth! Guido never painted that beautiful picture from her blanched face, as it appeared after this confinement. And how rejoiced she must have been to die at last, having already been in a sepulchre so long!" (*Italian Notebooks*, 137). Placed as she is in that "little upper chamber," James's Fuller recalls quite explicitly the saintly copiest, Hilda, the "Dove in her turret-home," where she copies Guido's mysterious painting in Hawthorne's *Marble Faun*. Of that painting, Hawthorne writes: "It was a sorrow that removed this beautiful girl out of the sphere of humanity, and set her in a far-off region, the remoteness of which—while yet her face is so close before us—makes us shiver as at a spectre."[21] In fact, the entire section of *William Wetmore Story* from which I have been quoting parallels quite minutely Hawthorne's tourist impressions in *The Italian Notebooks*. What James casually terms the "regular old pleasant things" of Italian tourism—Rospigliosi Casino to see Guido's *Aurora*, Barberini Palace to see Reni's *Beatrice Cenci*—are just the activities Hawthorne describes in his entries for February 20, 1858. What so perplexes and troubles Hawthorne is his sense of innocence violated, of femininity "unhumanized":

> I looked close into its eyes, with a determination to see all that there was in them, and could see nothing that might not have been in any young girl's eyes; and yet, a moment afterwards, there was the expression—seen aside, and vanishing in a moment—of a being unhumanized by some terrible fate, and gazing at me out of a remote and inaccessible region, where she was frightened to be alone, but where no sympathy could reach her. (*French and Italian Notebooks,* 505)

Three times in his notebook entries Hawthorne stresses the unrepresentable quality of this painting: "No artist did it, nor could do it again" (89). Certainly, its magical effect has to do with that fact that "we bring all our knowledge of the Cenci tragedy to the interpretation of it" (90). Of course, Hawthorne and James must try their hands at representing such an unmasterable mystery, and it is just the mystery of ambivalent sexuality—a young girl's innocence "unhumanized" by some "terrible fate"—that haunts both of them. For Henry James more explicitly than for Hawthorne, however, this mystery is implicated in his portrait of Margaret Fuller and nineteenth-century women's rights.

James's Margaret-ghost repeats this Hawthornesque portrait of tragical inhumanity, but not for the sake of emphasizing the violence of rape or incest. Quite to the contrary, James represents Fuller as exemplifying the very superficiality for which he had sometimes reproached Hawthorne and more regularly criticized the parlor reformers of transcendentalist Boston.[22] James reproaches Hawthorne for having written little, and he extends that judgment to Fuller: "It matters only for the amusement of evocation—since she left nothing behind her, her written utterance being naught; but to what would she have corresponded, have 'rhymed,' under categories actually known to us? Would she, in other words, with her appetite for ideas and her genius for conversation, have struck us but as a somewhat formidable bore, one of the worst kind, a culture-seeker without a sense of proportion, or, on the contrary, have affected us as a really attaching, a possibly picturesque New England Corinne?" (*Story,* 128).

James indicates that the "we" of the quotation are "of our own luminous age," and that we moderns are to decide whether or not she is "a candidate . . . for the cosmopolite crown" (*Story,* 127). As James makes so clear in *Hawthorne,* this was the crown reserved for him alone, and so it is in these impressions: "Mme. Ossoli's circle represented, after all, a small stage, and . . . there were those on its edges to whom she was not pleasing. This was the case with Lowell and, discoverably, with Hawthorne; the legend of whose having had her in his eye for the figure of Zenobia, while writing 'The Blithedale Romance,' surely never held water" (129). Earlier in this volume, James quotes James Russell Lowell's letter to Story, in which Lowell mocks Margaret Fuller for her political commitments. Here James can align Hawthorne with Lowell, even going so far as to contradict himself by dismissing the theory that Fuller was the model for Hawthorne's Zenobia—a theory to which James had subscribed enthusiastically in *Hawthorne* a quarter of a century before. Here is poetic repression on a grand scale, ending with the ugly bathos of James's little joke that the "legend . . . surely never held water," recalling Zenobia's suicide and the drowning of Margaret, Count Ossoli, and their infant son off Fire Island in May 1850. Woman in the nineteenth century is turned once by Hawthorne, twice by James into Auerbach's "mermaid" by an ugly twist of the "facts": "In her Boston days, . . . she had been as a sparkling fountain to other thirsty young. In the Rome of many waters there were doubtless fountains that quenched, collectively, any individual gush" (128). Intellectually drowned in the cosmopolitan Italy that only James, the master modern, could navigate, Fuller is thus relegated to the perverse poetic justice of her historical end. The extended metaphor of "drowning" is a joke in the poorest taste, of course, and for all its sexism a telling expression of this Boston son's deepest anxieties about the progressive woman.

Hawthorne's allegorical transfiguration of woman has become James's repression of what Fuller represents to his fathers and to him: woman no longer as the topic of patriarchal art, the character in its fictions, but woman as author, as master. What Hawthorne judged the "unhuman" remoteness in the gaze of Guido's *Beatrice Cenci* belongs to Victorian conventions of violated feminine innocence. Just as Melville reflected on the hideousness of the polar bear's ferocity "invested in the fleece of celestial innocence and love" in "The Whiteness of the Whale" chapter of *Moby-Dick,* so Hawthorne dwells on the incompatibility of good and evil as the essence of what so perplexes him in this representation of Beatrice. As he looks at the feminine innocence of Guido's Beatrice, Hawthorne cannot forget what invests this daughter with sorrow: her father's violation of her. "I wish, however, it were possible for some spectator, of deep sensibility, to see the picture without knowing anything of its subject or history; for, no doubt, we bring all our knowledge of the Cenci tragedy to the interpretation of it," Hawthorne writes in his *Italian Notebooks* (90). For James, however, Beatrice represents woman secretly contaminated with masculine desire; she is perversely and monstrously full of her father's violence. In fact, the count's unnatural lust has given birth to what for James must seem the ultimate *monstrum horrendum:* a woman with a masculine will. It is just such "unnaturalness" that leads to what this tourist looks for: the crime of *parricide,* rather than the crimes of rape and incest.

This is the threat, I would argue, that surfaces only to be buried again in James's early story from his own Roman days of that winter of 1873, "The Last of the Valerii." Like the other stories from *A Passionate Pilgrim,* "The Last of the Valerii" (1874) is obviously derivative of Hawthorne, and this one in particular a variation of Prosper Merimée's "La Venus d'Ille."[23] These traditional influences aside, "The Last of the Valerii" is full of the "Margaret-ghost." Martha, the American heiress, has married the Italian count Camillo Valerio for love, if we are to believe her godfather, the narrator, whose profession is genre painting. Martha has also married the count for his lovely, overgrown, run-down, perfectly Italian villa and its antiquities. Her mother knows better than the godfather: "It's the Villa she's in love with, quite as much as the Count. She dreams of converting the Count; that's all very well. But she dreams of refurnishing the Villa!"[24] Fuller, together with her husband, Count Ossoli, and Mazzini's followers, dreamed of a more encompassing and enduring political conversion of Italy from divided principalities to a unified republic.

The "cause" in "The Last of the Valerii," however, is far more conventional and trivial; it is conversion to the domestic authority of the modern American woman, embodied in Martha as "blonde prettiness, so tender, so appealing, so bewitching" as to make her godfather unable to "believe that [Count Valerio] must, like a good Italian," also "have taken the exact measure of" her equally "pretty fortune" (*V,* 260). The desperate financial circumstances of Margaret Fuller, Count Ossoli, and their son in Rome in the winter of 1848 are part of Fuller's legend, stuff of the scandalous "Margaret-ghost," but financial need is merely the conventional touch of James's decadent Italian aristocracy in "The Last of the Valerii."

It is European history in its full antiquity that Martha loves, and it is fetishized in her godfather's description of her lover's very head "as massively round as that of the familiar bust of the Emperor Caracalla, and covered with the same dense sculptural crop of curls." "Bronzed," with eyes like "a pair of polished agates," Count Valerio is already "une morceau de musée" for Martha and her godfather, who makes his living as "an unscrupulous old painter of ruins and relics" and "plants" his "easel in one of the garden-walks" of the villa early in the narrative (*V,* 262). At Martha's "urgency," the count begrudgingly "had undertaken a series of systematic excavations" at the villa, on her assumption "that the much-trodden soil of the Villa was as full of buried treasures as a bride-cake of plums, and that it would be a pretty compliment to the ancient house . . . to devote a portion of her dowry to bring its mouldy honours to the light" (265).

All this work continues despite the count's protestations, "If you can't believe in them, don't disturb them. Peace be with them!" (*V,* 266). They unearth "a majestic marble image" of Juno: "Her beautiful head, bound with a single band, could have bent only to give the nod of command, her eyes looked straight before her; her mouth was implacably grave; one hand, outstretched, appeared to have held a kind of imperial wand; the arm from which the other had been broken hung at her side with the most queenly majesty" (267–68). A "Juno," but of "the great Greek period," "a Juno of Praxiteles at the very least," the narrator tells us, as the count will say with a frown at the very end, "A Greek" (268, 283). The sculpture is of the Greek Hera, then, not the Roman Juno, and thus the sister and wife of Zeus, and the goddess known to antedate Zeus and the more familiar Olympians in Attica.

Hera was the protectress of women and of marriage. Such primal mythic women are the proper subjects of Fuller's *Woman in the Nineteenth Century,* where she writes: "Certainly the Greeks knew more of real home intercourse and more of Woman than the Americans. . . . The poets, the sculptors, always tell the truth. In proportion as a nation is refined, women *must* have an ascendancy. It is the law of nature" (210). It is a reflection that causes Fuller to relate Beatrice Cenci to her noble Greek precursors: "Beatrice! thou wert not 'fond of life,' either, more than those princesses [Greek tragic heroines in Euripides and Sophocles]. . . . Thou wert not so happy as to die for thy country or thy brethren, but thou wert worthy of such an occasion" (210). Unlike Shelley or Hawthorne, Fuller equates Beatrice with a true revolutionary, capable of turning her revenge against her father into rebellion against a tyrannical state.

The Greek statue of Juno works mysteriously on Count Valerio, who promptly "steals" the broken fragment of her hand as a private fetish and then neglects poor American Martha for the "atavism" that seems excavated with this sculpture. The few critical accounts of "The Last of the Valerii" take its romantic allegory at face value; it is an early tale of "the international theme" and thus an unproblematic version of European evil purged by the innocence and trust of American womanhood. In these respects, the story is sometimes cited as anticipating the themes of *The American,* Newman's innocence played out in "The Last of the Valerii" by the pure and naive Martha. Having "shuddered" for her husband's infidelity with a statue, Martha resumes command and orders it reburied. Count Valerio has "learned" something—just what, the critics never tell us, and domestic tranquillity is restored, save for the hand he keeps hidden in a cabinet of antiquities, "suspended in one of its inner recesses," under lock and key (*V,* 283).

James himself had seen his own Juno on April 27, 1873, at the Villa Ludovisi: "The sculptures in the little Casino are few, but there are two great ones—the beautiful sitting Mars and the head of a great Juno, the latter thrust into a corner behind a shutter."[25] Like the exotic and thus *Orientalized* "turbaned head" of Guido Reni's *Beatrice Cenci,* this "head of the great Juno" has some affinity with the "beautiful head, bound with a single band" of the Juno in "The Last of the Valerii," and all these tenuous connections return us by various psychic detours to the "Margaret-ghost." Most of the critics of the story agree with its conclusion that Martha's reburial of the statue of Juno is the healthy thing to do, given the sickness of her atavistic husband. But

James's reflections on the "head of the great Juno . . . hidden behind a shutter" cast a different light on the conclusion to "The Last of the Valerii." James reminds us that the Villa Ludovisi is the residence of King Victor Emmanuel and his morganatic queen, Rosina: "I had an opportunity to reconstruct, from its *milieu* at least, the character of a morganatic queen. I saw nothing to indicate that it was not amiable; but I should have thought more highly of the lady's discrimination if she had had the Juno removed from behind her shutter" (*Italian Hours*, 296).

Symbol of a united Italy, of the risorgimento's long struggle against the Austrians, the Russians (in the Crimean War), and the Papal States, Victor Emmanuel II is represented obliquely by James through his morganatic queen and what presumably the new Italy would do with its ancient heritage: hide it behind a shutter. What is hidden here as well as in "The Last of the Valerii" is the mythic source of feminine power: Juno's original, the Greek goddess, Hera. James seems to answer in his 1873 Roman notebook and his 1874 story "The Last of the Valerii" the question he asks of the "Margaret-ghost" in *William Wetmore Story*. In "our luminous" modern age, the "progressive" new woman would not only castrate man but cut herself off from her own rich, sexually fertile, mythic heritage. Or so James, co-opting Fuller's mythic woman, would like us to believe.

My admittedly tenuous conclusion here gains a bit of solidity when Victor Emmanuel's morganatic wife, Rosina, is considered. Rosina Vercellana, countess of Mirafiori, was a drum major's daughter, but she wielded considerable political power through the king and was generally at odds with Cavour. What scandalized the Italian court was hardly that Rosina was the king's mistress—Victor Emmanuel had numerous affairs with ladies at court—but that she wielded significant political power.[26] James's brief reference to Rosina clearly follows the popular gossip that she was a vulgar and ambitious woman intent on using her personal influence for the sake of political gain. In this regard, James's American Martha is a more attractive alternative for the modern woman, respecting as she does both history and the hearth.

In his own visit to the Villa Ludovisi, in March 1858, Hawthorne also commented on "a colossal head of Juno [that] is considered the greatest treasure of the collection, but I did not myself feel it to be so, nor indeed did I receive any strong impression of its excellence. I admired nothing so much, I think, as the face of Penelope (if it be her face) in the group supposed also to represent Electra and Orestes" (*French and Italian Notebooks*, 142). In keeping with the gendered rhetoric of his age, Hawthorne prefers a figure representing feminine patience and forbearance over the more imperious head of the goddess. What strikes Hawthorne especially, however, serves to conclude his entries for the day: "One of the most striking objects in the first casino was a group by Bernini,—Pluto, an outrageously masculine and strenuous figure, heavily bearded, ravishing away a little, tender Proserpine, whom he holds aloft, while his forcible gripe impresses itself into her soft virgin flesh. It is very disagreeable, but it makes one feel that Bernini was a man of great ability" (143). Close as James's visit matches Hawthorne's twenty-five years earlier, even down to their shared judgment that Guercino's *Aurora* is a "muddy masterpiece," James makes no mention of this group by Bernini. What Hawthorne uncovers in this moment is perhaps too explicit an image of the masculine will to power threatened by Hawthorne's Juno, James's Hera, and domesticated by their Penelopes and Marthas. Bernini's *Abduction of Proserpine* is the uncanny moment in which Hawthorne's "so puzzled and perplexed" gaze on Guido's *Beatrice Cenci* may be understood as Hawthorne's own terrified fascination with the masculine power that is the secret source of that "unhuman" element in Beatrice's gaze.

What James does not record in his Roman notebook of 1873, however, is recorded in "The Last of the Valerii." Rumors of the unearthed Juno having spread beyond the villa, "a German in blue spectacles, with a portfolio under his arm," visits the villa to inform the count: "Your new Juno, Signor Conte, . . . is, in my opinion, much more likely to be certain Proserpine." The count rejects the German's specious expertise, insisting, "I've neither a Juno nor a Proserpine to discuss with you. . . . You're misinformed" (*V,* 270). Quite clearly, Count Valerio has no interest in modern science, as well as no need to be told what his sculpture represents. "She" is simply the sexual power of myth and history from which the impoverished count has hitherto been alienated.

Like so many of James's tales from the 1860s and 1870s, "The Last of the Valerii" is full of images of an anxious, hardly sublimated sexuality. "Yes, by Bacchus, I am superstitious," the count protests of the original excavation. The workers are rewarded with wine when the Juno is discovered, then when it is reburied. The narrator and his goddaughter first sense that the count is cracking up when they watch him pour "a libation" at the foot of the statue (*V,* 269). They know he is nearly lost to them when they find traces of blood on a rough block, with "illegible Greek characters," improvised by the count as a kind of altar before the Juno. James's fantasy of atavistic revival reflects his own troubled fascination with castration. The fetish of the sculpture's hand is all that the hapless count is left once he has sold his birthright for Martha's fortune.

James's nearly comic account of Valerio's love affair with a Greek sculpture is a pastiche of the many stories derived from Ovid's Pygmalion in the *Metamorphoses,* who falls in love with his sculpture of Aphrodite. Indeed, the most celebrated modern version before George Bernard Shaw's *Pygmalion* (1913) was W. S. Gilbert's comedy *Pygmalion and Galatea,* which appeared in 1871, only three years before "The Last of the Valerii." James varies the themes of the classical legend by his curious transference of the rhetoric of feminine sexuality and maternity from Martha to Valerio. The story is, after all, an account of the *last* of the Valerii line, who retains merely nominal title to his history once he has married an American heiress. In this regard, the story is rather conventionally Jamesian, but the excavation of the long-buried statue, the libation of wine, the blood on the altar, and the hand secreted by the count all suggest some fantasy of his own process of giving birth to his family's forgotten past. Juno's "imperial wand," her commanding look, and "implacably grave" mouth suggest phallic power and masculine legal authority. It is, according to this fantasy, Juno who penetrates Valerio, spilling his virginal blood on the altar. Such rhetorical cross-dressing is by no means unusual in James and has obvious relevance for James's ambivalence about his own sexuality. At this early stage in James's literary career, the reversal of gender roles is threatening, and James works out the denouement not only to achieve a satisfactory fictional ending but also to allay his own anxieties regarding the improprieties his imagination has dug up. The violation of Valerio by his Juno also suggests a more general masculine fear of nineteenth-century women's bids for economic, legal, and political powers. What allows James to defend himself against what is a homoerotic fantasy of transvestism and sodomy is his caricature of Juno's power as merely a version of the New Woman. Valerio is virtually held "in thrall" by his private devotions to this Medusan lover, in keeping with the Victorian rhetoric of the independent woman's demonic powers.

Having uncovered such a threat to masculine authority, James reasserts the more attractive alternative of the domestic wife. Martha may unwittingly initiate this psychodrama by offering to use her fortune to improve the villa, but at the end, she returns to the drawing room, choosing to exercise a more disguised power over her husband in the familiar interpersonal dynamics of the Jamesian novel of manners. In her final appearance, after she has ordered the Juno reburied, Martha "wandered into the drawing-room and pretended to occupy herself with a bit of embroidery," as Catherine Sloper will do at the end of *Washington Square* (1881). As if to make sure we catch the classical references to Homer's Penelope and the Greek Parcae, James clumsily describes "the Count lifting the tapestried curtain which masked the door and looking silently at his wife" (*V*, 283). Unmanned, he surrenders to her: "The Countess kept her eyes fixed on her work, and drew her silken threads like an image of domestic tranquillity. The image seemed to fascinate him." Caught in the modern spell she has woven, the count anticipates Prince Amerigo's surrender thirty years later in *The Golden Bowl:* "At last she raised her eyes and sustained the gaze in which all his returning faith seemed concentrated. He hesitated a moment, as if her very forgiveness kept the gulf open between them, and then he strode forward, fell on his two knees, and buried his head in her lap" (*V*, 283).

"He never became, if you will, a thoroughly modern man," the narrator begins the concluding paragraph, in which we discover the count has kept his fetish of the Juno's hand, "suspended in" "his cabinet." Whatever sexual passion, Dionysian revel, or imaginative ecstasy of which he and his mythic past might have been capable has been reduced to this "marble hand," a mere phallic memento.[27] Yet in Count Valerio's symbolic castration, James has saved himself, even as he has controlled the "Margaret-ghost." James's "Margaret-ghost" appears best in the law-giving, angular, beautiful figure of Juno—both her head at the Villa Ludovisi and her nearly restored form in "The Last of the Valerii." In this way, James emulates the Attic authority that Fuller's Greek women possessed (somewhat romantically, no doubt) in myth, sculpture, and classical tragedy.

The Juno is just missing a hand, a trivial detail perhaps for this potent authority of woman buried in the Roman countryside for millennia. Yet a deformed hand is the singular feature of James's most terrifying ghost in a later story of psychopoetic defense, "The Jolly Corner." What Juno misses, Count Valerio fetishizes, and the "Margaret-ghost" used too little, it would seem, on the evidence of what James tells us she has left behind. All these failures and lacks, James claims to supplement with his own hand. Even so, the ghostly double for James's literary hand remains that of Spencer Brydon's ghost in "The Jolly Corner," one of whose "hands had lost two fingers, which were reduced to stumps, as if accidentally shot away."[28] The complex weave of references I have traced in James's hand, not all of which I wish to argue belong to James's consciousness, is James's "tapestried curtain," which he would contend far exceeds the "image of domestic tranquillity" woven by this much reduced modern woman, Martha.

The sexual power that so fascinated Hawthorne in Guido's *Beatrice Cenci* and Bernini's *Abduction of Proserpine* threatens James in the form of the political New Woman, intent on framing a new mythology beyond that of patriarchal domination. Such mythopoeia is not simply domesticated in the conventional "American girl," Martha, but sublimated in James's own narrative appropriation of sexual power. In "The Last of the Valerii," there is no question of choosing between Juno or Martha; the former is an elusive anachronism, a mere token of a lost matriarchy, and the latter is simply a well-intentioned, but sexless, modern wife. The revival of this Juno in the political aims of Margaret Fuller and the New Woman is by no means sublimated in Martha; James makes certain we understand how little she counts. At this early stage of his career, James anticipates those high moderns who figured their own literary powers in sexual metaphors, often claiming as T. S. Eliot would for poetry a certain hermaphroditic productivity. Beyond the hopeless grapple of the typist and young man carbuncular in *The Waste Land*, there is often the promise of the literary transumption of sexuality rather desperately offered by anxious masculine moderns from James to Eliot. If we are to comprehend James's relation to contemporary debates regarding women's rights and his relevance in the current feminist revisions of the literary canon, then we will have to take into account the complex entanglement of his own conception of his modernity and his characterizations of women—both fictional and real. Neither strictly intrinsic nor extrinsic accounts of James's attitudes toward women's rights are satisfactory. All James's ambivalences about sex, the past, woman, and his fathers are captured in "The Last of the Valerii" in a poetic bid for mastery that could be claimed only by trivializing the ghostly women of his fiction: figures liberated in his literature only to bury his own profoundest anxieties.

Nonetheless, James is unable to control the destabilization of gender boundaries and confusion of sexual powers that "The Last of the Valerii" dramatizes. Throughout the rest of his career, James would return to many of the same problems of sexual transgression mapped out in this early story. James's primary intention in the story is to write a "heterosexual containment narrative" that will address the threatening sexuality associated with women, such as Margaret Fuller, who insisted on greater civil and legal rights. Yet in the course of writing such a conservative story, James has undermined his own purpose by riveting the attention of the count and the reader on the mythic sexuality of Juno, with its phallic suggestion of homoerotic power, and trivializing the American "Martha," whom we associate only with a safe, but confining, domesticity. Throughout his career, James will repeatedly return to similar themes in which an otherwise threatening feminine figure becomes the object of desire precisely because she does threaten customary gender and sexual boundaries, offering thereby some promised emancipation from a social order James is often at such pains to criticize.

Thus Miriam Rooth in *The Tragic Muse* threatens the tidy gender divisions of British society, only to reveal how secretly perverse those gender roles already are. The dramatic situation of "The Last of the Valerii" also antici-pates James's little murder mystery of 1896, *The Other House,* by creating a "goddess" whose power is perverted in the later work into the murderous will of Rose Armiger, herself described at one point as "the priestess of a threat-ened altar."[29] As Priscilla Walton has argued, *The Other House* "works to sensationalize the threatening nature of a sexually assertive and lesbianized woman" in the character of Rose Armiger, but the novel ends up "covertly critiquing the heterosexuality it overtly works to affirm."[30] In *The Other House,* the reader can hardly be expected to choose Rose Armiger, the mur-derer of four-year-old Effie Bream, over the maternal and obedient Jean Martle, even if Rose is intended to seize our interest. But in "The Last of the Valerii," Juno's power is clearly pitted against the quiet but nonetheless com-manding manner of Martha, whose wealth supports her authority over the count. For these reasons, the reader is supposed to be far more attracted to the count's stony and long-buried Juno, whose violence is sacrificial, rather than merely murderous, than to her thoroughly modern counterpart, Martha. In the case of both texts, however, James seems the most interested in, perhaps even obsessed with, the very sexual transgressions of conventional nine-teenth-century gender boundaries that had so frightened his New England fathers. Repeating as he does their trivialization of their contemporary Mar-garet Fuller, James nonetheless creates the literary contexts in which he will increasingly identify with such feminine power, both in its association with the women's rights movement and its more spectral suggestions of lesbian and homosexual alternatives to heterosexual culture.

2 ᧥ A Phantom of the Opera: Christopher Newman's Unconscious in *The American*

> Everything was over, and he too at last could rest. . . . The most unpleasant thing that had ever happened to him had reached its formal conclusion, as it were; he could close the book and put it away. He leaned his head for a long time on the chair in front of him; when he took it up he felt that he was himself again. Somewhere in his mind, a tight knot seemed to have loosened. He thought of the Bellegardes; he had almost forgotten them.
>
> —Henry James, *The American* (1877)

My epigraph comes from the penultimate scene in the novel, just before Newman meets Mrs. Tristram for their final interview. In that closing scene, Newman burns the note given to him by Mrs. Bread and purported to have been written by the dying marquis, in which he incriminates his wife for his murder. As the note burns, Mrs. Tristram thinks aloud about what Newman has told her of his abortive revenge against the Bellegardes and their cool defiance of him: "My impression would be that since, as you say, they defied you, it was because they believed that, after all, you would never really come to the point. Their confidence . . . was not in their innocence, nor in their talent for bluffing things off; it was in your remarkable good nature! You see they were right."[1]

Newman's "remarkable good nature" is directly proportionate to his ability to repress "the most unpleasant" things, and the strange relation between his moral self-righteousness and his repression has much to do with the romantic melodrama that organizes the last half of *The American*. For some critics, it is easy to account for these matters; Newman is an incorrigibly good fellow who "forgives and forgets." In their view, his refusal to avenge himself either on his business associate in New York or on the Bellegardes in Paris is the perfect measure of his moral tone. I have a more perverse view. Somehow, every time

Newman does the "right thing," the world becomes strange and unfamiliar to him. Every time he follows his conscience, he has to get out of town.

Newman's boundless "good nature," then, is connected for me with strangeness and repression, the two most important elements in the literary and psychological fantastic. *The American* is generally treated as a formally divided work, which begins realistically enough and ends in a flurry of events drawn from the popular romance and supernatural thriller: a duel (Valentin and Kapp), a gloomy chateau (the Bellegardes' country estate, Fleurières), arranged marriages (Claire's marriage to M. de Cintré; her engagement to Newman), murder in the family, secret messages, a double agent (Mrs. Bread), and the like. Critics are fond of lining the realistic features up on the side of Newman, America, and our notoriously practical character; the melodrama and intrigue get associated with the snobbish and protective Bellegardes, the Old World, aristocratic decadence, and the deviousness of polite society. But like most of the other apparently clear oppositions between good and evil in *The American,* this crucial distinction between America and Europe does not hold up under close examination.

Newman's past is as murky and curious as the Bellegardes'. We know nothing of his parents, the place of his birth, the real source or extent of his fortune, or much else about his experience in America. He admits to telling "tall tales," having learned the style from cowboys out west. He can be as patronizing to Valentin, Tom Tristram, the Nioches, and the young marquise (Urbain's wife) as the Bellegardes are toward him. Newman is appalled that Claire's mother and older brother might use their authority to convince Claire to break off her engagement with him, and he generally relates the Bellegardes' aristocratic pretensions to their lust for power and control. Variously, however, he promises to take Claire, Valentin, and Mrs. Bread to America with him (not one of them will ever go), and he promises to remake the fortune of the Nioches. Newman is as explicitly willful and manipulative as Jay Gatsby, and yet he never seems to recognize in himself any of the negative traits that he shares with the more explicitly decadent (Valentin), hypocritical (the Nioches), or tyrannical (the Bellegardes, *mère et frère*) characters. This is passing strange in a novel by Henry James, who traditionally has been considered the modern master of the bildungsroman. As the epigraph suggests, Newman seems merely to *forget* his strange experiences in France, rather than to learn anything whatsoever from them. Indeed, it appears that his very character depends on such forgetting, perhaps in keeping with nineteenth-century stereotypes of the American as he who can happily escape the nightmare of history. Of course, Henry James goes to great lengths in his writings to remind us that such historical innocence is by no means an advantage, but instead the mark of an American fatality from which he is usually at some pains to save us.

How James does that in his fiction is to show us how profoundly Americans are involved in history and how little we are justified in claiming the "uniqueness"—today we term this "American exceptionalism"—that comes of forgetting the past. Elsewhere I have argued how deeply ignorant Newman is of the European political history that is so crucial to the Bellegardes' existence as a family.[2] History also plays itself out in personal relations, and James makes sure the reader does not miss how profoundly Christopher Newman repeats the very failings of those European characters of whom he is the most expressly critical. This pattern of doubling and repression is extremely interesting and so pervasive in the novel as to prevent any complete catalog here. It is not just that Newman criticizes the characters who serve as partial alter egos; he generally recoils in horror from such characters. He refuses to have anything to do with Valentin's duel, but Newman repeatedly refers to his contest with the Bellegardes in dueling terms: "Once in the street, he stood for some time on the pavement, wondering whether, after all, he was not an ass not to have discharged his pistol" (*American*, 292). When he learns that old M. Nioche has resigned himself to his daughter's ambitious immorality, Newman will have nothing more to do with him. But Newman himself finally accepts the "immoral" wrong the Bellegardes have done to him. Old Nioche, feigning bravado, tells Newman that someday he will punish his daughter: "You will see it someday in the papers" (300). Newman is amused, but he has made virtually the same idle threat to Urbain regarding his evidence: "I'm thinking of beginning with the duchess. . . . I thought . . . I shouldn't have much to say to her, but my little document will give us something to talk about" (284). And, of course, Benjamin Babcock, Newman's self-righteous traveling companion, reproaches Newman for just about the same moral laxity that Newman finds in Noémie: "You seem to hold that if a thing amuses you for the moment, that is all you need ask for it; and your relish for mere amusement is also much higher than mine" (72).

Newman's failure to recognize himself in others and his incapacity to comprehend criticism such as Babcock's are certainly measures of his "innocence." Newman's psychological and political ignorance are bound up together in *The American,* and they account for the fantastic world he enters after Claire has rejected him. The structure of James's transition from realism to melodrama is worth sketching at this stage. Although the actual change in dramatic mood in the novel occurs gradually, the most noticeable shift occurs in chapter 17, at the Paris Opera. Listening to Mozart's *Don Giovanni* for the first time, Newman runs into a cross section of the cast in the novel: Madame de Bellegarde, Urbain, his young wife, Noémie, Valentin, Stanislas Kapp (for the first and only time). It is at the opera—and such an opera!—that events turn genuinely strange for Newman. Noémie is with another man, thus betraying Newman's incorrect judgment of her goodness. Valentin and Kapp trade insults and plan a duel over this coquette. In short, the strangeness is introduced by the way in which the Nioche subplot (farcical to this point) and the main plot cross each other. The farcical Noémie will become the means of destroying Valentin. This crossing of plots is hardly incidental when we consider that it also involves a very explicit crossing of class boundaries. The confrontation between the aristocratic Valentin and the bourgeois Kapp is an exaggerated double of the main plot: the contest of wills between the aristocratic Bellegardes and the American capitalist, Newman.

James employs Mozart's opera to make this dramatic moment of transgression—of classes, cultures, ages, and personalities—even more explicit. *Don Giovanni* is an opera that swings rather wildly from opera buffa (the *dramma giocoso* of its title) to the tragic.[3] In its own divided dramatic action, then, the opera reflects nicely for James the contrary moods and tones of the different actions in *The American.* In the specific context of chapter 17, *Don Giovanni* appears primarily to function as a means of bringing diverse characters together and secondarily to further the comedy of Newman's clumsy efforts to appear cultivated. Discussing the opera with the marquis between the first and second acts, Newman sounds much like Quixote at Master Peter's puppet show:

> "What do you think of the opera?" asked our hero. "What do you think of the Don?"
>
> "We all know what Mozart is," said the marquis; "our impressions don't date from this evening. Mozart is youth, freshness, brilliancy, facility—a little too great facility perhaps. But the execution is here and there deplorably rough."
>
> "I am very curious to see how it ends," said Newman.

"You speak as if it were a *feuilleton* in the *Figaro*," observed the marquis. "You have surely seen the opera before?"

"Never," said Newman. "I am sure I should have remembered it. Donna Elvira reminds me of Madame de Cintré; I don't mean in her circumstances, but in the music she sings." (*American*, 200)

By contrasting the marquis's sophisticated concern for the performance with Newman's naive interest in the plot, James seems merely to reaffirm the conventional distinction between old-world experience and new-world innocence. Having just moments before listened to Donna Elvira, Donna Anna, and her fiancé, Don Ottavio, accuse Don Giovanni of having murdered Donna Anna's father (Don Pedro, the commendatore), Newman is either hopelessly ignorant or baldly insulting the marquis by comparing his sister and Newman's fiancée, Claire, with Donna Elvira, the woman of Burgos seduced and then spurned by Don Giovanni. Here, as elsewhere, the reader is encouraged to admire the marquis, stiff as he is, for his savoir faire in laughing away the unintended insults of his American guest: " 'It is a very nice distinction,' laughed the marquis lightly. 'There is no great possibility, I imagine, of Madame de Cintré being forsaken' " (*American*, 200). The "nice distinction" to which the marquis refers is Newman's—"I don't mean in her circumstances, but in the music she sings," and "nice" must here be taken to mean "very fine," when one considers how difficult it is to distinguish an operatic character's "circumstances" from her "music."

The opera is, however, considerably more significant as an ironic double for the dramatic action in the novel, especially at this crucial moment when realism begins to drift into romance. Having suffered Newman to compare Claire to the forsaken Donna Elvira, the Bellegardes playfully cast themselves in the roles they imagine might suit Newman's opinions of them. The young marquise says: "I suppose Zerlina reminds you of me." And the marquis concludes the discussion by saying: "I will go to the *foyer* for a few moments . . . and give you a chance to say that the Commander—the man of stone—resembles me" (*American*, 200–201). Comparing herself to the peasant girl, Zerlina, whom Don Giovanni unsuccessfully attempts to seduce and whose piercing scream brings the other characters to her rescue at the end of act I, the young Madame de Bellegarde mocks Newman's ignorance of the opera even as she suggests how patronizing Newman's comparison of her sister-in-law, Claire, to a character in an opera is. She also reminds Newman that she possesses some of the spirit and fidelity that allow Zerlina to resist Don Giovanni in the opera and may well allow her to resist the seductive allure of Newman's fortune. By comparing himself to the commander, Donna Anna's murdered father, the marquis acknowledges both the stiff formality others see in him as well as the responsibility of his position as the legal head of a noble family. Don Pedro insists on dueling with Don Giovanni at the beginning of the opera to defend the honor of his daughter and of his family. Reluctant to fight an old man, making light of his seduction of the daughter, Don Giovanni nevertheless kills the father in specious self-defense. Yet it is to "the man of stone" that the marquis compares himself, not the living Don Pedro, referring Newman to the subsequent action in act II, when the statue of the commander, Don Pedro, comes to life for Don Giovanni in the cemetery. It is this supernatural "father" who returns not only to haunt Don Giovanni but eventually to open the gates of hell for him.

On the barest surface level, *Don Giovanni* hardly fits the dramatic action of *The American,* especially as the Bellegardes sarcastically have assumed roles for the sake of reproaching Newman for his faux pas in comparing Claire with Donna Elvira. All their comparisons cast Newman in the role of Don Giovanni, an implication that he himself has unwittingly made at the very start of this witty but treacherous game. Christopher Newman as Don Juan is an analogy that certainly runs counter to the conventional critical accounts of Newman as the innocent and good-natured American abroad.

On closer examination, however, the opera doubles the action of the novel in a very curious manner. The dramatic event that motivates the subsequent actions in the opera is the duel between Don Giovanni and the commander, Don Pedro. On this very evening, under the influence of an opera with which he is intimately familiar, Valentin arranges a duel with Stanislas Kapp. Like Don Pedro, Valentin will fight to defend not only his personal honor but the class and family he represents. Valentin's only other accomplishment was similarly quixotic, but nonetheless based solidly on his sense of historical attachment to his family and its traditions. Fighting with the Zouaves, who defended the pope against Republican troops in Italy, Valentin was wounded in the battle of Castelfidardo and imprisoned for three years in the Castel' Saint Angelo in Rome (*American,* 93).[4] Valentin arranges the duel at the same time that Newman is offering to help Valentin make his fortune: "Come over to America with us, and I will put you in the way of doing some business. You have got a very good head if you will only use it" (199). Indeed, the seriousness with which Valentin treats both Noémie's coquetry and Kapp's insult is considerably more understandable when we read both as confusedly related by him to Newman's humiliating offer. Throughout the novel, Newman endlessly reminds Valentin of his uselessness and frivolity, virtually repeating Urbain's criticism of his brother. At least in one sense, Valentin arranges the duel with Kapp to satisfy his own sense that he is still a man, which is to say, still capable of representing his family's aristocratic honor. The real challenge to his manhood and honor, however, comes not from Kapp's jealous taunts but from Newman's condescension to help put him "in the way of doing some business" in America. Such an interpretation seems supported by the fact that Newman is clearly helping the Nioches financially while Valentin courts Noémie. Valentin's rebellious and deliberately reckless courtship of Noémie is intended to shock his family and declare thereby his independence. At the very moment he most desires to affirm his independence, however, he finds himself dependent on the patronage of a rich American, either in Newman's offers to Valentin himself or in his support of the Nioches.

This interpretation is in no way contradicted by the fact that Valentin initially accepts Newman's offer of help: "I make myself over to you. Dip me into the pot and turn me into gold" (*American,* 205). Like Donna Anna or Donna Elvira in the opera, Valentin has been seduced and risks becoming just another bauble on his seducer's chain. It is absurd to imagine Newman as Don Giovanni only if we think of the analogy in purely sexual terms. Babcock has already suggested in his letter that there is something licentious about Newman: "You put, moreover, a kind of reckless confidence into your pleasure which at times, I confess, has seemed to me—shall I say it?—almost cynical" (72). The description very aptly fits Don Giovanni in Mozart's opera, giving even more credibility to the Bellegardes' sardonic comparison of Newman with the operatic character.

What Babcock judges to be Newman's lack of seriousness and what Newman concludes is a judgment of his own "immorality" is a consequence of Newman's economic, rather than sexual, licence. The Bellegardes are less offended, I suspect, by his comparison of Claire with Donna Elvira (this bespeaks, after all, merely his lack of cultivation) than by the reminder that he is, after all, the best modern substitute for the seventeenth-century Don Juan. Whereas the mythic Don Juan represents a certain aristocratic decadence and abuse of power, Newman represents capitalist decadence, which is considerably more difficult to identify and combat. Valentin can fight Stanislas Kapp because the affront to his honor is direct and conventional. Yet Newman profoundly insults Valentin's honor and entire way of life at the very moment that he offers with genuine concern and interest to *help* Valentin. This may explain Valentin's refusal of Newman's offer to arrange the duel itself: " 'I will take charge of it,' Newman declared. 'Put it into my hands' " (*American*, 207). Even while attempting to do whatever a friend ought to do in such circumstances, Newman ends up reaffirming the very authority over Valentin that may well have helped fuel Valentin's rage against Kapp. Indeed, Kapp, the son of a Strasbourg brewer, is decidedly not an aristocrat; he represents the very class of capitalists to which Newman belongs.

Had Newman followed the plot of *Don Giovanni* with the personal involvement occasioned by the witty reproaches of the Bellegardes, he might have recognized in his own soul some trace of Don Juan's immorality. It is this oblique but nonetheless significant relation between art and life that Babcock tries to make Newman heed: "Art and life seem to me intensely serious things, and in our travels in Europe we should especially remember the immense seriousness of Art" (*American*, 73). Babcock's letter ends with a repetition of this very advice: "*Do* remember that Life and Art *are* extremely serious," as if Babcock anticipates that the lesson will be lost on Newman. Great art reflects the personality of the viewer, which is quite decidedly why Newman has so little appreciation of, or taste for, the fine arts. At the end of Mozart's *Don Giovanni,* Donna Elvira resolves to finish her days in a convent, anticipating Claire's fate at the end of *The American.* In a certain sense, then, Newman has blundered into the right interpretation of *Don Giovanni* as far as Donna Elvira and Claire are concerned, but Newman betrays no recognition at all of his modern affinities with his operatic double, Don Juan. The relation of life and art is, after all, one governed by psychological doubling, whether such doubling occurs as a consequence of reading ourselves in art or, as in this chapter in *The American,* by way of the wry manipulation of the artist, Henry James.

What follows this night at the opera is Claire's unexpected breaking of the engagement and her rapid departure from Paris. Newman intends to follow her immediately to Fleurières, but he is delayed by the urgent message requiring him to attend the dying Valentin. At this point, the two parts of the main plot—Valentin's friendship with Newman and Newman's engagement to Claire—double each other. The duel between Valentin and Kapp keeps Newman from engaging the Bellegardes in his own romantic duel, but the figurative relationship between the two unexpected events is clearly established by James. At Valentin's bedside, the doctor is reading a copy of Laclos's *Liaisons dangereuses,* which crosses political and amorous dueling in about the same way James has done. And in the gloomy inn where Valentin is dying, Newman receives his first significant "secret" communication: Valentin's deathbed testament that there is a skeleton in the Bellegarde closet. This links the duel between Valentin and Kapp, by way of Valentin's deathbed revelation, with the deathbed scene of the old marquis, who similarly issues an ambiguous but provocative message.

Suffice it to say that the melodramatic portions of *The American* seem structured primarily by such doublings, which widen like ripples in a pool to take in everyone in the narrative. By the end of the dramatic action, the reader is only faintly surprised when Newman stumbles on Noémie and Lord Deepmere (seventh cousin to the Bellegardes) strolling amorously together in Kensington Gardens, London, where Newman has fled yet again, as he did in departing America in the first place, to avoid misfortune and defer revenge. "Dear me! . . . Are you here, too?" Newman exclaims when he stumbles on old M. Nioche sitting on the bench next to him following his chance meeting with Noémie and Lord Deepmere.

Such coincidences belong properly to comic opera, not to the vicissitudes of life, unless such coincidences are understood as the effects of psychological phenomena. The doubling that multiplies so dramatically in these portions of *The American* is the psychological cause for Newman's experience of the fantastic. By the same token, such doubling is James's way of forcing the reader to recognize how much the fictional landscape functions as a psychic mise-en-scène for Newman. These doubles are the "real things," after all— what Newman has missed all along because of his stubborn refusal to take any event at any more than its face value (which is to say as an impression without psychic depth). Mozart's opera—indeed, any artistic performance or visual artifact—makes explicit the doubled character of ordinary experience. At once highly stylized and actually experienced in its performance, the opera reminds the viewer that the reality of experience depends on the relation between direct impression and the significance informing such an impression. That such significance necessarily involves our own psychological circumstances is a familiar lesson in James's dramas. Technically, this doubling causes the close bond between the reader and Newman's relative point of view (the narration follows the laws of *erlebte Rede* or *style indirect discours*) to split apart, so that the experience of reading becomes increasingly schizophrenic. Whereas our previous perceptions had followed Newman's lead, our reading experience is now constantly at odds with Newman's impressions. While we see nothing but reflections of Newman, Newman sees nothing but unaccountable events, strange coincidences, unexpected revelations. Whereas the reader is encouraged to read the psychological significance of the allegorization of *Don Giovanni* in terms of the novel's dramatic action—from Claire's repetition of Donna Elvira's fate to Valentin's reenactment of the operatic duel—Newman sees nothing but a night's entertainment.

This narrative schizophrenia in its purely technical dimension would be enough to account for how the melodrama of *The American* serves James's generally realistic aims. But there is considerably more significance to be read in all of these "coincidences" of romance than may be addressed by merely technical analyses. First of all, James suggests that these doublings are perfectly motivated by the psychic narrative that has unfolded. It is not the doubling in and of itself that is uncanny. Mozart's *Don Giovanni* does not cause the uncanny relation between Newman and Don Juan; Newman himself establishes that relation, only to deny its full significance for his own personality. By means of such repression, by way of his studied refusal to recognize himself in others, Newman renders the world around him uncanny.

The strangeness is a consequence of Newman's refusal to recognize such doublings—that is, Newman *estranges* by means of repression just those connections with others that he himself has already motivated. He is in part responsible for the Nioches' presence in Kensington Gardens, insofar as he has introduced Noémie to Valentin, who has in turn introduced Noémie to Lord Deepmere. Add to this, of course, that Noémie's coquetry, albeit there in embryo when Newman meets her, takes flight once Newman has offered the Nioches some hope of escaping their poverty. By the same token, he shares responsibility with others for Valentin's duel (again, he introduces Valentin to Noémie), for Claire's refusal and flight (his ignorance of the complications her marriage to him will bring, given the particular politics and religion of the Bellegardes), for Mrs. Bread's revelation (Mme. de Bellegarde is right when she claims, "I understand that he has bought her confidence"), and so on. Even more significantly, as I have already argued, Newman's friendly offer of help to Valentin plays a significant, albeit unrecognized, part in precipitating the duel with Kapp.

James thematizes the romance that structures the second part of *The American* in very specific ways. He makes it clear (as he would in so many other works, especially *The Aspern Papers, The Turn of the Screw,* and *The Sacred Fount*) that the romance is just what the deluded character *sees.*[5] It is Newman who characterizes his story as a "page torn out of a romance," Chateau Fleurières as a "Chinese Penitentiary," the plan for revenge as "theatrical," and Valentin's death as "unnatural and monstrous." It is Newman as well who selects the ruined castle on the hill above Fleurières as the site for his secret "twilight" meeting with Mrs. Bread. In a manner that would become habitual in his subsequent works, James makes a character (or characters) responsible for the fantastic, romantic world that emerges unexpectedly from everyday realism.

We know, of course, that the uncanny is perfectly familiar and known to us but "has been estranged only by the process of repression."[6] Indeed, the very oppressive familiarity of the object or experience causes us to repress it. And the more powerfully we repress it, the more certainly it will return, according to what Freud considers the instinct of the repetition-compulsion:

> It must be explained that we are able to postulate the principle of a *repetition-compulsion* in the unconscious mind, based upon instinctual activity and probably inherent in the very nature of the instincts—a principle powerful enough to overrule the pleasure-principle, lending certain aspects of the mind their daemonic character. . . . Taken in all, the foregoing prepares us for the discovery that whatever reminds us of this inner *repetition-compulsion* is perceived as uncanny. ("Uncanny," 145)

The Old World that Newman encounters is, in this reading, nothing other than the New World that he has repressed. That this Old World emerges at precisely the moment that Newman encounters in his "immortal hack" in New York "disgust" with the revenge he had contemplated should not surprise us. The Old World that Newman encounters is not the real Europe— "in all its thickness and complexity of evil," as R. W. Butterfield has described it in James's writings.[7] What Newman discovers as a strange, foreign land is precisely the America that he is helping to build and for which he experiences a moment of involuntary disgust that could appear to him only in some unconscious state such as sleep. After all, Newman is so utterly ignorant of French and European politics, of the history of French Catholicism and its relevance for Catholic legitimists such as the Bellegardes, and of European art history in general that it is absurd to suppose that what he experiences has anything to do with the reality of late-nineteenth-century Europe.

Like Strether in the country, during his little "experiment in French ruralism," Newman encounters his own distorted image, his own ghostly double in this "New World" of his psyche. In his faulty English, M. Nioche says of Newman's namesake, Christopher Columbus, "He invented America" (*American*, 21); Newman has "invented Europe," but in such a way that it becomes America's alter ego. For the sake of economy and a little rhetorical effect, let me exaggerate the case by concluding with a forced allegory of this psychic landscape, this schizophrenic America. The old marquis accuses his wife of having "killed" him, and in one sense, the truth of this accusation is confirmed in his insistence that this "murder" is linked with his wife's insistence on marrying Claire to M. de Cintré for the money: "My wife has tried to kill me, and she has done it; I am dying, dying horribly. It is to marry my dear daughter to M. de Cintré. With all my heart I protest—I forbid it" (268). Newman certainly understands that a similarly commercial arrangement is at least one attraction for the Bellegardes in his proposal. The old family ties and social relations have been turned into commercial transactions, which are compatible with the America that Newman represents. In short, the murder plot that Newman imagines he has uncovered in the Bellegardes' past is merely a romantic distortion of the fatality he brings to their house and line by not simply proposing to their daughter but rather proposing to buy their history for his own sake.

This does not mean that Henry James condemns Newman's modern commercialism for the sake of nostalgically yearning for the lost civilization of the Catholic and monarchist Bellegardes. Quite to the contrary, James stresses the extent to which the democratic promise of America has ended up merely repeating, if not compounding, the sins of the aristocratic Europe that his ancestors had hoped to escape. Nowhere is this doubling between America and Europe better represented than in the dreary fates of women in both social orders. The European women Newman meets are all servants of one sort or another, even if most of the women characters continue to assert their class privileges and deny the bondage that otherwise unites them as victims of patriarchal hierarchies. Every married woman is unhappy for this very reason: Mme. de Bellegarde with her husband (to the desperate pass of murder?), the young marquise with Urbain, Mrs. Tristram with Tom. In many ways, just this depressing image of a "married woman" may be said to motivate Noémie's coquetry as one of the few powers available to women in this patriarchal culture: power to manipulate by way of romance. So would Newman have marriage; he would "save" Claire, keep her "safe," be a "father" to her—otherwise make her a dependent. Once again, the fate of woman in capitalist America, where the spheres of commerce and society revolve in different galaxies, seems to repeat even more insidiously the bondage of the European woman to her class and its male representative.

Thirty years later, in *The American Scene,* James stresses the difference between European women and the new American woman: "The result elsewhere, in Europe generally, of conditions in which men have actively participated and to which, throughout, they personally contribute, she has only the old story to tell, and keeps telling it after her fashion. The woman produced by a women-made society alone has obviously quite a new story—to which it is not for a moment to be gainsaid that the world at large has, for the last thirty years in particular, found itself lending an attentive, at times even a charmed, ear."[8] This great change in the social independence of women, however, is for James only an illusory revolution, just another trap by which women are held captives:

> For why need she originally, he wonders, have embraced so confidently, so gleefully, yet so unguardedly, the terms offered her to an end practically so perfidious? Why need she, unless in the interest of her eventual discipline, have turned away with so light a heart after watching the Man, the deep American man, retire into his tent and let down his flap? She had her "paper" from him, their agreement signed and sealed; but would she not, in some other air and under some other sky, have been visited by a saving instinct? Would she not have said "No, this is too unnatural; there must be a trap in it somewhere—it's addressed really, in the long run, to making a fool of me?" (*AS,* 348)

The "women-made society" in America still makes its "bargain" for independence in precisely the economic terms of the American man, so that her new story turns out to be simply a novel version of the "old story" that the European woman "keeps telling . . . after her fashion." For all its great difference from Europe, James's America and its Newman have repeated the old sins. This passage from *The American Scene* even seems to carry specific memory traces of *The American*. The military metaphor of the American man retiring "into his tent," like some Achilles, suggests that the changes in gender relations in modern America have in fact involved a battle of epic proportions, but the war has clearly been won by "the Man." In a similar fashion, the macropolitical battles and conflicts of the European powers in *The American* are reflected in the personal conflicts of the dramatic action, which are often metaphorized as "battles," literalized in the duel between Valentin and Stanislas Kapp. The "paper" she has won is presumably in the extended metaphor the treaty by which her enemy concludes the overt battle and thus retires into his tent, but by which he has more profoundly cheated her of more expansive rights to full social, political, and economic participation in American society, thereby winning the war. In a similar fashion, Newman offers to "save" both Noémie and Claire from their respective bondage, but the liberation he promises turns out to be simply a more modern version of feminine subordination.

It is this sort of "seduction" of woman for which Newman may be held accountable in the curious analogy *The American* makes between him and the legendary Don Juan. Newman seduces not only Noémie and Claire with unfulfilled promises of freedom; he also tantalizes Valentin with the possibility of escaping his fate as the younger son in a conservative Catholic family. The results for all three are versions of the very historical fatality they had hoped to escape by way of Newman's promise of democratic opportunity. Noémie merely turns to another aristocrat, Lord Deepmere, once her chances for either the French noble, Valentin, and the American, Newman, have been dashed. For her, the cynicism behind Newman's democratic promise becomes the ironic principle of her conduct. Claire withdraws from the world into the Carmelite convent in complete abjection to the moral rigor of her Catholic family.[9] Noémie's cynicism is perfectly modern, and Claire's obedience is thoroughly traditional; both behaviors reflect, however, the persistence of masculine authority in determining the conduct and identity of women. Such patriarchy is even more insidious because it so often exercises its authority through other women. The old marquis accuses his wife of trying to "kill" him for marrying Claire to M. de Cintré. Valentin dies only nominally by the shot from Kapp's pistol in their duel; the text suggests that he has been killed as effectively by Noémie's infidelity. Mrs. Bread conspires with Newman to expose the Bellegardes' crimes in large part out of her hatred of Madame de

Bellegarde and the hint of her love for the old marquis. And it is Mrs. Tristram who initiates the sad sequence of events that ends with Valentin dead, Claire entombed, and Noémie lost.

These women are not, however, the real agents of the destruction wrought in the novel; they are all victims of the larger powers represented by Newman's capitalist America and the Bellegardes' Catholic monarchism. Carolyn Porter has pointed out how woefully undeveloped Claire de Cintré is as a major fictional character, arguing that James is as guilty as Christopher Newman and the Bellegardes of using her blankness to substitute his own symbolic value: "She is reified as a symbol in proportion to the erosion of what she symbolizes—a noncommercial, uncontaminated, and incorruptible value."[10] But James has made clear throughout the novel not only that Claire's "blankness" is an effect of the willful efforts by others—Newman, the Bellegardes, the Tristrams—to impose their own values, but that her own value as a person is thus relatively impoverished. The very fact that she is undeveloped fictionally, then, is precisely because she has been so thoroughly infantilized and commodified by all the characters who have claimed responsibility for her upbringing, from her mother and brother to Newman.

Porter argues further that what allows both Claire and Noémie to be circulated so shamelessly as commodities is what James judges to be the "decay" of "patriarchal authority and protection."[11] Much as this conclusion contradicts my own interpretation of the novel, there is some evidence to support it. Porter points both to the old marquis, who dies trying to prevent Claire's marriage to M. de Cintré, and to the financial and emotional ruin M. Nioche has apparently suffered as consequences of his wife's infidelity.[12] Without strong father figures, young women such as Claire and Noémie appear to be adrift, prone to the whims of a modern society that recognizes "no value except cash value."[13] According to Porter, then, women are doubly stereotyped in *The American*—first, as symbols of transcendent value, in keeping with the nineteenth-century ideology of the "domestic angel"; second, as representatives of the worst commercial impulses of the modern age, in keeping with the mass cultural rhetoric that often connected liberated women with moral decadence. To be sure, such myths about women are traded back and forth by most of the men in *The American*, especially Newman and old M. Nioche, but James appears to indulge such stereotypes precisely to show how deeply they are tied to patriarchal values in general.

What reader can believe M. Nioche's false bravado when he declares to

Newman his rage on discovering his wife's infidelity "at last": "I have only been once in my life a man to be afraid of . . . it was in that hour" (*American*, 57)? As he emulates the passionate jealousy of the stereotypical Frenchman, M. Nioche only reminds us how far he has fallen from such youthful vigor. When he declaims against his wife's infidelities, we are encouraged to class such memories with his many other exaggerations and distortions of an otherwise trivial life.[14] A Frenchman ruined by his unfaithful wife is the very romance that lends M. Nioche's life the bit of grandeur it so clearly lacks. That Newman believes the old man, even to the point of entertaining M. Nioche's concerns that Noémie may have inherited such immoral tendencies from her mother, only betrays Newman's deeply patriarchal and equally naive ideas about women. When he tells M. Nioche casually, "Oh, we'll marry her, . . . since that's how you manage it," Newman betrays his own belief in marriage as a system of moral constraint and control, rather than as the path to freedom he will later promise Claire.

In her own way, Noémie seems to understand Newman's ignorance and even tries to educate him. As she shows him paintings in the Louvre that she might copy for him, she selects paintings that display the historical variety of women's roles, ranging from the sacred offices of the Virgin and Saint Catherine (of Genoa?) to the secular power of Marie de Médicis to the mere respectability of the unidentified "Italian portrait of a lady," who is little more than her "golden hair," "purple satin," "pearl necklace," and "two magnificent arms" (*American*, 61). All these paintings represent explicitly or implicitly the masculine authority sustaining such women, and at least two are specifically marriage portraits.[15] Even within the confines of Western patriarchy, Noémie seems to suggest, women have exercised various powers and escaped the narrow stereotypes to which her father and Newman are so inclined. Noémie's efforts to teach Christopher Newman are short-lived, perhaps because he seems so insensitive to her subtle hints regarding the personal significance of these paintings in the Louvre.

Nevertheless, this little history of art teaches the reader that women have for centuries been commodified, either as idealized Virgins or as "golden hair" with "two magnificent arms." There is thus little reason for us to imagine that the old marquis de Bellegarde might have protected Claire from such a fate had he survived his wife's treachery, whether it be actual poison or a bad alliance for their daughter. The old marquis would hardly have given Claire the freedom that Porter argues attracts her first to Newman; the marquis undoubtedly would have married her "better" than to M. de Cintré, meaning thereby to a more aristocratic and wealthier husband.[16] James's point in all these respects seems to be that the patriarchal domination of women is a long-standing practice that will require more than mere legislation to reform.

In this latter respect, James displays his limitation as a critic of such patriarchy. Revealing the power of patriarchal values, as well as showing how these values are reproduced both by men and by women, James offers little opportunity for rebellion or social transvaluation. American democracy, at least insofar as it is represented by Christopher Newman, is unlikely to offer any radical departure from the social and psychological confinement of women in Europe displayed so bleakly in *The American*. What is worse, Newman shows not the slightest understanding of how his conduct reproduces class and gender hierarchies of an Old World that it was the purpose of American democracy to overturn. Having gone this far, however, James is unable to offer the women in the novel any viable alternatives to a patriarchal ideology that not only has a venerable history—dating at least from the Catholic Mariolatry of the Latin Middle Ages—but also pervades the ostensibly different social orders of nineteenth-century America and Europe.

Noémie's cleverness in attempting to teach Newman about such important matters is only a distant reminder of James's far more sustained and subtle education of the reader; she is finally caught up in the general irony of the social game and becomes the very coquette her father so feared she would become. Claire may try to refuse to be commodified either by Newman or her family, but when she enters the Carmelite convent she merely follows the proper path for an unmarried Catholic woman in difficulties. At some level, every woman in the narrative seems to understand how profoundly she is imprisoned by the patriarchal order, but none shows any ability to escape what James represents as an ideology that is both historically established and socially comprehensive. Left only with self-destructive rebellion (Noémie), powerless irony and sarcasm (the young marquise), vicarious pleasures (Mrs. Tristram), fantastic dreams of freedom (Claire engaged to Newman), or abject obedience to an unjust social order (Claire when she enters the convent), the women in the novel are offered no genuine agency by James. Like the paintings Noémie paints in the Louvre, these women are all copies of someone else's artistic or social representation.

This problem is by no means isolated to James's early fiction, such as *The*

American; James's entire oeuvre is variously haunted by the question "What, then, can a woman *do?*" Noémie plainly tells Newman in the Louvre, "I don't understand how a man can be so ignorant" (63), and many of James's most promising women characters will struggle to find ways of educating men and other women to recognize the folly of their confidence in established gender and class roles. They are, however, rarely successful and are often ruined for their generosity. In the end it must be James who reveals and educates, leaving us only with the option of his high aesthetic standard, to which virtually none of his women characters is capable. This strikes me as a flaw in James's fiction, not just in the plot of a formally conflicted novel such as *The American* but in the entire Jamesian project, whose moral tone depends finally on the promise of some liberation from what James understands so clearly to be the unjust class and gender hierarchies of both an older Europe and the flawed promise of the new America.

In entangling the historical experience of Europe in the only apparitional futurity of America, however, James brilliantly criticizes the growing immorality of American society for failing to realize its democratic promise. For James, the profoundest sin grows secretly within the apparent virtue of that innocence by which Newman avoids his responsibility for the world around him. The political situation in France and Europe on the eve of the Franco-Prussian War seems utterly alien to Newman, even though he insists on being "informed" and voraciously devours the daily papers. It is the dilemma of modern America that James will treat again and again: the capitalist takes no cognizance of politics, except as an occasionally bothersome interference with the free enterprise he pursues in his entrepreneurial zeal. In the place of political and social issues, the personal dominates. The modern cult of personality is precisely what Newman represents for America—a form of debased "self-reliance" transformed from Jeffersonian or Emersonian man (that is, *representative* man) into anarchic individualism, in which only the fittest survive: in sum, a cynical Don Juanism. That this modern Don Juan "seduces" men as well as women (Valentin, Noémie, M. Nioche, Claire, Tom and Mrs. Tristram, Mrs. Bread) is some measure of his modernity as well as his voracious appetite for power and control.[17] As a consequence, interpersonal relations have all the subtlety and sensitivity of the other that one encounters in a duel. Above all, man works only to produce the hollow self, never to build a social context in which to discover himself in and through others. Others have only exchange value for the commercial self, intent on turning every friendship into "gold" or some commodity by which the self's capital grows. Tom Tristram moves from one immediate gratification to another without really knowing quite what would please him.[18] By the same token, this expatriate merely reveals what works more insidiously in Newman's commercial life. Turning from the manufacture of washtubs to the sale of leather goods, from copper mining to railroads, Newman's capitalism is always a form of speculating, a version of the stock market transaction he is about to undertake on that ride in his "immortal hack."

The dilettantes for whom Newman has so much contempt are doubles for the American capitalist, who merely follows his whims, who prizes the novelty and originality of a thing. What Newman represents is a kind of aestheticism that has little to do with works of art but makes entertaining and merely distracting the human relations that ought to be the basis for real social value. For Newman, *everyone* should be feminized to bask in the aura of his triumphal paternalism. However much Henry James might have been criticized over the years for his own aesthetic indulgences, he never aestheticized human relations in this manner. For Henry James, an aesthetic consciousness ought to bring the complexities of human relations more clearly into view, accomplishing for the viewer or reader a better understanding of his own complicity in the world so represented. It is precisely this "aesthetic consciousness" that Christopher Newman so fatally lacks, and nowhere more obviously than in his encounter with Mozart's *Don Giovanni.*

Like Columbus, Newman wanted to go east but ended up in the West—the "Wild West" that James envisioned as the dangerous territory mapped by the modern American: the self-reliant, apolitical, patriarchal heir to all the tyrannical tricks and hierarchical laws of his aristocratic forebears. "For West is where . . . you go when you get the letter saying: *Flee, all is discovered.* It is where you go when you look down at the blade in your hand and see the blood on it," Jack Burden says in *All the King's Men.*[19] The West is the place for criminals. But James's American has one talent that makes him uniquely powerful; he has the power of forgetting who he is. Newman forgets himself and thereby creates a strange, fantastic world that strikes him as utterly "foreign," evil, better left well enough alone. He has caused us to go on calling it "Europe," even though James tells us that it really is home.

3 ❧ Acting Lessons: Racial, Sexual, and Aesthetic Politics in *The Tragic Muse*

> My dear father, only people who look dull ever get into the House of Commons, and only people who are dull ever succeed there.
>
> —Lord Goring to his father in Oscar Wilde,
> *An Ideal Husband* (1895)

> The fuller treatment of the English national character that his theme invites is among James's happiest achievements in this book: it is chiefly remarkable . . . for what one may call his loving discrimination in respect to the English, the discrimination being always exact and severe as the love is sincere and tender.
>
> —Dorothea Krook, *The Ordeal of Consciousness in Henry James* (1962)

Dorothea Krook opens her chapter on *The Tragic Muse* in *The Ordeal of Consciousness in Henry James* (1962) by noting that it is "perhaps the most distinguished novel . . . of James's 'middle period,'" even though "there has been a tendency to neglect it among James's works of this period—a neglect wholly undeserved in view of the rich and varied interest it offers."[1] Krook offers no explanation for this neglect, which has continued to our own day, but I think the novel baffles readers who think they understand James as the faithful Anglophile deeply imbued with the values of British culture and its aesthetic ideals. Maxwell Geismar long ago tried to attack the novel on just these grounds by arguing that its weaknesses are typified by its endorsement of such fatuous British snobs as Peter Sherringham and the "tedious" aesthetes Nick Dormer and Gabriel Nash.[2] What Geismar fails to understand is that James fully shares Geismar's judgment of Peter Sherringham as a pretentious and hypocritical man of feigned cultivation, who is repeatedly the object of James's withering critique of an increasingly outmoded British ruling class. In regard to Dormer and Nash, Geismar never suspects that their relationship combines aesthetic and sexual identities that challenge the rigid patriarchal values of late Victorian culture. Hardly tedious, both are particularly threatening to the strict gender roles and other behavioral proprieties of British society.

There is still another important reason for the critical neglect of this novel by traditional James criticism: Miriam Rooth. She answers every criticism that has been directed at James's other heroines; quite simply, Miriam Rooth is James's most successful and emancipated feminine character. Although surrounded by characters who offer to "help" her succeed as an actress, Miriam is clearly self-reliant, even though she cheerfully acknowledges others' assistance. Besieged by moonstruck admirers, she never succumbs to false flattery or to romantic deception; she is always in control of herself and her destiny. Although her talent as an actress is frequently questioned, especially in her younger years, Miriam never doubts her ability and confidently seeks to develop a career she had chosen primarily for altruistic reasons, even as she is fully aware of the possible personal advantages success on the stage might bring her. She manages and is never managed *by* the media, especially the popular press. She is thoroughly modern without being vulgar; she is enthusiastically professional without being meretricious. Above all, Miriam triumphs over every character and circumstance that would have misled or doomed any other heroine in Henry James's writings. In the end, she does play the part of Juliet, and she does it with the artistic grace that James clearly equates with that of great artists in other media, including his own. In a novel notable for its irony with respect to virtually all the areas of British and French society represented in it, Miriam Rooth escapes the satire James elsewhere levels at "career women," such as Henrietta Stackpole in *The Portrait of a Lady,* or "liberated women," such as Miss Birdseye and Olive Chancellor in *The Bostonians.*[3] In a host of ways that I will discuss in this chapter, Miriam Rooth is a magnificent example of what the New Woman can do once she has freed herself from the delusions of romantic love, nineteenth-century femininity, national character, and family heritage.

Why, then, should the critics have so neglected her or so repeatedly misinterpreted Miriam Rooth as the "ruthless," "scandalous," "gauche," "vulgar," "opportunistic," "Jewish" actress?[4] It is precisely Miriam Rooth's capacity to challenge popular stereotypes of race, class, gender, ethnicity, and nationality that so disturbs critics, even those who make no effort to comment on these aspects of her extraordinarily interesting character. For example, she is neither American nor English, thus scandalizing those who insist that James's new cosmopolitan virtues are primarily Anglo-American. In addition, she occupies no clear class position, either in her initial appearance as struggling actress, promoted by her impoverished and opportunistic mother, or her final triumph as a celebrated actress on the English stage, playing such serious roles as Shakespeare's Constance in *King John* and Juliet in *Romeo and Juliet.* Finally, her ethnic background is rendered deliberately unclear, both by James and by Miriam herself, so that the "Jewishness" that various characters seek to confirm in her appearance, her ancestry, her career, and her social behavior is far more the consequence of Victorian anti-Semitism than anything intrinsic to the character or ancestry of Miriam Rooth.

Even the rare critic who recognizes Miriam's unique qualities among James's heroines cannot avoid qualifying James's realization of such a character by calling attention to her relative "blankness" as a central character. Thus Geismar points out how James fails to develop Miriam's character, as if he is afraid of the challenge she might pose to his own artistic authority, a charge differently developed by Sara Blair in her more recent study of the roles of race and nationality in James's writings: "The 'blank[ness]' associated with her history and performances constitutes, at least in part, a power of transformative self-invention to which the author of *The Tragic Muse* continues to aspire."[5] Miriam is presented to us primarily as she is seen by others, as James notes in his preface: "We have no direct exhibition of [her consciousness] whatever, . . . we get at it all inferentially and inductively, seeing it only through a more or less bewildered interpretation of it by others. The emphasis is all on an absolutely objective Miriam."[6] What Geismar views as a technical failure in character development, Blair judges as James's criticism of a modernity represented by Miriam Rooth that he at once abhors and envies.

Blair may well be right about James's ambivalent attitudes toward modern culture, which is very much the target of James's irony in this novel about a theatrical celebrity. But Miriam herself, insofar as readers get to know her at all, seems nearly exempt from the satire James levels at such thoroughly modern characters as the narrator of *The Aspern Papers,* Mr. Morrow in "The Death of the Lion," or Mona Brigstock in *The Spoils of Poynton.* Even though he does not himself "go behind" Miriam, he may claim in his preface that she remains the "center" of fictional interest; Miriam is "central in virtue of the fact that the whole thing has visibly, from the first, to get itself done in dramatic, at least in scenic conditions . . . that . . . move in the light of *alternation*. This imposes a consistency other than that of the novel at its loosest, and, for one's subject, a different view and a different placing of the centre."[7] James's famous claim to "scenic development" as a feature of the modern novel thus aligns his own experimental technique in *The Tragic Muse* with Miriam's dramatic medium. In a sense, Miriam is represented in the novel as nothing more than her passion and talent for the stage, as her eventual marriage to the actor and theater manager Basil Dashwood seems to confirm. There is simply never a scene in which Miriam is *not* acting, whether she is actually on the stage or receiving visitors in her dressing room or staging social gatherings at Balaklava Place. For James, this complete identification of the artist with his or her medium is consistently a measure of artistic success.[8] Richard Salmon points out that Miriam's studied "theatricality" represents quite accurately the success of Victorian actresses, such as Ellen Terry, who were able to project "personalities" with which the public could identify them and thus played on "private" identities that contributed to their celebrity.[9] In our own postmodern era, when celebrities (and their agents or other delegates) carefully engineer publicity stunts to simulate "private" identities for public purposes, we have grown accustomed to what in the late nineteenth century was the relatively novel interrelation of public and private selves in the construction of a public figure.

This technical innovation is related to James's moral purpose in the novel to test social mores in terms of the disturbance that such a "public character," a "supposed particular celebrity," will produce when added to "the contemporary social salad."[10] Just what Miriam Rooth adds to English society is her cosmopolitan, polyglot, ethnically hybridized character. That such a "character" is so adaptable to English theater, providing a virtual revitalization of it, is some indication that James imagines English society ready for modernization. Blair interprets James's representation of Miriam's cosmopolitanism as both a challenge to provincial English culture and at the same time James's own defense against the threatening elements of modernity: "But even as the narrator conducts this kind of cosmopolitan exposure, he embodies a certain involuntary movement of defense against the 'contagion' inherent to cosmopolitanism itself, linked metonymically with the activities of decadents, anarchists, homosexuals, aliens and Jews."[11]

The reader of *The Tragic Muse* is challenged to distinguish between Henry

James's view of Miriam Rooth and the English characters who stereotype her variously as Jew, New Woman, actress, foreigner, lower class, and immoral. Acknowledging James's satire of English snobbery in the characters of Peter Sherringham, Lady Agnes, and Julia Dallow in the ways they either love or detest Miriam, Blair nonetheless concludes that James himself exploits his character even more thoroughly by making her revitalize English society even as James's narrator "partially shares Sherringham's *horror vacui* with regard to Miriam's public performances: . . . a veritable 'monster' with 'no countenance of her own' save 'the one that came nearest to being a blank.' "[12] In Blair's view, James uses Miriam's cultural blankness to *Anglicize* her, thereby subtly stripping her of her Jewish heritage, reorganizing her many different cultural influences into a cosmopolitan Englishness, and putting her "half a dozen languages" to the single task of brilliantly performing Shakespeare's English: "By the end of the novel, James's identifications with cosmopolitan alterity will collapse into the well-made ending, with the requisite marriages and reversals of fortune, of the distinct English literary tradition he has attempted to redirect."[13]

Miriam's extraordinary success on the English stage does suggest a general narrative of cultural assimilation and the late-nineteenth-century rhetoric of the "melting pot," but we should be cautious about treating reductively the very different ideas of cultural assimilation and transformation debated at the turn of the century. Nowhere is this caution more appropriate than when we reconsider James's fictional treatment of Miriam's supposedly Jewish ancestry. Liberal assimilationist rhetoric regarding the "acceptance" of Jews into Victorian society is typified by Anthony Trollope's fictional representation of Jewish lawyers such as Solomon Aram in *Orley Farm* (1862), whose outward respectability is accompanied by a residual unscrupulousness, or of Jewish entrepreneurs such as Melmotte in *The Way We Live Now* (1875), who represents the worst excesses of modern financial speculation. Trollope generally counsels the Victorian reader to be patient and tolerant of the "foreign" traits of Jews, who will inevitably be assimilated, especially as they are "civilized" by their contact with English culture. Allowing himself to indulge the worst anti-Semitic fantasies of Victorian culture, Trollope will stress the "dark" skin, "greasy" black hair, "greedy" lips, and "beaked" or "hooked" noses in his descriptions of English and European Jews, as well as their "usurious" ways and excessive "love" of property. Assimilation of the European Jew into English society means for Trollope a gradual process of socialization and "cultivation" by which the Jew will be deracinated and Anglicized. The ugliness of this putatively "liberal" cultural attitude becomes thoroughly repugnant in works such as Trollope's *Nina Balatka* (1867), which focuses on intermarriage between a Christian woman and a Jew. Set nominally in Prague, the novel really deals with the new urban mobility across religious and ethnic lines that is occurring, according to Trollope, in the great European cities. Although Nina and Anton eventually do marry, they leave Prague forever, presumably for one of those European cities such as London where Trollope repeatedly tells us there is greater religious and ethnic tolerance.[14]

James's treatment of Miriam's conquest of London differs drastically from Trollope's anxious fables of Jewish assimilation into the English bourgeoisie, even though Blair is right to characterize Miriam's success as ultimately one of assimilation. Whereas Trollope expects "foreigners" to follow the role models for individual behavior and community organization established by English society, James imagines Miriam as challenging and ideally transforming English society. Trollope's Jews and Irish are happy merely to be accepted into "civilization." In Trollope's *The Landleaguers* (1883), the Irish American singer Rachel O'Mahony must choose between the impoverished Irish gentleman Frank Jones, the Jewish tenor Mahomet M. Moss, and the British Lord Castlewell. Trollope gives his heroine every "feminine charm," but this doesn't prevent her from hurling the ugliest anti-Semitic invective at her Jewish admirer, despite his theatrical talents, cosmopolitanism, and her grudging acknowledgment that he is "by no means an ill-looking man."[15] In the end, Rachel makes good on her promise early in the narrative to "kill" Mr. Moss if he does not cease pursuing her; when he tries to embrace her after proposing marriage, Rachel stabs him to death. Trollope's chapter title, "Mr. Moss Is Finally Answered," seems to indicate that Trollope believes Mr. Moss has earned his fate.[16] In Trollope's social scale, the Orientalized tenor—Jews and Moslems are for Trollope irrationally equated in his naming—is far beneath the Irish gentleman in eligibility for her love. The penniless and provincial Frank Jones competes successfully with Lord Castlewell for Rachel's love, and Rachel politely but firmly breaks her engagement with the lord, who has insulted her by criticizing her radical father. Mr. Moss, however, does not even figure in Rachel's romantic equation; his attentions are from the outset viewed by Rachel as the equivalents of sexual assaults.[17] On the other hand, James's Miriam refuses to join English society unless it will acknowledge the difference she represents. James's drama may still be as profoundly nationalist as Trollope's, but James's conception of the modern nation departs drastically from Trollope's strictly English bourgeois model. Instead James represents in *The Tragic Muse* cultural assimilation as the utopian means by which a society ought to adapt to cultural and historical influences. It is a model that is finally more appropriate to James's ideal America than England.

In his interpretation of James's response to American immigrants in *The American Scene*, Ross Posnock stresses James's identification with the alien and his openness to the new social relations produced by the influence of immigrant populations in America: "James acknowledges that the alien must be honored as alien, as other, unassimilable to one's own needs. . . . With typical capaciousness, James seeks to respect various conflicting conceptions of citizenship—the alien's, his own, and even the official American one—for 'in the happiest cases' the converted alien has acquired an American identity of 'all apparent confidence and consistency.' "[18] What Posnock terms "James's devotion to heterogeneity" in *The American Scene* seems anticipated by Miriam Rooth and the changes in social relations she prompts in the dramatic action of *The Tragic Muse*. Like Christopher Newman, Miriam Rooth has an extremely ambiguous family history. Unlike Newman, she never capitalizes on such ambiguities, even as she allows others to indulge their wildest fantasies about her past. What such imaginings do, in typical Jamesian fashion, is reveal the unconscious social assumptions and prejudices of those with whom she comes into contact.[19]

Of course, Miriam Rooth is not an American, no matter which different account of her family background we accept. She is decidedly not French, Swiss, or Alsatian, despite her initial training in Paris and her emulation of the nineteenth-century French actress Rachel.[20] If we accept the bare elements of Gabriel Nash's fanciful account of Miriam's backgrounds early in the novel, Miriam is thoroughly English, although "she has spent her life on the Continent," where "she has wandered about with her mother."[21] On her mother's side, Miriam is descended from an apparently aristocratic English family. "What connexion is *not* a misalliance when one happens to have the unaccommodating, the crushing honour of being a Neville-Nugent of Castle Nugent?" Gabriel Nash sardonically remarks to the Dormers and Peter Sherringham. By his account, her father is a German Jewish immigrant to England: "The father's . . . only a Jew stockbroker in the City" (*TM*, 1:61). Nash refers to Miriam as "the *jeune Anglaise*," despite the apparent difficulties Miriam has with idiomatic English, and later Miriam will respond to Peter

Sherringham's challenges, "But you're not English" and "You're a Jewess—I'm sure of that," by insisting, "I beg your pardon. You should hear mamma about our 'race' " and "My name's Jewish . . . but it was that of . . . my father's mother. She was a baroness in Germany. That is she was the daughter of a baron" (1:204–5). Although James problematizes Miriam's Jewish ancestry, it is probable that he also wishes to retain it as one among several elements that lend her interest. James is, after all, a product of his time and place, and nineteenth-century Anglo-American cultures treated Jews as a "racially" distinct group.[22]

In short, Miriam's "foreign" qualities are her wide experience of the world and her Jewish background, each of which criticizes in turn the provincialism and the anti-Semitism of the English characters who so identify her. In fact, her English and German backgrounds align her closely with the Anglo-Saxon identity so prized by the English ruling class.[23] What Blair terms "the racial logic of Jewishness" in the novel is exclusively represented by those characters who variously fear or exoticize her Jewish background.[24] Their "racial" construction of Miriam's Jewishness is, however, implicitly criticized by the narrator, who refers to such English types as Peter Sherringham, Nick Dormer, and Lady Agnes Dormer as belonging to the "English race," effectively confusing ethnic and national identities. In the narrator's initial description of Nick Dormer, for example, he writes: "He was the sort of young Englishman who looks particularly well in strange lands and whose general aspect—his inches, his limbs, his friendly eyes, the modulation of his voice, the cleanness of his flesh-tints and the fashion of his garments—excites on the part of those who encounter him in far countries on the ground of a common speech a delightful sympathy of race" (*TM,* 1:6). Any good tourist should recognize the irony in this passage, which suggests how members of the same nation, otherwise strangers, will claim nearly familial bonds when meeting in a foreign land. As if James wants to underscore his irony, he continues, "This sympathy may sometimes be qualified by the seen limits of his apprehension, but it almost revels as such horizons recede" (1:6). In short, Nick does not always return this sympathy, in keeping with what will be his growing rebellion against English respectability and obedience to his "racial" type.

Unlike Nick, Peter Sherringham remains faithful to all such national stereotypes, even to the point of accepting the confusion of racial, national, and religious identities. After Miriam has explained that her German grandmother was Jewish, Peter smugly concludes that she is therefore the "Jewess" he has named her: "Peter accepted this statement with reservations, but he replied, 'Put all that together and it makes you very sufficiently of Rachel's tribe'" (*TM*, 1:205). Peter imagines he is wittily punning on the names of the biblical Rachel and the great French actress, but Miriam specifies her identification with the latter and rejects his racial logic: "I don't care if I'm of her tribe artistically. I'm of the family of the artists—*je me fiche* of any other! I'm in the same style as that woman—I know it" (1:205). Miriam strategically chooses a French idiom (*je me fiche*, "I make fun of; I don't care about") at this moment to reject Peter's English anti-Semitism, gracefully reminding him that people are properly identified by what they do, rather than by some specious identification with a "racial" or "national" heritage. The great actress Rachel's "tribe" can only be that of other tragedians, rather than the Jewishness of her Alsatian father by which Peter identifies this celebrity.[25]

Indeed, the general theme of art's universality is used by James to undercut any efforts by the characters to promote art's role in supporting national, racial, and religious identities. James may be succumbing to an aesthetic ideology that has its own dangers, as we know from the critique of modernity's tendency to universalize its own values; but from within such modernity, James rejects provincial ideas of nationality, especially when they are based on the exclusion of foreigners and hysterical appeals to national identity as a "tribal" or "racial" bond.[26] The nineteenth-century Rachel achieved success on the French and English stages playing roles in the classic French dramatic repertoire. Miriam's career is framed by two performances of Shakespeare: her dramatic reading of Constance's despairing speech at the opening of act 3 of *King John* that convinces her teacher, Madame Carré, that Miriam can act, and her triumphant role as Juliet in *Romeo and Juliet* at the end of the novel. Both roles realize her earlier ambition, declared to Madame Carré as: "I want to play Shakespeare" (*TM*, 1:135).

Blair argues that "Miriam remains unnaturally free to adopt and adapt the resources of race and nation in a richly cosmopolitan form of cultural theater."[27] What Blair means is that Miriam brings her cosmopolitanism to the English stage in keeping with Peter Sherringham's conservative hope of revitalizing English theater and purifying a corrupted English language. If so, then Miriam's two Shakespearean roles are oddly selected for the national project of revitalizing English theater. *The Life and Death of King John* certainly poses considerable challenges to any nationalist project, since it focuses on legitimate French claims to the English crown during John's reign (especially the claims of Constance's son, Arthur, the duke of Brittany) and focuses on King John's corruption and immorality. In a similar sense, *Romeo and Juliet* uses the dramatic situation of feuding families of Verona to address domestic conflicts within Elizabethan England. Both plays may contribute to the growing internationalism of Elizabethan England, but they are hardly the most patriotic or nationalist of Shakespeare's texts. Blair is right to call attention to Sherringham's desire to use Miriam to revitalize English drama and culture, but she neglects both the extent to which Miriam escapes Sherringham's influence and the degree to which James's narrative satirizes Sherringham's uncritical nationalism.

Throughout the novel, Sherringham's anguished choice between his love for Miriam and his devotion to his career in the British foreign service is counterpointed by the rhetoric of colonialism. When Sherringham decides he must leave London to avoid the "temptation" Miriam poses to him and thus the possible "damage" she will do to his diplomatic career, he asks for and receives from his superior a new posting to "a little hot hole in Central America" (*TM*, 2:232). Much as Sherringham imagines that he distinguishes between the important work of British imperialism and the theater, he nonetheless repeatedly confuses the rhetoric of one for the other. When he encourages Miriam to take advantage of her talents as an actress, he describes her in terms of a conquering army: "You must forage and ravage and leave a track behind you; you must live upon the country you traverse" (2:359–60).[28] By the same token, Sherringham thinks of Miriam as the object, rather than agent, of colonial domination, and he frequently confuses his professional work for the Foreign Office with his ambivalent interest in her person and acting career. Reflecting on how readily Miriam expresses her appreciation to him for his admittedly amateurish tips about acting, "Sherringham was amused with the liberal way she produced it, as if she had been a naked islander rejoicing in a present of crimson cloth" (2:134). Still elsewhere, as Sherringham reflects on the potentially global reach of Miriam's fame, he explicitly connects her worldliness with his own diplomatic career, finding the latter wanting in the face of her sublimity: "He was most conscious that, at the best, even the trained diplomatic mind would never get a grasp of Miriam as a whole. She was constructed to revolve like the terraqueous globe; some part or other of her was always out of sight or in shadow" (2:195).

The entire plot of Peter Sherringham's courtship of, and ultimate proposal to, Miriam is couched in the rhetoric of the territorial conquests of British imperialism. His experiment in the English theater is simply another aspect of the larger imperial project to which he has dedicated his career, rather than the distraction or diversion he imagines such art to be. Yet Sherringham fortunately remains an amateur in the theater and a minor, albeit aspiring, officer of the British foreign service throughout the novel. We must never lose sight of the fact that the plot turns critically on Miriam's splendid refusal of Sherringham's proposal that she marry him, give up the stage, and become his "ambassadress" in that "little hot hole in Central America." Miriam does more than merely politely decline Sherringham's offer; she gives him an eloquent lecture on morality, both personal and national. When Sherringham asks Miriam to abandon her profession at the very moment of one of her greatest theatrical triumphs, he explicitly compares the theatricality of diplomacy with the English stage: "The stage is great, no doubt, but the world's greater. It's a bigger theatre than any of those places in the Strand. We'll go in for realities instead of fables, and you'll do them far better than you do the fables" (*TM*, 2:340). In effect, Sherringham tries to convince Miriam to transfer her talent from the stage to the ambassador's salon, turning English theater into an explicit tool of British imperial ideology.

Thus when Miriam eloquently reveals Sherringham's "sophistry," she does far more than merely reject his proposal and expose the contradictions in his character. Arguing that Sherringham would kill the very dramatic talents for which he loves Miriam, she also points out how selfish his desire is to "possess" what he terms "the very essence of your being" (*TM*, 2:341). At this moment, the rhetoric of imperialism that has playfully connected Sherringham's diplomatic career and his romantic attraction to Miriam reveals their more profound complicity as Sherringham's possessive desire mirrors the larger desire of England to control foreign territories and peoples. As woman, celebrated actress, and exotic foreigner, Miriam experiences the possessiveness of masculine desire, political will, and imperial conquest. In this context, she challenges Sherringham to "prove" his love for her and for the theater by sacrificing his own career and following her onto the stage he professes to love so dearly. As Miriam points out, "Surely it's strange . . . the way the other solution never occurs to you" (2:342).

Peter Sherringham never understands what Miriam means, blustering instead that "the cases are not equal. You'd make of me the husband of an actress. I should make of you the wife of an ambassador," but it is just this apparent inequality of art and diplomacy that Miriam challenges (*TM*, 2:342).

What she accomplishes is a little revolution in the astute reader's understanding of the proper hierarchies of English social life, including those that subordinate art to politics, woman to man, a title to talent. She also points out in the most tactful ways imaginable that Sherringham's inflated sense of his own achievements in the Foreign Office hardly matches the great celebrity she has achieved in her own field; whereas she has triumphed in London and helped revitalize English theater, Sherringham has managed to get himself posted to a "little hot hole in Central America."

From the beginning to the end of the narrative, Miriam remains true not only to her theatrical art but also to what she so clearly recognizes is the theatricality of modern culture. Virtually every other character either admires or condemns Miriam for her quality of always being onstage, but unlike so many frauds in James's fiction, Miriam is in this manner only more true to herself. Richard Salmon concludes that James abandons in *The Tragic Muse* the nineteenth-century convention about the immorality of actresses—a convention James had used in earlier works: "James appears to challenge the cultural association between the theatrical exhibition of the female body and the figure of the courtesan." One way he does this, Salmon argues, is to show how male spectatorship is challenged by the active, critical "look" of the actress herself, who is no longer a commodity or extension of masculine desire, but an active presence on stage and in society.[29] James seems to understand more clearly in *The Tragic Muse* than in his earlier works that society is itself already an elaborate theatrical production and that every actor or actress in it is equally prone to manipulation by its design—that is, to a certain commodification. What women experience more immediately in the scopic logic of masculine desire in the theater or in the rituals of courtship and marriage is more subtly operative in all social relations. In his desire to marry Miriam and take her away from the stage, Sherringham hopes to "restore a conventional sexual division of labour within a normative conception of the public sphere," but James suggests that in modern Anglo-American society, such a desire involves a fond nostalgia for an earlier age in which public and private were clearly delineated along gender lines.[30]

Peter Sherringham never imagines that his fine sentiments about duty, honor, and country are as much postures as those of his beloved theater. Even when he acknowledges that Miriam would play a role as the "ambassador's wife," he still fails to comprehend the fiction of English nationalism and British colonialism on which his trivial career is based. Indeed, Miriam's cosmopolitanism is crucial to her sense of all identities as performances with varying degrees of value. Blair is right to point out that "Miriam achieves a power of cosmopolitan self-invention that James himself cannot afford to concede," primarily because it is just this sort of cosmopolitanism to which James aspires in his own work as a novelist.[31] On the other hand, Blair's contention that Miriam's "successful evasion of the fixed selfhood on which assignments of race, class, and nation crucially depend mounts the clear and present danger of identity denatured, reduced to an infinite regress of roles or signs," confuses James with conventional Englishmen such as Peter Sherringham.[32] If James competes with Miriam, it is because she embodies so thoroughly those qualities of alterity, foreignness, and modernity to which James himself aspires.

Miriam not only rejects Peter Sherringham but then marries her fellow actor and theater manager Basil Dashwood. Although critics complain that this marriage of convenience typifies Miriam's impropriety, it is nonetheless perfectly in keeping with Miriam's morality. If she is nothing but her roles and her career on the stage, then only another actor could love her truly. Dashwood's stage name is either a comment on his fast modern lifestyle or an allusion to the English literary tradition that includes the Dashwoods in Austen's *Sense and Sensibility* (1811); in all likelihood, James intends the name to evoke both reckless abandon and traditional respectability.[33] Dashwood does consistently support Miriam's career goals and makes the business arrangements for the theater that will allow them both some independence from the popular melodramas to which she seems doomed in her early London days. Julia Dallow accepts Nick Dormer's initial proposal because she imagines he will be the perfect candidate for the parliamentary seat for Harsh that she controls. Nick's mother, Lady Agnes, and sisters not only agree but immediately benefit from the engagement when Julia lends them her country house, Broadwood. And when Peter Sherringham learns Miriam has married Dashwood, he turns promptly to Nick's sister, Biddy, for yet another marriage of convenience. Whether arranged for financial or emotional security, then, all of the marriages in *The Tragic Muse* are marriages of convenience; the only difference between Miriam and the other characters is that she makes no pretense about marrying "for love."

Today such pragmatic reasons for marrying may seem hardly revolutionary, but in Victorian society, Miriam challenges the elaborate fiction of romantic love that helps prop up bourgeois respectability. The Victorian novel in general revolves around the conflict between romantic love and property rights; typically, as in the majority of Anthony Trollope's novels, fortune (or at least "a living") and romantic love are made, however improbably, to coincide. Miriam does not subscribe to strictly practical ends in selecting a partner. If she loves any other character in a passionate, romantic manner, then it must be Nick Dormer, whose passion for painting compels him to give up his parliamentary seat and lose both his inheritance from Mr. Carteret and, at least temporarily, his fiancée, Julia Dallow. What Miriam loves in Nick Dormer is what she would like to love in Peter Sherringham—a common passion for art, a love of what she terms the Idea:

> The way we simply stir people's souls. Ah there's where life can help us . . . where human relations and affections can help us; love and faith and joy and suffering and experience. . . . They suggest things, they light them up and sanctify them . . . they make them appear worth doing. . . . I must tell you that in the matter of what we can do for each other I have a tremendously high ideal. I go in for closeness of union, for identity of interest. A true marriage, as they call it, must do one a lot of good! (*TM*, 2:354)

Miriam discovers finally that Peter Sherringham utterly lacks such idealism, wanting instead merely to possess her: "What I want is you yourself" (*TM*, 1:371). But Miriam understands perfectly well that an actress is nothing but representation, that the spectator falls in love with what he or she imagines on the stage. Even Sherringham understands this in those moments when he is still inspired by her extraordinary theatrical performances: "Her character was simply to hold you by the particular spell; any other—the good nature of home, the relation to her mother, her friends, her lovers, her debts, the practice of virtues or industries or vices—was not worth speaking of. These things were the fictions and the shadows; the representation was the real substance" (2:118).

As a novelist struggling to assert his authority in modern society, James has his own motives for insisting that "representation" is "the real substance" behind the various fictions of social organization. In this regard, Miriam is his surrogate in the novel, and she is unusual among his other heroines insofar as she not only follows but succeeds in an artistic career. What Sherringham wants selfishly only for himself, Miriam offers to the wide world every time she performs. It is the reverberations of her performances, both on and off the stage, that are of real interest to the reader of *The Tragic Muse*. At the most basic level, Miriam causes the ruling classes to withdraw back into their own provincial insularity and thus refuse the very modern message she brings. Julia Dallow views Miriam as her rival for Nick Dormer's love and professional devotion, imagining that Miriam has caused Nick to abandon his parliamentary seat for a frivolous career as a portrait painter. Julia thus detests and stereotypes Miriam as a vulgar and immoral actress, whose display of her body onstage seems evidence of more private revelations. Nick's mother, Lady Agnes, can only view Miriam as embodying the artistic decadence that threatens her family's prospects for fortune and position. In the end, the threat to social stability and class propriety that Miriam presents to the Dallows, Dormers, and Sherringhams appears to be defeated. As Blair writes: "By the end of the novel, James's identifications with cosmopolitan alterity will collapse into the well-made ending, with the requisite marriages and reversals of fortune, of the distinctly English literary tradition he has attempted to redirect."[34] The two cousins, Nick Dormer and Peter Sherringham, will marry into each other's families, Peter marrying Nick's sister, Biddy, and Nick rumored at the end to be on the verge of renewing his engagement to Peter's sister, Julia.

Geismar concludes that James uses this theme of "cousinly affection" to use Miriam as an "attractive but vulgar" scapegoat whose social function is to reaffirm the bonds "shared by an ingrown and vaguely incestuous group of characters."[35] But Geismar and Blair neglect the changes in social relations that Miriam has effected. Unlike other Jamesian narratives, such as *Daisy Miller,* in which the threatening woman is exiled by proper society, in *The Tragic Muse,* Miriam quite clearly rejects the Dormers, Sherringhams, and the Dallows. One reason James devotes so much attention to the scene in which Miriam decisively rejects Peter Sherringham's selfish and hypocritical marriage proposal is to prevent the reader from forgetting that Miriam, now a public celebrity with great wealth, has rejected Sherringham, not the other way around. Brilliant actress that she is, Miriam brings out of others both their best and worst qualities; she *changes* interpersonal and social relations.

On the stage, Miriam can play the part of "a beautiful actual fictive impossible young woman of a past age, an undiscoverable country, who spoke in blank verse and overflowed in metaphor, who was exalted and heroic beyond all human convenience" and yet for these very fantastic reasons "was irresistibly real and related to one's own affairs" (*TM,* 2:327). In this sense, Miriam's cosmopolitanism becomes just what the English audience "recognizes" as part of its "own affairs," and thus she begins to do the work of broadening English interests to include the wider world, yet she does so by means of sympathetic identifications, rather than colonial conquests. When she is at her best, "it was easy to feel a fine universal consensus and to recognise everywhere the light spring of hope. People snatched their eyes from the stage an instant to look at each other, all eager to hand on the torch passed to them by the actress over the footlights" (2:323). Such a scene of audience recognition seems to me very much in keeping with the Aristotelian idea of the social function of drama to create a shared recognition in responding to the moral problem presented on the stage.

Blair suggests that Miriam's theatrical success is merely the incorporation of the foreign and exotic body into the normative discourse of Victorian culture, epitomized by her ultimate success in playing Shakespearean roles. Yet Miriam's conduct on and off the stage has more revolutionary consequences, especially for gender and sexual roles in Victorian society. In general, her most important challenge to English conventionality is her constant reminder that "art *makes* life, makes interest, makes importance," to borrow from James's own aesthetic manifesto, and that the best and worst ideas of race, nationality, and society depend on some sort of aesthetic representation or persuasive rhetoric (*Letters,* 4:770). Beyond that, the very freedom she exercises in her own artistic career and performances comes to encompass the other characters on whom she has had such an influence. Peter Sherringham may react to her refusal by returning to the respectability of the foreign service and marrying Biddy Dormer, but in the meantime, Biddy Dormer is no longer the obedient, submissive, younger daughter of Lady Agnes Dormer. Although Miriam tries to argue Nick out of giving up his parliamentary seat, she nonetheless inspires in him a freedom that includes his choice of an artistic career and changed relations with men and women.

James often uses conventionally feminine metaphors to emphasize Miriam's power and authority; she is a "Queen," a "mild Medusa," and an "angel" (*TM,* 2:325, 336). In other contexts, however, the power of a "queen on her accession" and Medusa are more explicitly gendered in masculine metaphors, as when Miriam's play is compared to a ship and she is clearly the captain who has brought it successfully "in port" (2:325). Miriam's beauty is almost always tied to her power, so that the reader is often confused when trying to apply Victorian conventions regarding feminine weakness and passivity and masculine strength and assertion. Peter Sherringham finds Biddy Dormer "pleasant" because she is typically "a young bright slim rose-coloured" woman, but Miriam's beauty is never described in this manner (2:96). Instead, she appears to the reader by way of Nick Dormer's unfinished portrait of her:

> Unfinished, simplified and in some portions merely suggested, it was strong, vivid and assured, it had already the look of life and the promise of power. . . . Miriam, seated, was represented in three quarters, almost to her feet. She leaned forward with one of her legs crossed over the other, her arms extended and foreshortened, her hands locked together round her knee. Her beautiful head was bent a little, broodingly, and her splendid face seemed to look down at life. (*TM*, 2:112–13)

In her strong, commanding pose, Miriam appears to be a later manifestation of the Juno unearthed in "The Last of the Valerii."[36] Both feminine figures recapture the power of ancient Greek goddesses. The confusion of gender conventions is one of Miriam's appeals to the viewer and to her fans, who follow diverse accounts of her, many engineered by Miriam and her mother, in the popular press: "The whole case was remarkable, was unique; for if the girl was advertised by the bewilderment of her readers she seemed to every sceptic, on his going to see her, as fine as if he had discovered her for himself" (*TM*, 2:385).

Insofar as Miriam brings out of her fans their own unconscious desires and fears, she increasingly exhibits in this manner the arbitrariness of Victorian gender boundaries. Reflecting on her future success, Gabriel Nash generalizes about the special power of such celebrity in the modern period: "Her greatest idea must always be to show herself, and fortunately she has a great quantity of that treasure to show. I think of her absolutely as a real producer, but as a producer whose production is her own person" (*TM*, 2:198). This idea that Miriam is an authentic producer of a product that is her "person" accords well with a certain rhetoric of narcissism and even masturbation that the narrative associates with her. When he visits Madame Carré's and witnesses Miriam playing Constance in Shakespeare's *King John*, Peter Sherringham metaphorizes her sudden display of talent in the following terms: "She had found the key to her box of treasures. In the summer, during their weeks of frequent meeting, she had only fumbled with the lock. One October day, while he was away, the key had slipped in, had fitted, or her finger had at last touched the right spring and the capricious casket had flown open" (1:338). Even if the eroticism of this extended metaphor is ignored, the rhetoric nonetheless suggests how much more powerful Miriam is when she relies primarily on herself, calling attention to a self-reliance usually associated with male characters.

Nowhere is this slippage of gender boundaries more evident than in Miriam's relations with Gabriel Nash and Nick Dormer. Part of the plot revolves crucially around Julia Dallow's unexpected arrival at Nick Dormer's studio and her fancy that she has "surprised" Nick and Miriam together. Of course, Nick is only painting Miriam's portrait, although Nick's fascination with his subject is a reasonable motive for Julia's jealousy. Add to this possible romantic triangle Miriam's apparent interest in Nick Dormer, and the reader is drawn into a plot that can be read in two radically different ways. If Julia Dallow breaks her engagement with Nick primarily because his artistic career has drawn him into a romantic affair with the actress Miriam Rooth, then the conflict between art and politics seems merely a pretense for a nineteenth-century melodrama. For all of Nick's sacrifices for art, there is the shabby explanation that he has been motivated primarily by his romantic interest in Miriam. By the same token, Julia Dallow's termination of her engagement with Nick is not based on her own deep commitments to public service and political life; it is simply the result of blind jealousy. James's point in concocting such a trivial plot could only be that "love conquers all," for better or for worse, and that art and politics hardly deserve as much attention as individual romantic passions.

Such an interpretation hardly sounds like Henry James's other fiction, so the other reading of the plot deserves at least some consideration. From this view, Julia Dallow utterly misunderstands Nick's interest in Miriam Rooth, failing to see that Nick's passion for the actress is entirely aesthetic, in large part because Nick's romantic interests are far more engaged by Gabriel Nash. Nick's infatuation with Gabriel Nash is not quite sexual, just as his fascination with Miriam Rooth is not entirely abstract; both Gabriel Nash and Miriam Rooth represent ambiguous, at times androgynous, sexual identities. Critical efforts to sort out Gabriel's and Miriam's "proper" places in Victorian social psychology (and its literature) are doomed to failure because both characters transgress such conventions. Kaja Silverman tries to treat Gabriel Nash as surrogate "father" and Miriam Rooth as "mother" in the "fantasmatic" structure of authorial desire in the novel.[37] But Miriam quite consistently refuses to play the "mother" function in the heterosexual Oedipus complex not only for Henry James but for any and all of his male characters in the novel. Just as she refuses to be conventionally "courted," so she refuses to behave as the medium through which Peter or Nick will construct his identity at the expense of her own. In a similar fashion, Gabriel Nash refuses to play the "father," even though he will be repeatedly identified as Nick's aesthetic "muse." Repeatedly feminized, Gabriel Nash cannot perform the Victorian psychological function of surrogate father; repeatedly masculinized, Miriam Rooth refuses to act out the complementary maternal function. Indeed, both characters seem self-consciously designed parodies of other characters' *needs* for paternal and maternal surrogates. This confusion of conventionally masculine and feminine roles attracts Nick, explicitly because of his own love for arts that by definition challenge such conventions and implicitly because he is himself in doubt about his own sexuality. Indeed, Julia Dallow dislikes Gabriel Nash as much as she does Miriam Rooth; both of them represent aesthetic decadence, vulgarity, and a snide disregard for the English propriety that Julia and Peter Sherringham so typify. That Julia can be jealous of both in her romantic relationship with Nick Dormer is further evidence that these two characters transgress conventional Victorian boundaries of gender and sexuality.

Eric Haralson has argued convincingly not only that Gabriel Nash is modeled on Oscar Wilde but that Nash also embodies the traits of sexual and aesthetic "queerness" that late Victorian culture identified with the Decadents.[38] In his biography of Wilde, Richard Ellmann draws several comparisons between Wilde's familiar expressions and those used by Gabriel Nash in the novel.[39] Fred Kaplan speculates that Wilde's *The Picture of Dorian Grey*, "which began appearing in *Lippincott's Magazine* in July 1890, . . . may have been in part a contrapuntal, slanted response by Wilde to *The Tragic Muse*, whose serial publication was completed in May 1890 and which was published in book form early in June."[40] That Henry James did not like Oscar Wilde and refused to sign Stuart Merrill's petition for clemency for Wilde that was circulated widely among intellectuals and artists in 1895 should not distract us from interpreting Gabriel Nash as a positive representation of a character who is homosexual and represents many of James's aesthetic views in *The Tragic Muse*. It is also fair to say that Nash represents several views that are inimical to James, including Nash's patronizing attitude toward most characters, his personal affectations, and his studied laziness. But behind these disguises of the conventional aesthete so reviled in the popular press of James's day, Gabriel Nash serves as a spokesman for many of James's most important claims for the social functions of art, including: art as the medium for expressing the cultural unconscious; art as a mode of being, rather than of any specific utility; the artist as possessing a special consciousness on which "nothing is lost."

In representing the relations among Gabriel Nash, Nick Dormer, and Miriam Rooth as founded primarily on aesthetic interests, even as he uses a highly erotic style to express those interests, James was following what Haralson terms "his tendency to treat (homo)sexuality by implication and indirection," especially in his writings of the 1890s.[41] Even in this cautious manner, however, James carefully distinguishes between the dominant homosocial bonding of the English ruling class and the "queer" community established by his aesthetically sensitive characters. Nick Dormer's political and social future depends not only on Julia Dallow's aid in providing him with the parliamentary seat for Harsh that she controls but also on his father's close friend and adviser, Mr. Carteret, whose promise of a bequest to Nick on the day he marries Julia Dallow assures him of the economic means to support his political position. The relationship between Nick and Mr. Carteret is constantly shadowed by Nick's father, Sir Nicholas. Like Julia Dallow, Mr. Carteret lives vicariously his political passions by advising others. Never married, attended by the faithful servant, Mr. Chayter, and his dutiful solicitor, Mr. Mitton, Mr. Carteret epitomizes the deeply repressed homosexual panic at the heart of English patriarchy. When Nick visits him at the old Abbey of Beauclere to tell Mr. Carteret that he has given up his parliamentary seat, Mr. Carteret responds by insisting that Nick should be "ashamed" and that he has "been bad," much as a father might scold a child and much as the ruling class trivializes art as a childish distraction from serious work (*TM,* 2:167, 174). Nick defends himself against such charges by claiming, "I'm not bad. But I'm different. . . . Different from my father. Different from Mrs. Dallow. Different from you" (2:167).

Nick's "difference" is both his commitment to art and his dim understanding of what interests him in other people. What he loves in Miriam Rooth is what he equally loves in Gabriel Nash, and it is just the excitement of their iconoclastic honesty, their refusal to obey the sober proprieties of English society, that is also full of erotic hints for Nick Dormer. The supposed honesty of both Gabriel and Miriam seems to contradict their mutual commitment to telling stories and playing parts, but it is just this honesty with regard to the fictionality of everyday life that makes both seem so appealing to Nick.[42] Just after his election to the parliamentary seat of Harsh, Nick describes himself to his mother as "two men": "The difficulty is that I'm two men; it's the strangest thing that ever was. . . . I'm two quite distinct human beings, who have scarcely a point in common" (*TM,* 1:244). Nick is referring to himself before and after the election, and he knows well that the consequence of his victory is subordination to Julia Dallow. After all, she has provided the vacant parliamentary seat and organized his campaign to ensure his victory. Earlier his mother had asked Nick, "Aren't you her member. . . ?" to which Nick replies, "*Her* member—am I hers?" (1:243). There is no need to read into this exchange any phallic double entendre to understand how Nick feels the conventional gender hierarchies have been reversed at precisely the moment of his political success. Nick remains divided between the man who is capable of representing himself as an artist and the man who represents someone else. Lady Agnes puts the case precisely in terms of the metaphor of "representation," thus calling attention to the distance separating artistic from political representation for Nick: " 'Well, if the place is hers and you represent the place—!' she began. But she went no further, for Nick had interrupted her with a laugh. 'What a droll thing to "represent," when one thinks of it!' " (1:243).

Julia clearly disempowers, even castrates, Nick, but he consistently takes strength from his relationship with Gabriel Nash. Early in the novel, Nick explains to Peter Sherringham just what he finds so appealing in Nash:

> "His means, his profession, his belongings, have never anything to do with the question. He doesn't shade off into other people; he's as neat as an outline cut out of paper with scissors. I like him therefore because in dealing with him you know what you've got hold of.[43] With most men you don't: to pick the flower you must break off the whole dusty thorny worldly branch; you find you're taking up in your grasp all sorts of other people and things, dangling accidents and conditions. Poor Nash has none of those encumbrances: he's the solitary fragrant blossom."
>
> "My dear fellow, you'd be better for a little of the same pruning!" Sherringham retorted. (*TM,* 1:80–81)

In the rhetorical play between phallic "branch" and vaginal "blossom," Nick turns Gabriel Nash into a hermaphroditic figure in order to stress Nash's self-sufficiency. In these respects, Nash resembles Miriam, whose artistic powers give her the aura of one capable of self-engenderment. Despite romantic banter between Miriam and Gabriel early in the novel, as well as Sherringham's fear that he may have to compete with Nash for her affections, James makes it clear that Gabriel and Miriam are kindred spirits. When Miriam first appears at Nick's studio for her sitting, she is brought to him by Gabriel Nash. Miriam explains that Gabriel's companionship is "a relief to her mother": "When I take him she has perfect peace. . . . People think he's my 'companion'; I'm sure they fancy I pay him. I'd pay him, if he'd take it . . . rather than give him up, for it doesn't matter that he's not a lady. He *is* one in tact and sympathy, as you see" (*TM*, 2:38).

Peter Sherringham thinks that Gabriel Nash "sounds like an Elizabethan dramatist," referring explicitly to his surname's evocation of Thomas Nashe, who is also considered one of the Renaissance originators of the modern English novel, as well as hinting at the bisexuality of so many Elizabethan males, especially those in the theater (*TM*, 1:77). This analogy is equally important in establishing Gabriel's aesthetic affinity with Miriam Rooth because Nash seems to take less interest in Miriam's actual performances than Sherringham and Nick. Gabriel repeatedly claims to have "invented" Miriam—a claim he can support primarily on the bases of having introduced her to Nick and Peter and having contributed to the costs of her training by Madame Carré. Yet insofar as Miriam succeeds on the London stage and in the press, she has invented herself, much as Nick imagines Gabriel distinguishes himself from the usual rank and file of men. What Gabriel and Miriam share is imaginative power sufficient to transcend and often overturn conventional social realities. It is just this power that inspires Nick Dormer, and it is why the title of the novel remains ambiguous to the end.

On the one hand, of course, the title of "tragic muse" refers merely to Miriam's ambition to pass from melodramatic and comedic roles to the role of tragic heroine. In another sense, Miriam is Nick Dormer's "tragic muse," both as the subject of the two portraits he paints of her and as the occasion for his difficult decision to give up fortune and respectable marriage for his art. The latter reading of the title is further complicated by Gabriel Nash's role as Nick's "muse"—a part Nash plays even more explicitly toward the end of the novel in those chapters in which critics note he begins to fade from the dramatic action.[44] Nick's fictional disappearance is described in the narrative as akin to some event in a "delicate Hawthorne tale," and it is anticipated, even predicted, by Miriam in her final sitting for Nick (*TM*, 2:412). Concerned that he is losing his primary source of inspiration, Miriam suggests that he "find other models. Paint Gabriel Nash. . . . It will be a good way to get rid of him." And then, as if to stress for the reader that she is referring here to the competition between aesthetic and romantic passions, Miriam adds: "Paint Mrs. Dallow, too, . . . if you wish to eradicate the last possibility of a throb" (2:398).

The next chapter (49) opens with the narrator confirming that Miriam "had guessed happily in saying to him that to offer to paint Gabriel Nash would be the way to get rid of that visitant" (*TM*, 2:400). Before Nash vanishes, however, he offers his own prediction that "Mrs. Dallow will send for you. . . . To paint her portrait. She'll recapture you on that basis. . . . Take care, take care . . ." (2:406). The picture Nash paints of Julia and Nick reunited is clearly one of social respectability, in which Nick will "sketch" "on days you can't hunt" and will be regarded by "bishops and ambassadors . . . as if you were a 'well-known' awfully clever amateur" (2:406). Having made his prediction that Nick will return to the respectable and very insular circle of the English ruling class, Nash obligingly vanishes, "without a trace," like "a personage in a fairy-tale or a melodrama," leaving Nick with the fantasy that "in the portrait he had begun" Nash's image had "an odd tendency to fade gradually from the canvas" (2:412).

The strange coincidence of Miriam's and Gabriel's contradictory predictions about the consequences of Nick's attempt to paint Julia Dallow—that it will end forever his love for Julia or that it will guarantee that "she'll put up with the palette if you'll put up with the country-house"—leaves the conclusion of *The Tragic Muse* strangely suspended between opposite possibilities (2:406). When the call does come from Julia for Nick to paint her portrait, Nick does not readily agree before arranging "with the former mistress of his fate the conditions, as they might be called, under which she should sit to him" (2:440). The result appears to be Nick's success in painting at least one more portrait: "Every one will remember in how recent an exhibition general attention was attracted, as the newspapers said in describing the private view, to the noble portrait of a lady which was the final outcome of that arrangement" (2:440). Much as this account seems to confirm Nash's prediction, James is elusive to the very end of the novel, leaving the future of Julia and Nick's relationship in tantalizing suspension: "I may finally say that his friend Nash's predictions about his reunion with Mrs. Dallow have not up to this time been justified. On the other hand, I must not omit to add, this lady has not, at the latest accounts, married Mr. Macgeorge. It is very true there has been a rumour that Mr. Macgeorge is worried about her—has even ceased at all fondly to believe in her" (2:441).

Blair argues that the two characters who radically challenge the proprieties of English society, including its imperialist ambitions and racist sense of its own superiority, do so by means of a cosmopolitanism that James claims for his own narrative authority. Thus Miriam Rooth, the Jewish actress, and Gabriel Nash, the worldly aesthete, must vanish from James's center of interest, the English ruling class: "The racial logic he appropriates from popular contexts enables but ultimately limits the range of his performances in the cosmopolitan mode."[45] There are, however, at least two other ways to read the ending of *The Tragic Muse,* even as we acknowledge the truth of Blair's interpretation that James remains deeply conflicted regarding the political significance of the avant-garde forces he has unleashed in the novel. The safest reading of the conclusion would be that Nick has internalized the authority of both Miriam Rooth and Gabriel Nash; he has learned from both of them and thereby gained confidence in his artistic vocation. On such a basis, he may properly return to Julia Dallow, who must now recognize that their interpersonal differences will be the bases for a successful marriage: "You'll eat your cake and have it," as Nash says (*TM,* 2:406). This is certainly a conventionally happy ending, but it does not mean that either Miriam Rooth or Gabriel Nash has been banished. Miriam has made her own choice of Dashwood, the theater, the popular press, and a celebrity that already exceeds the increasingly diminished authority of an older ruling class. By the same token, Nash now circulates inside the otherwise closed world of that ruling class by virtue of his influence on Nick. What Christopher Lane has judged to be Nash's function as "never . . . *more* than a fantasy" still has the potential to change heterosexual relations.[46]

On the other hand, Miriam may be right that Nick's successful portrait of Julia will "eradicate the last possibility of a throb" and that only social gossips have imagined that Julia will marry Nick, rather than Mr. Macgeorge. If so, then there is at least the hint that Nick's relationship with Julia is, like his friendship with Miriam, primarily an aesthetic one, and that Nick recognizes his need to remain a bachelor, like his creator, Henry James. In this case, we must also conclude that James has caused Nash to "disappear" primarily to control the homoerotic passions and rhetoric that characterize his relationship with Nick. Nevertheless, the fictional representation of a man as another man's artistic muse, together with the hint that such a relationship may have undertones of the "tragic," strikes me as decidedly modern for 1890.

Up to the very end of the novel, James gives hints that the new social relationships he has described—Nick and Gabriel, Miriam and Nick, Miriam and Basil Dashwood, Miriam and Peter—have had some positive effects on more conventional social relations. In the final paragraph of the novel, the narrator offers just a hint "that in glancing about the little circle of the interests I have tried to evoke I am suddenly warned by a sharp sense of modernness" (*TM*, 2:440). Among the several examples of modernity that James offers in the novel, Biddy Dormer's relationship with Florence Tressilian, Julia Dallow's sometime companion, is often forgotten because Biddy ends up marrying Peter Sherringham. Yet before she accepts Peter's proposal, Biddy first spends a week in London with "Florry Tressilian, who had lately taken the dearest little flat in a charming new place, . . . with all kinds of lifts and tubes and electricities" (2:417–18). Florence is indeed a very modern woman, who "could by this time do without a chaperon—she had two latchkeys and went alone on the top of omnibuses, and her name was in the Red Book" (2:418).

Biddy refers to her time with Florence Tressilian as her time of "enlightened spinsterhood," causing her brother, Nick, to be "immensely abashed and humiliated, for, modern as he had fatuously supposed himself, there were evidently currents more modern yet" (*TM*, 2:418). Biddy's relationship with Florry is insufficiently developed to justify any conclusions regarding their lesbianism, but it is fair to conclude that Biddy gains strength by her association with another independent woman.[47] It is just this confidence in herself that enables Biddy to accept Peter Sherringham on her own terms, rather than as the "young bright slim rose-coloured woman" Sherringham meets in her brother's studio (1:96). Acknowledging that homosocial relations may be means of building confidence in both men and women in their respective same-sex relations may only confirm the ideology of homosociality that informs much of Victorian and nineteenth-century American cultures. Nevertheless, James aligns himself with more modern twentieth-century women writers when he recognizes how women rely on their own homosocial bonds in the work of socialization.

Whatever his relationship with Julia Dallow may entail, Nick Dormer does not forget the influences of Miriam Rooth and Gabriel Nash. In a similar manner, James suggests that Biddy Dormer can accept Peter Sherringham only with the confidence she gains from other independent women. To be sure, the vague associations of Miriam's Jewish backgrounds with the iconoclasm of the aesthetic avant-garde do not quite constitute a cosmopolitanism that effectively challenges the more insidious global reach of British imperialism. Unlike *What Maisie Knew* and *The American Scene, The Tragic Muse* does not engage the racial questions so fundamental to British imperialism, substituting instead a religious heritage for a wide range of questions regarding ethnic, racial, and national identities. But James still manages to distinguish between the transnational ambitions of modern art and the will to power that lurks behind the facade of English ruling-class worldliness. He also hints that change is in the air, that modern relations on the interpersonal level might also be followed by more enlightened political possibilities. In the "large bright picture of her progress through time and round the world" that Gabriel Nash paints of Miriam Rooth's growing celebrity, James makes it clear that the only "race" affected by her success will be the "human race":

> She's a big more or less directed force, and I quite admit that she'll do for a while a lot of good. She'll have brightened up the world for a great many people—have brought the ideal nearer to them and held it fast for an hour with its feet on earth and its great wings trembling. . . . Blest is he who has dropped even the smallest coin into the little iron box that contains the precious savings of mankind. Miriam will doubtless have dropped a big gold-piece. It will be found in the general scramble on the day the race goes bankrupt. And then for herself she'll have had a great go at life. (*TM*, 2:198–99)

It may be mere wishful thinking on James's part to imagine that modern art might challenge the commercialism of modern society by offering a contribution to the human economy rather than selfishly taking its due. Unlike the political and social economies that James criticizes in *The Tragic Muse*, successful art earns more by virtue of what it gives; its generosity is itself wealth for both the artist and the viewer. Struggling valiantly to found modern social relations on just such aesthetic reciprocity, James engages the modern age that elsewhere baffles and frustrates him.

4 ꙮ Textual Preference: James's Literary Defenses against Sexuality in "The Middle Years" and "The Death of the Lion"

> There had been a big brush of wings, the flash of an opaline robe, and then, with a great cool stir of the air, the sense of an angel's having swept down and caught me to his bosom. He held me only till the danger was over, and it all took place in a minute.
>
> —Henry James, "The Death of the Lion" (1894)

Until Eve Sedgwick's 1984 English Institute essay "The Beast in the Closet: James and the Writing of Homosexual Panic," discussions of gender and sexual preferences in James's writings focused primarily on his attitudes toward nineteenth-century women's rights politics and his characterizations of women in his fiction.[1] Whether James's works are part of the patriarchal ideology of Victorian culture or constitute modes of resistance to the gender stereotypes of his times remains a crucial question for scholars and theorists, in part because James continues to occupy such a central position in the history and theory of the modern novel. However we answer this question, Sedgwick's work encourages us to consider the history of attitudes toward homosexuality and homosociality in the assessment of James's literary representations of gender.

What was once celebrated as the aesthetic indeterminacy of James's modernism must now be interpreted in relation to James's ambiguities regarding the gender and sexual identification of his most compelling characters and, of course, himself. I shall not attempt to address the biographical Henry James in this chapter, but instead the literary "master" who is unquestionably among James's most carefully crafted characters and whose elusiveness, like that of James's Shakespeare, must be counted one of his singular marks of genius.[2] For the moderns so influenced by James, literary genius was often figured as sexual potency, erotic energy, and Dionysian excess that transcended the natural limits of ordinary human sexuality. From Eliot's "typist and young man carbuncular" or "Lil and Albert" in *The Waste Land* to Beckett's characters anonymously coupling, modern literature commonly represents physical sexuality as repulsive, degrading, and (perhaps most importantly) unproductive. The modern artist often claims his creative potency by transfiguring ordinary sexuality into aesthetic expression either by demonizing or caricaturing the feminine as the radical other of a more genuine poetic productivity.[3]

Feminist scholars and literary historians have demonstrated convincingly how patriarchal ideology worked hard in the early modern period to minimize women's productivity, often in specific reaction to the struggles by women to achieve legal, political, and economic recognition of their work.[4] Aesthetic theories and practices certainly contributed to the perpetuation, even intensification, of patriarchal social hierarchies, often by sophistically attempting to refute the self-evidence of women's work and by fantastic distortion insisting on the "unnaturalness" of such work. But less attention has been devoted to the ways such patriarchal ideology constructed stereotypes of the feminine to deal with what Sedgwick terms the "homosexual panic" so fundamental to the homosocial practices of modern Western patriarchy.

Gay studies have attempted to change the often binary assumptions of gender studies by arguing that there are other possibilities for relations among men than the homosexual panic hiding behind the fundamentally homosocial practices of patriarchy. If gay scholars are right, then we ought to consider these alternatives as potential modes of political and cultural resistance that should be interpreted in a coordinated fashion with any successful feminist criticism of modern literature, culture, and politics. In *Masculine Desire: The Sexual Politics of Victorian Aestheticism*, Richard Dellamora acknowledges the importance of Sedgwick's work for his own study of nineteenth-century homophobia and homosexuality, but he distinguishes his work from what he terms "Sedgwick's female-centered, heterosexually determinate focus" by arguing for the possibilities of a wide range of "relations between men" that *resist* the homophobia and homosexual panic of the Victorian period.[5]

Dellamora's approach makes good historical and theoretical sense, as demonstrated by a study that richly illustrates the range of "masculine desires" in Victorian culture from Tennyson to Wilde. But Dellamora's work also poses a significant theoretical problem for critics interested in relating gay and feminist theories as necessary complements.[6] Granting the unstable relation between the patriarchal functions of homosociality and the oppositional potential of homosexual behavior and cultural expression in the Victorian and early modern periods, what criteria of judgment—that is, of *criticism*—are we to use to assess the ideological functions of the cultural representation of relations between men?

Since Foucault, gay studies have addressed this problem in part by pointing out how the criminalization of male homosexuality in the late nineteenth century, with the passage of such legislation as the Criminal Law Amendment Act of 1885 in England, gives public visibility to an ideology distinguishing homosocial from homosexual in a way that allows subsequent expressions of relations among men to be judged quite clearly. To be sure, the passage of laws declaring certain relations among men to be criminal significantly affects the possibilities for resistance in the political, social, and cultural spheres. But the mere facts of such legislation do not in and of themselves divide neatly all expressions of possible "relations between men" as either "for" or "against" the ideology of homophobia.

Another way to situate "relations between men" in terms of ideology is to consider lesbian relations as critical to our theoretical and historical understanding of same-sex relations and representations. This connection may seem self-evident in the 1990s, but Sedgwick argues that in the two previous decades, "separatist-feminist" assumptions informed "the lesbian interpretive framework" in ways that excluded "commonality between gay male and lesbian experience and identity."[7] Sedgwick goes on to argue: "Since the late 1970s, however, there have emerged a variety of challenges to this understanding of how lesbian and gay male desires and identities might be mapped against each other. Each challenge has led to a refreshed sense that lesbians and gay men may share important though contested aspects of one another's histories, cultures, identities, politics, and destinies."[8] Sedgwick wisely includes "contested aspects" of gay and lesbian histories as crucial to any utopian project of establishing what has been and can be *shared* by lesbians and gays.

The contested cultural space of gays and lesbians has to a large extent, however, remained an issue of contemporary gender and sexual politics. Scholarly and critical work such as that of Dellamora and Sedgwick encourages us to reconsider the sites of historical contestation from which many contemporary lesbian and gay politics and theory derive. A great deal of important historical recovery has been accomplished by gay and lesbian studies, especially in what Sedgwick terms "the reclamation and relegitimation of a courageous history of lesbian trans-gender role-playing and identification," but the actual contestation, conflict, and even cultural *confusion* between lesbians and gays has not been addressed adequately in historical and cultural terms.

Nowhere is this more evident than in the new studies of Henry James as a gay writer. The renaissance of work on Henry James as a crucial figure in the cultural self-definition and ideological demonization of homosexuals in the early modern period has covered virtually every aspect of James studies. Not only have previously neglected works such as *In the Cage* and "The Death of the Lion" and "The Middle Years" been rediscovered as tours de force of a gay aesthetic, but James's biography and his autobiographical works have been reinterpreted. Yet gay studies of Henry James have flourished, so that the once-traditional consideration of James's late Victorian demonization of lesbians and their cultural identification with the politics and aims of the "New Woman" has disappeared from our intellectual conversation.[9] This chapter is an effort to restore to the exciting discussions of James now under way the historical conflict and contest between gays and lesbians at the historical moment both groups were struggling to establish their *political* identities in reaction to legally authorized cultural phobias regarding same-sex relations.

Reading these conflicts in James's fiction must be carefully historicized in his career unless we want simply to essentialize a radically playful but effectively unconscious figure we shall call "Henry James," constructed as it were from our desires as readers to discover a "gay Henry James" as an author function. This is a delightful and attractive Henry James, but this Henry James also allows us to forget how same-sex politics did not always rely on the sorts of coalitions between gays and lesbians for which Sedgwick rightly appeals. This Henry James also allows us to forget the Henry James who lent credibility to the cultural stereotype of the New Woman as "unnatural" or "deviant" lesbian.[10] Although this Henry James has traditionally been identified as the "master" of the familiar aesthetic ideology of Western patriarchy, we must look closely at the ways the gay Henry James also developed in conflict with these stereotypes of lesbians and emancipated women.

In his writings of the 1880s, James emphasizes the demonic effects of lesbian feminist identity. From *The Portrait of a Lady* (1880) to *The Bostonians* and *The Princess Casamassima* (1886), the emancipated woman threatens the established order and the cultural values James is intent on upholding, even when he recognizes how such cultural conservatism can be abused. Henrietta Stackpole, Olive Chancellor, and the Princess Casamassima (Christina Light) are clear warnings in the 1880s. They are excesses that their doubles must somehow avoid while not ignoring the changes these new women announce as ineluctable. Isabel Archer must avoid the careerism and pragmatism of Henrietta Stackpole without accepting the false patriarchal authority revealed in Gilbert Osmond. Verena Tarrant must be "saved" from the political hysteria and paranoia of Olive Chancellor, but only if Verena can avoid the southern romance plotted by Basil Ransom. And perhaps most interesting of all, Hyacinth Robinson cannot simply "switch" from the corruptions of the patriarchal class system to the equally hierarchical authority represented by the anarchists and the princess. In reading the complex rhetoric representing the homosexual subcultures of London in *The Princess Casamassima,* we should thus be reminded that Hyacinth's suicide has as much to do with his inability to identify his proper gender role and sexual identity as it does with his revolutionary politics.[11] In this latter regard, the princess has helped lead him astray as successfully as any of the anarchists of "The Sun and Moon."

In chapters 1 and 2, I argue that James's fiction in the 1870s questions patriarchal ideology, but in ambivalent ways that leave James in considerable doubt about how men and women should overcome such domination. The gothic conclusion of *The American*—both the revelation of the Bellegardes' secret and Claire's withdrawal into a convent—is James's own evasion of the alternative available to him to grant women the power not only to question but to overturn patriarchal ideology. In both "The Last of the Valerii" and *The American,* however, any such feminine rebellion is subordinated to James's own author function, and the women characters either accept their subordinate social roles or mime grotesquely the power of patriarchal ideology. In the 1880s, James seems intent on experimenting with the fictional possibilities of various types of the "New Woman" as if to prove to himself that none will satisfy the requirements of his imagination. In short, no feminine character in his fiction of the 1880s succeeds in approaching the complexity, cultivation, and self-reliance of his own narrative voice. In the 1880s, James subordinated the feminine, stereotyped as it certainly was in his typology, to his own aesthetic power, much in the manner of his male modernist heirs, many of whom claimed James as a significant influence.

In the early 1890s, James still measures his protagonists against "dangerous" women characters, who variously represent some violation of James's aesthetic and cultural values. But the change initiated in the character of Hyacinth Robinson—ambivalent in his gender role and sexual identity—now assumes the appearance of explicit homosexual identity. Homosexual and homoerotic representation is often affirmed by setting male friends in opposition to socialite women, often also represented as couples. The resulting contests and combinations not only signal a departure from James's earlier studies of social and psychological relations but also offer him a certain aesthetic and intellectual liberty to explore new and alternative social roles and identities. This tone of emancipation at the level of style is manifest in a certain overt playfulness, which ranges from homoerotic punning to irony. Such comedy should by no means be taken to mean that James happily adjusts to the new fluidity in gender roles and sexual behaviors occurring in the 1890s; James's ironies bespeak his deep conflicts regarding his changing attitudes toward same-sex relations and to the general issue of sexual propriety in early modern culture.

Among the many possible reasons for such a change in James's representation of gender roles and sexual identities, the most plausible is Fred Kaplan's argument in *Henry James: The Imagination of Genius:*

> Something extraordinary began happening to James in the mid-1890s, and more frequently in the next decade. He fell in love a number of times. He established intimate relationships, beyond his usual friendships, that for the first time provided him with the feeling of being in love. If it was a feeling more than an articulated awareness, it was a powerful feeling. He had a need for intimacy. . . . In each case, he fell in love with a younger man. . . . Each time he fell in love, he placed the emphasis on friendship, not on physical consummation, which remained as dangerous, as threatening, as morally and culturally difficult for him as it had always been.[12]

What Kaplan describes as Henry James "coming out," insofar as this was possible in the ferociously homophobic Victorian culture of the 1890s, I think begins a few years earlier in James's short fiction of 1893 to 1894. It should not surprise James scholars that he would first have worked out his personal desires in fictional form; what is most interesting, however, is the way in which his defenses regarding sexual desire involve the demonization of the already available lesbian feminist stereotype of the 1880s.

My two examples, "The Middle Years" and "The Death of the Lion," have been rediscovered in recent years, thanks to the new critical attention paid to homosexuality in James's fiction. "The Middle Years" was the only story James published in 1893; it appeared in *Scribner's* magazine in May. "The Death of the Lion" was published in *The Yellow Book* in April 1894. Both were published in the collection *Terminations* in 1895. Previously, these stories were considered minor contributions to the "stories of writers and artists" theme; both deal centrally with the relation between an aging male writer and a younger male admirer.

The two stories are virtual doubles of each other, both in their plots and the pairing of two men and two (or more) women in their respective denouements. This doubling between the stories is complicated by the doubling of the male characters within the story: Dencombe, the author of *The Middle Years,* and Doctor Hugh, one of Dencombe's admirers who is also attending physician to "the Countess," parallel quite neatly the writer Neil Paraday and the worshipful journalist who narrates "The Death of the Lion." This sort of internal doubling is complicated further by James's use of the title "The Middle Years" for the third volume of his autobiography, published twenty-four years later in 1917. The two stories James wrote at the age of fifty, and James's own changing attitudes toward his work, his personal life, and his friendships, are complexly twinned. Indeed, as I try to sort out the relations between homosexual and lesbian relations in the two stories, I want to keep in play the doubling within James's own authorial and personal identity. Edel and Powers have pointed out in *The Complete Notebooks* that James was prone to referring to his inspiration or imagination as a "guardian spirit," sometimes addressed as "*mon bon*" and at other times as "*caro mio*" in his notebook entries.[13]

At least at some level, James falls in love fictively with himself in these two stories, but this may well be his own defense against the more obvious expression of homoerotic passion between men. I want to be careful not to reduce such aesthetic "self-love" to the narcissism so frequently and often erroneously attributed to same-sex relationships, both for the sake of respecting the complexity of James's artistic representations and the variety of same-sex behaviors and psychologies. As Kaja Silverman points out in her neo-Freudian interpretation of James's fiction, "narcissistic object-choice" is "the libidinal economy which Freud most frequently associates with homosexuality."[14] There is unquestionably some element of narcissism evident in the mutual relations between the male couples in "The Middle Years" and "The Death of the Lion"; each character projects onto the other his particular desires, including very erotic passions. Silverman concludes that such narcissism acts out the "self-love" that she identifies "with sodomitical identification," which "permits the subject to participate at the imaginary level in the 'father's' phallic sexuality—to penetrate by identifying with the one-who-penetrates."[15] But in James's somewhat different psychic triangulation, both male characters constitute themselves in relation to a third term that is *literature*. Although we have been conditioned as readers to expect the "author" and "reader" parts played by the respective male couples in these stories to perform the "active" and "passive" roles of the Freudian family romance, James causes both male characters to "sacrifice" themselves for "art." At a certain level, the psychopoetic scenario is quite conventionally romantic, but there is another sense in which their mutual sacrifices allow them to help James defend against his own homoerotic anxieties by displacing them into aesthetic concerns and to offer alternative subject positions to the customary roles of masculine self-assertion. By figuring homoeroticism carefully and consistently in terms of the male characters' shared interests in literature, James may represent their passion as perfectly *textual* not only to disguise his own narcissistic homosexuality but also to consider psychic triangulation *apart from* the customary narrative of heterosexual subject formation. Yet the cost of this experiment is that the respective bonding of the two male characters in each story occurs by virtue of a dramatized struggle with female characters, who are themselves ultimately expelled from the "family romance." In his effort to substitute "literature" for both the "father" and the "mother," the textual for the sexual, James ends up reinstating gender binaries by demonizing lesbian sexuality as he affirms homosexuality.

In "The Middle Years," Dr. Hugh meets the middle-aged writer Dencombe at the health resort of Bournemouth, where Dencombe has come to recover his health following the ordeal of finishing his finest and just published work, *The Middle Years*. Doctor Hugh, who "looked like a German physiologist" and is "enamoured of literary form," has managed to get an advance copy of *The Middle Years* from "a friend of his, a journalist," who has "lent him his copy . . . sent to the office of the journal and already the subject of a 'notice' which . . . it had taken a full quarter of an hour to prepare."[16] Dr. Hugh is at the moment employed by the Countess, a "large lady, an Englishwoman by birth and the daughter of a celebrated baritone, whose taste *minus* his talent she had inherited" and "widow of a French nobleman" ("Middle," 88).

"Taken ill on a journey in Switzerland the Countess had picked" Doctor Hugh "up at an hotel," and "the accident of his happening to please her had made her offer him, with her imperious liberality, terms that couldn't fail to dazzle a practitioner without patients and whose resources had been drained dry by his studies" ("Middle," 89). Also accompanying the Countess is Miss Vernham, a pianist and traveling companion, who has hopes of benefiting from what she believes is the inheritance Dr. Hugh may expect on the death of the Countess, who suffers from "a grave organic disorder" (89).

Although attended by his own physician, Dencombe increasingly depends on Doctor Hugh, from the moment that the young doctor saves Dencombe from a fainting spell occasioned by an embarrassing confusion of their respective copies of *The Middle Years*. In the same paragraph in which James describes the Countess virtually "picking up" Doctor Hugh, Dencombe in effect captures the doctor's heart by swooning away:

> [Doctor Hugh] had taken up as it lay on the bench Dencombe's copy instead of his own, and his neighbour at once guessed the reason of his start: Doctor Hugh looked grave an instant; then he said: "I see you've been altering the text!" Dencombe was a passionate corrector, a fingerer of style; the last thing he ever arrived at was a form final for himself. . . . He was amused at the effect of the young man's reproach; for an instant it made him change colour. He stammered at any rate ambiguously, then through a blur of ebbing consciousness saw Doctor Hugh's mystified eyes. . . . Later he knew he had fainted and that Doctor Hugh had got him home in a Bath-chair. ("Middle," 90–91)

Ostensibly the onset of an old illness unconnected with this moment of embarrassment, Dencombe's "fainting" is in fictive fact the consequence of this confusion of texts and thus of proper ownership and authority. This is not merely a jeu d'esprit but a serious point in the narrative: what makes Dencombe such a great writer is the *reader's* capacity to carry the text further, to make something more than what is literally given.

It is, of course, the Jamesian aesthetic, and the literary Doctor Hugh is in love not so much with the enfeebled, albeit middle-aged, *body* of Dencombe as with the body of Dencombe's work, especially since that "body" is in large part Doctor Hugh's own as reader. All of this rhetorical dodging about is not just avoiding the homoeroticism of the tale; it is a certain aestheticizing that is impossible to disentangle from the issues of homosexuality in the narrative. These same questions are addressed, however, only in the context of the specific vulgarization of the two women who make increasingly brusque demands on Doctor Hugh and Dencombe. The Countess begins to suffer for the lack of Doctor Hugh's attendance on her, and in some anticipation of the "sacred fount" theme, she deteriorates in health as Dencombe and Doctor Hugh spend more time together.

The Countess is "so jealous that she had fallen ill," and Dencombe even emulates the familiar nineteenth-century (and very Jamesian) rhetoric of feminine sacrifice when he advises Doctor Hugh, "Stick to the Countess— don't mind me" ("Middle," 97). Indeed, the entire plot of the story revolves around the choice Doctor Hugh will make—between the meretricious Countess or the ethereal Dencombe. Doctor Hugh has, of course, already made his choice from the moment he secured an advance copy of *The Middle Years,* and there is an extraordinary scene of textual consummation that has all the qualities of homoerotic fantasy that Eve Sedgwick finds in James—"this half-conscious enforcing rhetoric of anality, numbness, and silence" of James's address to his "male muse."[17] In this passage, Dencombe describes for Doctor Hugh the work he would write with more time, another "go":

> Even for himself he was inspired as he told what his treasure would consist of; the precious metals he would dig from the mine, the jewels rare, strings of pearls, he would hang between the columns of his temple. He was wondrous for himself, so thick his convictions crowded, but still more wondrous for Doctor Hugh, who assured him none the less that the very pages he had just published were already encrusted with gems. This admirer, however, panted for the combinations to come and, before the face of the beautiful day, renewed to Dencombe his guarantee that his profession would hold itself responsible for such a life. ("Middle," 99)

The anality of the metaphors of mining, together with the fetishism of the "treasures" mined, is only superficially disguised by this rhetoric, which sounds very much like that of the French Symbolistes and their Anglo-Irish imitators. Like James, these early moderns often used images that condensed scatological, gemological, and corporeal referents. Often connected with savage, threatening femininity, this symbolist imagery is not exclusively homosexual; it more frequently serves to reinforce homosocial bonds.[18] In "The Middle Years," the eroticism of the rhetoric clearly reinforces same-sex desire, rather than serving more conventional homosocial purposes.

At the very moment Doctor Hugh makes his "choice" of "the consequences of my infatuation" ("Middle," 104), Miss Vernham arrives to ask Dencombe "to leave Doctor Hugh alone" to avoid doing "him a terrible injury." The injury turns out to be tangible enough: the Countess dies and leaves him "never a penny" (99, 104). Dencombe will also die in the final paragraphs of the story, uttering those famous words so often associated with James's ideals: "We work in the dark—we do what we can—we give what we have. Our doubt is our passion and our passion is our task. The rest is the madness of art" (105). But Dencombe and Doctor Hugh have mined the pearls of the writer's and reader's passion.

Left behind are Miss Vernham—"an odd creature but an accomplished pianist" ("Middle," 89)—and the Countess, the latter dead for want of Doctor Hugh's "attentions" and bereft of what Dencombe is so "lucid" in understanding about the two women: "He . . . had a characteristic vision of Miss Vernham's great motive. The Countess hated women of course . . . so the hungry pianist had no personal hopes and could only console herself with the bold conception of helping Doctor Hugh in order to marry him after he should get his money or else induce him to recognise her claim for compensation and buy her off" (101). Richard von Krafft-Ebing's *Psychopathia sexualis* was published in 1886 and gave scientific legitimation to nineteenth-century stereotypes of lesbians as sexual "deviants" whose "inversion" was typified by "masculine behavior." Carroll Smith-Rosenberg concludes that "Krafft-Ebing's lesbians seemed to desire male privileges and power as ardently as, perhaps more ardently than, they sexually desired women."[19]

Just such masculine miming characterizes the Countess, whose hatred of women is matched by her drive to dominate Doctor Hugh and Miss Vernham in the manner of hired servants. The passage describing Doctor Hugh's employment by the Countess quoted earlier sounds decidedly like a Victorian man soliciting a prostitute. And, of course, the other connotation of lesbianism throughout the nineteenth century was its "dangerous" association with the "deviance" of prostitution, as well as the association of lesbianism with what nineteenth-century medical writing imagined to be the "sexual pathology" of "primitive," especially African, women. Martha Vicinus points out how medical treatises in the first half of the nineteenth century link "the lives of prostitutes with those of cross-dressed lesbians. Both represented possibilities and fears for men, for each embodied an active, independent, uncontrollable sexuality."[20]

I am tempted to argue that Doctor Hugh, who "looked like a German physiologist," is a fictive version of the German neurologist Richard von Krafft-Ebing, whose *Psychopathia sexualis* was a cause célèbre as it was translated and republished in countless editions in the changing sexual culture of late-nineteenth-century Europe and America. Such a detail I cannot prove, but it is not by any means the important point. What matters here is the degree to which James is able to express a passionate homoeroticism not simply because it has been fully *textualized* in the relation of Dencombe and Doctor Hugh but also because it has been rendered different from the "deviance" so clearly represented by the Countess and Miss Vernham.

This lesbian "deviance" appears in "The Middle Years," however, to be little more than the projection onto these two meretricious women—one using inherited wealth and the other feeding parasitically on that wealth—of James's customary rage against the superficial commercialism of the modern age. This is just what prompts James's germ for "The Death of the Lion" (1894). As James wonders in his notebooks: "Could not something be done with the idea of the great . . . artist . . . who is tremendously made up to, . . . written for his autograph, portrait, etc., and yet with whose work, in this age of advertisement and newspaperism, this age of interviewing, not one of the persons concerned has the smallest acquaintance? It would have the merit, at least, of corresponding to an immense reality—a reality that strikes me every day of my life."[21] This donnée is virtually what James develops, adding a "journalist" who narrates the story of Neil Paraday's death at the country house of Prestidge as the melodrama of a master brought down by the murderous forces of the age unleashed by celebrity.

The nameless narrator might as well be Doctor Hugh's friend who provided the advance copy of Dencombe's *The Middle Years,* for the journalist who undergoes "a change of heart" begins as the mere underling of Mr. Pinhorn, "chief" of a "weekly periodical" he is determined to "bring up" by whatever means possible.[22] Young enough not to have been quite spoiled by the commercial press for which he works and old enough to know the glories of a truly literate culture, the narrator begins with the quixotic purpose of "writing up" the great writer Neil Paraday, whose works have been until this fictive moment virtually neglected.[23]

As in "The Middle Years," so here the modern age is characterized by the false celebrity fed by the newspapers and weekly magazines, as well as by meretricious women. In "The Death of the Lion," however, this modernity is connected explicitly with what Mr. Morrow, a publisher controlling the syndication of stories in thirty-seven journals, terms "the larger latitude," by which he explicitly means alternative gender roles and sexual identities ("Lion," 119). Vaulted to fame by a column (not a review or notice) in *The Empire,* Neil Paraday finds himself and his new book in unexpected competition with the latest sellers by Guy Walsingham, "the brilliant author of 'Obsessions'" and "a lady who goes in for the larger latitude," using a male pseudonym because "men are more naturally indelicate," and Dora Forbes, the male "author of 'The Other Way Round,'" who writes under a woman's pseudonym despite his bushy red mustache because "the larger latitude has simply got to come" and because "his sex makes him a less prejudiced witness" (113–15).

In this tale, a demanding and authoritative princess, who matches the Countess in "The Middle Years," is the eventual cause of Neil Paraday's death. However, a somewhat lesser socialite, Lady Augusta, also contributes to his death by borrowing his new manuscript, lending it out, and then losing it. These aristocratic women are virtual stock types and thus replaceable fictive parts; they mark in their characters and idle chatter the moral laxity of the modern age. That decadence is curiously entangled, however, with the "larger latitude," not so much because of the mannish behavior of these women— literal, materialistic, unsubtle, and selfish—but more to the degree that they mistake the writer's work for his person, the corpus for the corpse.

The loss of Paraday's unfinished manuscript is quite explicitly treated as a death-dealing castration. The narrator first hears the manuscript in a reading by Paraday that has the same romantic consequence as the textual consummation between Dencombe and Doctor Hugh in "The Middle Years." On first hearing "the written scheme of another book" read to him by Paraday, the narrator describes it as "a great gossiping eloquent letter—the overflow into talk of an artist's amorous plan," and soon the familiar images—"a mine of gold," "a precious" work—from the description of Dencombe's hopes in "The Middle Years" come flooding back: "The Idea he now communicated had all the freshness, the flushed fairness, of the conception untouched and untried: it was Venus rising from the sea and before the airs had blown upon her. I had never been so throbbingly present at such an unveiling" ("Lion," 106–7). The imagery of the birth of Venus carries over in this scene to the rhetoric of Paraday's description of his own desire for the time and privacy to complete the manuscript so planned. As the narrator exclaims, "My dear master, how, after all, are you going to do it? . . . Oh for a lone isle in a tepid sea!" Paraday replies quite candidly, "Isn't this practically a lone isle, and aren't you, as an encircling medium, tepid enough?" (107).

Like Dencombe, Paraday is recovering from an illness strangely tangled up with his previous book project and hanging over his new work: "Of course my illness made, while it lasted, a great hole—but I dare say there would have been a hole at any rate" ("Lion," 107). From this moment on, the narrator will serve as his protector, often figuring his role as that of a doctor.[24] All this homoerotic rhetoric suggests that the two mutually satisfy their sexual needs, even if both refuse to answer Mr. Morrow's insistent inquiries regarding Neil Paraday's views on the "larger latitude": "Mr. Morrow remarked invitingly that he should be happy to make a note of any observation on the movement in question, the bid for success under a lady's name, might suggest to Mr. Paraday. But the poor man, without catching the allusion, excused himself, pleading that . . . he suddenly felt unwell. . . . His young friend might be trusted to answer for him" (116).

Amid this banter, what I term in chapter 6 the rhetorical cross-dressing that would come to distinguish much of James's work from the second half of the 1890s to the end of his career, the socialite women who eventually pester Neil Paraday to death are curiously represented as figures of pain, if not outright sadomasochism.[25] Of Mrs. Weeks Wimbush, the brewer's wife, the narrator writes: "She was constructed of steel and leather, and all I asked of her for our tractable friend was not to do him to death. He had consented for a time to be of india-rubber, but my thoughts were fixed on the day he should resume his shape or at least get back into his box" ("Lion," 123). The box to which the narrator refers is clearly the form of Paraday's text, the frame of his writing that protects him from such attacks.

It is not surprising, then, that the text becomes the narrator's primary weapon in defending Paraday against these attacks by grasping, modern, celebrity-hunting women. "Defense" is the proper word, because James develops the "lion hunt" as an extended metaphor in this story, in the same manner he would develop the "hunt" in "The Beast in the Jungle," a story anticipated in many respects by "The Death of the Lion."[26] In this case, however, the narrator assumes more textual authority than Doctor Hugh in "The Middle

Years," and the narrator does so precisely in terms of a narrative of seduction that curiously appears to be intended as a romance of conversion. In this case, it is the conversion of a young American woman to the "larger latitude" represented by the homoerotic aesthetic of Paraday and Henry James.

The young American woman's name is Fanny Hurter. Recalling the comedic actress Fanny Rover in *The Tragic Muse* (1890) and anticipating Fanny Assingham in *The Golden Bowl* (1904), the name belongs to a fictive chain that certainly expresses James's obsessive anal humor. In one of his early notes for *What Maisie Knew* (1897), James names Maisie's parents "the Hurters," subsequently changing their surname to Farange.[27] Fanny Hurter's name does not suggest sodomy as much as the sadomasochism implied in the representations of "masculine" women such as Mrs. Weeks Wimbush and later the princess (or the Countess from "The Middle Years"), who would convert Paraday and the narrator to their "inverted" version of the commercial, homosocial world these homoerotic men wish to avoid, if not transcend.

At the end of the story, Paraday is dead, and the narrator claims either to have married or to be affianced to Fanny, now on the verge of taking his unmentioned name. What permits this conversion is itself another version of textualizing sexual relations. Shortly after joining Neil Paraday at the country house of Prestidge, the narrator begins to write letters and keep a "notebook" for the young American woman. He initially met Fanny Hurter when she came for Paraday's "autograph," but she surprises him as one of the rare fans to have read the master's work. She claims she wants to "see" Paraday, "Because I just love him!" and because his books have "been everything to me and a little more beside—I know them by heart. They've completely taken hold of me. There's no author about whom I'm in such a state as I'm in about Neil Paraday" ("Lion," 129).

Initially, the narrator does everything possible to keep Fanny Hurter from his lover, insisting that the "homage really sublime" would be to "succeed in never seeing him at all" ("Lion," 131). The rationale for such sacrifice, of course, is familiar to readers of James: the absence of the person of the author means the "presence" of the text in its true value and integrity. From the moment Fanny agrees to this preposterous idea, the narrator begins to court her, even convincing himself that he is in love with her. He is, of course, in love only with Paraday and what Paraday's works represent, but from the moment that she, as a willing reader, agrees to be part of that literary narrative, she becomes an object of love as well. This is not entirely cynical on the part of the narrator, I think, although James is clever enough to represent one important scene in which the narrator sadistically taunts her with a glimpse of the great author. The relationship between Fanny Hurter and the narrator is a more sadomasochistic version of the amorous relation between the critic Corvick and his fiancée, Gwendolyn Erme, in James's "The Figure in the Carpet" (1896), a tale in which the love relation is similarly sealed by a more profound love of literature.

At the opera one night with Fanny and her sister, Mrs. Milsom, the narrator points out to them "Mr. Paraday . . . in the stalls." And while Fanny's sister "devoured the great man through a powerful glass," the narrator "torment[s] tenderly" Fanny by pressing "the glass upon her, telling her how wonderfully near it brought our friend's handsome head." Fanny's response, even as she refuses to look at Paraday through the opera glass, is erotic in its bittersweetness even as it is a bit of operatic melodrama: "By way of answer she simply looked at me in charged silence, letting me see that tears had gathered in her eyes. These tears, I may remark, produced an effect on me of which the end is not yet" ("Lion," 134).

Perhaps because her tears have such a powerful effect on the narrator, he responds by including her as the specific reader of the final parts of "The Death of the Lion." While at Prestidge, where Paraday has no time at all to write between social demands and his growing illness, the narrator begins to write Fanny letters regarding the lost manuscript. Like Corvick and Erme in "The Figure in the Carpet," the narrator and Fanny establish their romantic relationship by way of this correspondence. The last two chapters (9 and 10) of the story are literally written by the narrator to Fanny, and quotations indicate where the actual letters begin and end. At the end of chapter 8, the narrator tells us: "It adds to the gratitude I owe her on other grounds that she kindly allows me to transcribe from my letters a few of the passages in which that hateful sojourn is candidly commemorated" ("Lion," 139).

Given this denouement, it would appear that the confrontation between James's nineteenth-century caricatures of "mannish" lesbians and gays in "The Middle Years" has been transformed into a more pedestrian denouement in "The Death of the Lion"—homosexual love entertained, textualized, repressed, and displaced by old-fashioned heterosexual romance. Yet what has occurred is just the opposite: the homoeroticizing of a threatening lesbian feminism by way of the customary Jamesian aesthetic. Fanny Hurter and the threatening "masculine" women in "The Death of the Lion," who otherwise would "hunt" Paraday down and "eat" him alive, are controlled by the textualization of sexuality that permits an apparent "larger latitude"—a slippage, that is, of sexual identities and gender roles—but only with the appearance of flexibility.

Michael Cooper reads the triangular relations among Neil Paraday, the narrator, and Fanny Hurter as a dramatization of James's homosexual panic and its resolution by recourse to conventional homosocial hierarchies: "By standing between Miss Hurter and his master, the narrator prevents his dispossession as Paraday's principal disciple and enjoys the sexual attentions of Miss Hurter that would . . . be directed at Paraday. . . . In effect, by seducing a woman attracted originally to Paraday, he sexually usurps Paraday's subject position."[28] "The Death of the Lion" problematizes such Oedipal triangulation, in which woman merely facilitates the struggle for masculine authority, by granting women genuinely threatening sexual and textual authority. To be sure, James demonizes this authority by way of associating it with either lesbian or sadomasochistic "deviance," both of which become metaphors in this story for modern decadence. Such psychotextual work has as its end not so much the restoration of homosocial relations as the protection of the relationship between the reader and the writer, both of whom figure James's own homoerotic desire in the protected space of the literary text. In his desire to constitute reader and writer as distinct from physically and thus sexually embodied subjects, James resists the rhetoric of Victorian homosociality. Paraday "dies" so that the narrator may "live," but the relationship is represented by James as lovingly sacrificial, rather than adversarial, and the Oedipal struggles of contemporary social life are projected onto women such as Mrs. Wimbush.

James has, then, entertained his own homosexual desire in these stories, but only to the extent that he has subscribed to some of the most egregious myths of lesbian sexual identity and feminist politics. In converting such dangerous women back to the fold of aesthetic propriety, as opposed to social conventionality, James has done the work of Victorian and early modern ideology. Yet there is always a certain excess, a certain "overflow," as the narrator would say of Paraday's writing; and in this regard, it affects James's own attitudes toward gender and sexuality. Guy Walsingham and Dora Forbes swap genders with an ease that disturbs James and his doubles, in part because the latter are just beginning to understand their own sexual identities as homosexual. These men longing to affirm their gay and homoerotic identities are still part of the system of gender roles and sexual identities that have been essentialized by ideology, which includes the arts (Dencombe's and Paraday's beloved forms). Nonetheless a certain destabilizing of gender and sexuality has occurred, even at the cost of the feminine identities and sexualities so represented. In the fiction of the 1870s such as "The Last of the Valerii" and *The American,* James criticizes patriarchal ideology and its arbitrary gender hierarchies even as he seems incapable of imagining alternatives to such an established system other than the occasional social ripples produced by a rebellious Daisy Miller or Noémie Nioche, an ironic Marquise de Bellegarde or sacrificial Claire de Cintré. In the fiction of the 1880s, he entertains the openly rebellious and thoroughly "new" woman, only to conclude that she merely reproduces the power dynamics of patriarchal ideology, whether in the mode of Olive Chancellor's possessiveness, Madame Merle's dishonesty, or Henrietta Stackpole's naïveté.

In the 1890s, James begins to play with more flexible ideas of gender roles and sexual identities, as I have suggested in my discussion of *The Tragic Muse* (1890) in chapter 3 and in the even more explicit stories of homoerotic passion, "The Middle Years" and "The Death of the Lion." Nevertheless, James remains a conflicted writer when it comes to such emerging sexual preferences and new gender possibilities, and the possibility of genuinely homoerotic passion must be disguised both by James's demonization of lesbian relations and by his insistence on an aestheticized male desire that mediates the passion for another man through the literary text.[29] Even aestheticized homosexuality made James uneasy, although his fiction after 1890 increasingly deals with situations that allow him to reflect on the entanglement of aesthetic values and sexual identity. Joseph Bristow recounts how in 1893 James would respond ambivalently to Edmund Gosse's gift of "one of the few copies of [John Addington] Symonds's privately printed study of homosexual desire, 'A Problem in Modern Ethics' (1891)," by thanking "Gosse for bringing him 'those marvellous outpourings'" but nevertheless finding "Symonds's work 'a queer place to plant the standard of duty.'"[30] For all of these reasons, it should not surprise us that a writer as personally involved in homosexual feelings, however conflicted, and as attentive to social change as Henry James would represent in his work the dramatic changes occurring in English and American society in regard to gender and sexual identity from the 1870s to the 1890s.

By the late 1890s, James could genuinely imagine endorsing the "larger latitudes" so sneeringly named by Mr. Morrow in "The Death of the Lion." In *The Spoils of Poynton* (1897), *What Maisie Knew* (1897), *In the Cage* (1898), *The Turn of the Screw* (1898), and *The Awkward Age* (1899), homosexual panic no longer informs James's obsession with "the other way round" of new gender roles and sexual identities. Whatever the other social problems discussed in these texts from the late 1890s, they are collectively working out a theory of gender and sexual preference different from any James had hitherto entertained seriously in his fiction. Women find each other as genuine alternatives to men, sometimes as companions such as Fleda and Mrs. Gereth at the end of *The Spoils of Poynton,* sometimes in mother-daughter relations as Mrs. Wix and Maisie share in *What Maisie Knew.* Men and women, gay and straight, have reason to look to each other for coalitions against the continuing forces of social and economic exploitation, often loosely associated with processes of modernization. Even marriage and courtship are no longer the same as they once were for James, at least if we take seriously the relations among Mr. Mudge, the telegraphist, and her friend, Mrs. Jordan, in *In the Cage,* or the possible alternative family structures tried out in *What Maisie Knew.* To be sure, these are "other" stories, and I think they go well beyond what Sedgwick analyzes as "homosexual panic" in James's writings. Throughout the 1890s there is another narrative, more flexible and less essentialized in its stylistic commitments (less realist, let us say), which has often been considered to anticipate the style of the Major Phase. Here it is a textuality that allows alternatives, combinations, and swaps. In his ability to consider these possibilities, Henry James anticipates the de-essentialized sexual identities and roles of our own postmodern era.

5 ꝛ The Portrait of a Small Boy as a Young Girl:

Gender Trouble in *What Maisie Knew*

I at once recognised, that my light vessel of consciousness, swaying in such a draught, couldn't be with verisimilitude a rude little boy; since, beyond the fact that little boys are never so "present," the sensibility of the female young is indubitably, for early youth, the greater, and my plan would call, on the part of my protagonist, for "no end" of sensibility.

—Henry James, preface to *What Maisie Knew* (1907)

I took on, when I had decently, and all the more because I had so retardedly, recovered, the sense of being a boy of other dimensions somehow altogether, and even with a new dimension introduced and acquired; a dimension that I was eventually to think of as a stretch in the direction of essential change or of living straight into a part of myself previously quite unvisited and now made accessible as by the sharp forcing of a closed door.

—Henry James, *A Small Boy and Others* (1913)

In "The Middle Years" and "The Death of the Lion," James satirizes the instability of gender roles, sexual preferences, and psychological identities in the modern age from a narrative perspective that seems nostalgic for the stabilities of an earlier age in which moral value was more conventionally identifiable with social position. Such aristocratic pretense is disguised as an aesthetic elitism that is by now one of the hallmarks of Anglo-American high modernism. The "new" aristocrats will be those "happy few" capable of seeing through the illusions of the modern age and preserving the enduring values of a cultural heritage otherwise being lost in the tawdriness and evanescence of fashion—the "neo-Nietzschean clatter" and "prose *kinema*" Pound would denounce in *Hugh Selwyn Mauberley*. The "antimodern" sentiments of high modernism are very much in evidence in James's writings, especially when we confuse his narratorial personae with his authorial stance—a confusion that James frequently encourages, although not always for such reactionary purposes.[1]

As I argue in the preceding chapter, however, the conservative pose of James's narrative perspective is often subtly transformed by the modernity it engages. James's withering satire of the literary transvestism represented by Dora Forbes and Guy Walsingham in "The Death of the Lion," for example, marks only the extremity of a gender slippage that is more discreetly and decorously displayed in the literary exchanges of Neil Paraday and his narratorial muse. James only appears to reject the new social and individual circumstances of modernity; what he does instead is to *adapt* his aesthetic to these new conditions, claiming thereby to redeem modern society from its decadence. In his stories of writers and artists, James has relatively little difficulty substituting his aesthetic for the corrupt values he condemns. No reader will take very seriously Guy Walsingham or Dora Forbes as a rightful challenger of the aesthetic standards upheld by the narrator and his author, Neil Paraday; no one is supposed to prefer the domineering and meretricious Countess and her submissive companion, Miss Vernham, to the more mutually supportive couple, Dr. Hugh and the writer Dencombe. The corruptions of the modern age are broadly satirized in both stories, whereas the complex relationship of two men bound together by their intellectual and aesthetic interests is represented by a subtle irony. It is nearly a formula in James's prose in the late 1880s and throughout the 1890s: burlesque and satire identify the aspects of the modern to be rejected; irony becomes the modern style that will endure. Appealing repeatedly for a renewal of "historical consciousness," James often strikes the note of the cautious and aging intellectual, familiar in every generation, who gloomily warns us away from the immoralities of the new. In another sense, James appeals to such historical consciousness as the primary means of legitimating and thus rendering moral otherwise strange and alien aspects of the new age.

I do not want to represent James as managing such a historical consciousness in a dispassionate and detached manner, as if it were some technical aspect of his craft of fiction. His obsession with the "sense of the past" certainly dominates his entire career, but it is especially notable in his writings from *The Aspern Papers* (1888) to *The Turn of the Screw* (1898). If I am simply concluding that James's historical consciousness is achieved by the means of an ironic tension between the conventions of the past and the novelties of the present, then I am merely rediscovering what the New Critics prized in James. I want to suggest instead that James's ideal of the historical consciousness increasingly reflects his anxieties and instabilities as an author attempting to adapt his aesthetic values to the conditions of modernity. Nowhere is such anxiety more evident than when the problems facing the author are also entangled with those confronting the biographical person.

James often identifies modernity with its changing attitudes toward gender roles and sexuality. His public posture seems that of the strict moralist who vigorously condemns the masculinized woman or feminized man—that is, the manifest transgression of conventional gender boundaries—as a sign of immorality, even as his own most admirable characters consistently dramatize their unique qualities by transcending the narrow limits of conventional stereotypes of gender and sexuality. In his notebook entries for February 27 and March 4, 1895, the year in which he was writing *What Maisie Knew,* James comments at some length on the pseudonymous Brada's *Notes sur Londres,* in which the author "speaks of in particular, as the 2 most striking social notes to him [in contemporary London], are *Primo,* The masculinization of the women; and *Secondo,* The demoralization of the aristocracy—the cessation, on their part, to take themselves seriously; their traffic in vulgar things, vulgar gains, vulgar pleasures—their general vulgarization."[2] Brada was the pen name for Henrette Consuelo Samson, contessa di Pugala, who bemoaned the decline of the European aristocracy and blamed its breakdown on the modernization process, chief among its examples being "New Women." James appears to be unaware that the author to whom he refers repeatedly as "he" is in fact a woman, but what most interests James in Brada is her insistence on "the Revolution in English society by the *avènement* of the women, which he sees everywhere and in everything. I saw it long ago—and I saw in it a big subject for the Novelist."[3] Just what James means by *agreeing* with Brada is difficult to say, even though the relative privacy of James's notebooks and the fact that James copies four long paragraphs in French from Brada's *Notes sur Londres* make the reader think that James is writing about a kindred spirit. Nevertheless, the aristocratic and patriarchal values endorsed by Brada seem far too crude for Henry James in the late 1890s.

We may never know whether James personally endorsed the cranky and reactionary views of this Italian contessa or simply found those views apt expressions of the modern problem. What is clear from these passages in his notebooks is that James viewed his own career—"I saw it long ago"—as concerned centrally with the ways in which the entrance of women into the public sphere constitutes a "Revolution in English" and American societies that is a "big subject for the Novelist." It is also clear that for James this revolution involves more than simply women gaining greater access to legal, political, and economic powers, but a "confusion" of conventional gender boundaries, which James goes on to generalize as an important part of the subject for a "great, broad, rich theme of a large satirical novel" that would focus on

> the great modern collapse of all the forms and "superstitions" and re-
> spects, good and bad, and restraints and mysteries—a vivid and mere
> showy general hit at the decadences and vulgarities and confusions and
> masculinizations and feminizations—the materializations and abdica-
> tions and intrusions, and Americanizations, the lost sense, the bru-
> talized manner—the publicity, the newspapers, the general revolution,
> the failure of fastidiousness.[4]

In rhetorical rapid fire, James lists the characteristics of the modern age that would be at the center not simply of "one large satirical novel" but of several of his novels and stories in the second half of the 1890s.

What Maisie Knew (1897) explicitly links the "confusions and masculiniza-tions and feminizations" of the modern age with the class confusions ("Ameri-canizations") of a changing economy ("materializations") and its transgres-sion of the old boundaries between public and private spheres ("abdications and intrusions"), so typified by the new dominant media ("the publicity, the newspapers"). I want to focus on this novel because it has not received much sustained critical attention in regard to its gender instabilities and its more general critique of the entire process of modernization, including the conse-quences of imperialism for national identity. Critics have traditionally consid-ered James's satire of the adults in *What Maisie Knew* to focus directly on the worst aspects of modern social disorder. There is little subtlety in his portraits of the former minor diplomat Beale Farange, for whom "contemporary his-tory had . . . no use," and who scrapes by on "only twenty-five hundred"; his first wife, Ida, the billiards champion and abusive mother; the sympathetic but pathetically weak aristocrat Sir Claude; and the social climber Mrs. Beale, also known as Maisie's governess at Maisie's father's house under the impressive title of "Miss Overmore," then as Maisie's stepmother when married to the father, and finally as Sir Claude's lover.[5]

For most critics, this social satire is the donnée of the novel, and it hyperbolically sets the stage of adult corruption for the sake of focusing all the more exclusively and minutely on the epistemological, moral, and finally aesthetic drama of Maisie's education as either poisoned by, or cure for, these social ills. This critical position leads many critics to conclude that Maisie's final choice to abandon both Sir Claude and Mrs. Beale in Boulogne and take the steamer back to England with Mrs. Wix aligns Henry James with the "moral sense" for which Mrs. Wix so hypocritically and yet tirelessly appeals in her miseducation of Maisie.[6] To be sure, Mrs. Wix may not live up to her own moral standard, but it is often assumed by such critics that the standard so maintained by her represents James's own ideal: the moral consistency and absolutism of premodern England and the United States. Equating Henry James's moral judgment of his fictional situation with Mrs. Wix's old-fashioned moral sense is to conclude that his response in his notebooks to the "revolution" of our modernity is distinctly reactionary. We must entertain at the outset that this is a possibility, even though it is one that I hope to show is rejected by James as he works his way through the full implications of this modern revolution. To be perfectly clear, I want to suggest that James begins with his own serious doubts about a social world of utter flux and instability—one commonly figured in the novel with metaphors of the puzzle, game, circus, exhibition, and show—only to end up adapting his own aesthetic values to this new and at times baffling modern world. What he gives us in the end is neither the lost innocent Maisie, fleeing the impossible choices offered by her equally impossible parents and surrogates, nor the dependent Maisie who must cling to the old moral sense of Mrs. Wix, constantly adjusting her "straighteners" (glasses) to focus this bleary social world, but the Maisie who works through the very failings of all her thoroughly modern parents and governesses (including Mrs. Wix) to find the means of living in the modern age with enthusiasm and courage.

In particular, Maisie will come to accept and even celebrate the instabilities of gender, class, race, and age that distinguish the modern age even as these same instabilities incapacitate the adults around her. At the outset, the adults seem outrageously modern, but by the end, we realize how sadly old-fashioned they all are. In his extensive notebook entries for the composition of *What Maisie Knew,* James refers to Mrs. Wix repeatedly as "the old frumpy governess," who in the end will try to "rescue" Maisie by effectively abducting her ("*taking* Maisie") to "her own poor, bare shabbiness of home," echoing thereby so many other fatal rescue efforts by such characters as Basil Ransom, Mrs. Gereth, the governess in *The Turn of the Screw,* even Isabel Archer as she returns to Rome for the sake of Pansy.[7] In the place of these efforts by his characters to possess and control each other, James offers Maisie the possibility of new, modern kinds of love. In *What Maisie Knew,* love comes to mean considerably more than the allowed Victorian conventions regarding parents' love for their children, marital love between consenting adults, and the general love for one's fellow human being at the heart of romantic social theories.

Late in the novel, in Boulogne, where the dramatic crises are reached, Maisie describes Mrs. Beale as "making love" to Mrs. Wix. Just a few sentences earlier, the narrator has made the point that Mrs. Beale is the most handsome woman at the hotel's luncheon, just "as Mrs. Wix foretold" Maisie. The attention Mrs. Beale attracts thus makes *her* attentions to "frumpy" Mrs. Wix all the more significant. The narrator's play with Maisie's and our different understandings of the idiom "making love" is one example of the many odd displacements of conventional meanings that marks this novel as one of the great language experiments of modern literature. In this context, Maisie uses this phrase to describe the manner in which Mrs. Beale is flattering Mrs. Wix in hopes of bringing her "round" or "squaring" her with Mrs. Beale's and Sir Claude's plans to divorce their respective spouses (Maisie's natural parents) and carry Maisie off with them as the step-child who would legitimate their scandalous relationship:

> There was a phrase familiar to Maisie, so often was it used by this lady [Mrs. Beale] to express the idea of one's getting what one wanted: one got it—Mrs. Beale always said *she* at all events always got it or proposed to get it—by "making love." She was at present making love, singular as it appeared, to Mrs. Wix, and her young friend's mind had never moved in such freedom as on thus finding itself face to face with the question of what she wanted to get. (*M,* 300)

The irony here seems easy to read: Mrs. Beale's idea of "making love" is thoroughly selfish and negates any proper idea of love, whereas Maisie longs for parental love of some sort and thus is encouraged by Mrs. Beale's bad example to misdirect her desires. The narrator ironizes Maisie's misunderstanding of the idiom "making love" by calling attention to its misuse by modern adults and Maisie's need for some proper education about the true meanings of such crucial words as "love." "Making love" implicitly should mean the complete opposite of Mrs. Beale's idea of "one's getting what one wanted"; it should mean the mutual satisfaction of needs and desires.

Beyond these determinate meanings for "making love" in the modern age, there is the more general sense that love is unmoored from its conventional referents. It is not just the child, Maisie, who is confused about the meaning of love, but virtually all of the other characters. Of course, all of the adults are selfish and "make love" to each other for the sake of "getting what one wanted": Beale Farange and Ida make love for money, Sir Claude for an heir, and Mrs. Beale to improve her social position. These are traditional corruptions of love in modern literature, but there are a wide variety of other possibilities available for "making love," and it is possible that this destabilization of the meaning of love will also lead to other freedoms.

We are told early in the narrative that Mrs. Wix is quite "attached" to Sir Claude, who protects her and Maisie from Ida's spiteful neglect and gives them moral support in their isolated and barren schoolroom. Just after Sir Claude has left Mrs. Wix and Maisie alone in Boulogne and only moments before Mrs. Beale appears, as if by magic, Mrs. Wix confesses to Maisie that she loves Sir Claude, in a moment that ends with the passionate communion of the governess and her student:

> "I adore him. I adore him."
>
> Maisie took it well in; so well that in a moment more she would have answered profoundly, "So do I." . . . what Maisie at last said was simply and serenely, "Oh I know!"
>
> Their hands were so linked and their union was so confirmed that it took the far deep note of a bell, borne on them on the summer air, to call them back to a sense of hours and proprieties. They had touched bottom and melted together, but they gave a start at last: the bell was the voice of the inn and the inn was the image of luncheon. (*M*, 289)

It is the very luncheon at which Mrs. Beale will "make love" to Mrs. Wix. Neither Maisie's relation to Mrs. Wix nor Mrs. Wix's relation to Mrs. Beale can be understood in any way as lesbian, but both relations must be understood to involve powerful passions, even if those employed by Mrs. Beale in "making love" serve thoroughly Machiavellian purposes. This scene with Mrs. Wix and Maisie, who is somewhere between eleven and fourteen years old at this stage of the narrative, is erotically charged with their common passion for Sir Claude, but the eroticism of the narrator's rhetoric also suggests the passions available to a young girl and an older, morally proper governess for each other, as well as for men.[8]

Amid the limited romantic conventions for love in the Victorian novel, James here adds the "amours" of young girls and older women not just for dashing young aristocrats such as Sir Claude but for the compassion he has shown them and then for their common plight, which is to say for each other. Such "passions" should not be too easily separated into those belonging "properly" to relations of mothers (or their surrogates, such as governesses) and daughters, sisters, and friends from those erotic feelings between women demonized in modern cultures. It is quite possible, of course, that James has no idea of what his narrator's rhetoric accomplishes in such passages, but one consequence for the modern reader (and not exclusively the late-twentieth-century reader) is the transgression of such proper boundaries. The close bond between Maisie and Mrs. Wix at the end of the novel is not, I think, the final note James wants to play, but it successfully makes the point that love between women helps broaden the cultural definition of romantic love to encompass something more akin to the "love" on which a more harmonious society should be built. Whether or not this is Henry James's intention is a very difficult question to answer, but it remains an important effect of the novels James wrote about the possible relations available to women in the early modern period. The relationship between Mrs. Wix and Maisie resembles in this regard the supportive relationship Mrs. Gereth and Fleda Vetch will develop in *The Spoils of Poynton,* also published in 1897, and written just before James began in earnest composition of *What Maisie Knew.*[9] Neither relationship is quite accurately described as a "romantic friendship" because both involve significant age differences between the women; neither is exactly characterized as a "mother-daughter" relation, although this may come closer to the truth. Both relationships nevertheless involve deep and abiding feelings that are passionate. Mrs. Gereth's and Fleda's final relationship in the novel may be as inadequate an alternative to women's active roles in the public sphere as Mrs. Wix's and Maisie's final relationship fails to compensate for a proper education or family, but both relationships affirm the importance of relations between women in Victorian culture and how those relations involve different forms of "love" than those presumed to govern parental and marital relations.[10]

Sir Claude is another notable example of how gender slippages help James both satirize a corrupt society and think about alternative possibilities for love and for passion in the modern age. Isabel Archer has very few choices available to her in *The Portrait of a Lady;* Casper Goodwood and Lord Warburton are far better men than the self-serving Gilbert Osmond, but they still represent the dominant values of patriarchal culture. The few possible alternatives, such as Ralph Touchett or Henrietta Stackpole, are either killed off or caricatured; neither poses a real alternative to the passionate attachments of marriage available to Isabel. As Habegger writes: "*The Portrait of a Lady . . .* represents marriage as a house of bondage yet never supports the obvious idea that Isabel would be wise to escape."[11] By the mid-1890s, however, James is willing to entertain socially viable alternatives to traditional heterosexual marriage and the bourgeois family.

Sir Claude has been treated variously by critics as a sex-crazed rake bent on seducing Ida, Mrs. Beale, and even Maisie, or as a hopelessly weak example of the declining aristocracy, still outwardly charming and appealing but lacking the real substance of the ruling class.[12] In James's writings, such male aristocrats are often feminized, even when they are heterosexually active, as are Count Valerio in "The Last of the Valerii," Valentin de Bellegarde in *The American,* Miles in *The Turn of the Screw,* and Prince Amerigo in *The Golden Bowl.* Such "feminization" takes several forms, including fantasies of gender reversals of power in "The Last of the Valerii," the equation of the younger son's economic powerlessness with that of women (Valentin de Bellegarde), the infantilization and perversion of aristocratic sexuality in the manner of gothic romances (Miles), and the domination of socialite men by the "feminine" values presumed to govern high society (Prince Amerigo). Sir Claude is feminized in all of these ways. Afraid of both Ida and Mrs. Beale, he identifies with Maisie and Mrs. Wix as victims of these domineering women. He is both trivialized and victimized by a name that is always a first name in our ears and sounds homophonically as if he has been *clawed* by the Furies, Ida and Mrs. Beale.[13] Different characters and the narrator describe Sir Claude as a "slave" either to the women who dominate him or to his own "passions," which may come to the same thing in James's estimation.[14] There is something decidedly childish about Sir Claude, which is reinforced by the facts that he is considerably younger than Ida and that he is a man of leisure, who has the time and inclination to take Maisie to the National Gallery, to Baker Street for "tea and buns," and to the park (*M*, 113).

One of Sir Claude's strangest behavioral patterns is his tendency to confuse genders in reference to both Maisie and himself. In what appears to be merely his affable familiarity with Maisie, Sir Claude refers to her as "an awfully good 'chap,'" "old boy," "my dear old woman," "old man," "woman," "my dear fellow," "my dear man," "dear boy," "old girl," "Maisie boy!" and "my dear child" (*M*, 76, 78, 122, 136, 233–34, 257, 262, 330–32). The few critics to comment on Sir Claude's rhetorical confusions have concluded either that they "can be read as attempts to deny the sexual differences between them that would sooner or later result in mutual sexual attraction" or that they represent Sir Claude's "delicate homosexuality."[15] Sir Claude is thus either trying to normalize his relationship with Maisie along homosocial lines or trying to accommodate her to the "delicate homosexuality" often confused with just such homosociality in Victorian culture.[16] Taken by themselves, these familiar names for Maisie would mean little beyond this characteristic confusion of homosocial and homosexual identification among many Victorian males, especially those for whom male social groups at school and at home are their primary frames of reference from early schooling through the university.

Sir Claude follows the same pattern of gender confusion in reference to himself. In addition to his tendency to represent himself as a victim, weak sinner, and generally abject person, he also contributes to his general feminization in the course of the novel. Protesting to Mrs. Beale early in the novel that he is "the most unappreciated of—what do you call those fellows?—'family-men,'" he defines what he means by a "family man": "I'm an old grandmother. . . . I like babies—I always did. If we go to smash I shall look for a place as responsible nurse" (*M*, 61, 63). The reason he gives for equating "grandmother" and "family-man" is that maternal women no longer exist. In reply to Mrs. Beale's impatient "Then why on earth . . . didn't you marry a family-woman," Sir Claude calmly answers: "There *are* no family-women— hanged if there are! None of them want any children—hanged if they do!" (61). Sir Claude's practical motivation in marrying Ida is to produce an heir, and this motive also helps explain his tendency both to masculinize Maisie and to feminize himself. Ida is clearly no "family-woman," so whatever children their marriage produces will be the result of Sir Claude's efforts. We are tempted by James's style in these passages to sympathize with Sir Claude and condemn these new, fashionable women, for whom marriage is a matter of economic convenience and their husbands mere tokens of respectability behind which such women may continue to pursue their own sexual and social pleasures—that is, to "make love" in that self-serving way Maisie understands Mrs. Beale to be making love to Mrs. Wix in Boulogne.

In at least one sense, Sir Claude is making love in much the same self-interested manner, since the production of heirs is the traditional work of aristocrats, both male and female. Such a claim for Sir Claude may seem odd in light of his apparent lack of financial means, although James is much vaguer in respect to Sir Claude's economic circumstances than he is with regard to those of Beale Farange and Ida. Nevertheless, Sir Claude still commands the capital of his title, which the reader of Victorian novels knows has considerable social and economic credit attached to it. He can afford a life of leisure with Maisie that includes visits to the National Gallery, trips in cabs, teatime together, and even more expensive ventures, such as their journey to Boulogne, with the costs of travel and hotels for themselves and Mrs. Wix. Even if he is impoverished, then what remains to him can be only the hereditary rights of his family name and the distant hope it might be redeemed by an heir, especially a male one.[17] In this latter respect, however, Sir Claude begins to understand by the end of the novel that Maisie might well take the place of the traditional male heir, especially in a modern world where the old proprieties and legalities, especially those defining the waning aristocracy, seem to be concerned. When he takes Susan Ash and Maisie to Folkestone and Boulogne, then brings Mrs. Wix across the Channel to join them, Sir Claude is quite serious about making a family out of the ruins of his failed marriage to Ida. Once Ida has effectively "sold" Maisie to him, Sir Claude seems intent on finding some way of making Maisie his proper heir, whether this means granting her legal rights to his modest means or simply recognizing her as his descendant.

At the end of the novel, Sir Claude reminds Mrs. Wix (and the reader) that Mrs. Wix will not have to "work" her "fingers to the bone" to take care of Maisie: " 'You needn't do that,' she heard him say. 'She has means' " (*M,* 359–60). The reader is supposed to remember here what the narrator has told us in the legalistic frame tale that precedes chapter 1: "The child was provided for, thanks to a crafty godmother, a defunct aunt of Beale's, who had left her something in such a manner that the parents could appropriate only the income" (8). Mrs. Beale "shrieked" when Sir Claude makes this claim, "Means?—

Maisie? . . . Means that her vile father has stolen!" but Sir Claude insists, "I'll get them back—I'll get them back. I'll look into it" (360). James's hints in moments like this that Sir Claude may well be interested in Maisie for *her* estate, however modest or entangled by other claims as her means might be. Indeed, Sir Claude is always on the verge of slipping into the immoral world inhabited by Ida, Beale, and the other parvenus of the dramatic action.

Yet our judgment of Sir Claude's intentions with respect to Maisie's "means" should be made in light of his *human* conduct toward her: his sense of Maisie as a young girl in need of parental authority and a young woman just beginning to recognize her sexuality. In his bid to serve as a proper parent to Maisie in the absence of others, Sir Claude encourages Maisie to make her own decision about her future, offers to help redeem her economic means of independence, and displays thereby his commitment to her, despite his inability to break his destructive connection with Mrs. Beale. In this climactic scene of the novel, when Maisie is compelled to choose between Mrs. Wix or these preposterous stepparents, Mrs. Wix accuses the vacillating Maisie of having "lost" her moral sense and Sir Claude of having "killed it when it had begun to live" (*M*, 354). Flushed with her power, Mrs. Wix appears "newer . . . than ever" and "high and great," but Sir Claude is for once "not after all to be treated as a little boy with a missed lesson: 'I've not killed anything . . . on the contrary, I think I've produced life. I don't know what to call it—I haven't even known how decently to deal with it, to approach it; but, whatever it is, it's the most beautiful thing I've ever met—it's exquisite, it's sacred'" (354). The rhetoric here is that of James's customary celebration of the aesthetic process, but in this case it is no painting or novel that Sir Claude admires: it is *his* child who is beautiful, exquisite, and sacred.

Sir Claude has figuratively "produced life" not as a male and aristocrat intent on a male heir to carry his name and perpetuate his fortune; he has created more in the manner of the parent who finds in his or her child the potential for independent agency, especially as these qualities can be distinguished from the failings of the parents. Sir Claude is described in a religious posture the moment he utters the word "sacred": "He had his hands in his pockets and, though a trace of the sickness he had just shown perhaps lingered there, his face bent itself with extraordinary gentleness on both the friends he was about to lose" (*M*, 354). Throughout their tours of Boulogne as they await Mrs. Beale or Sir Claude, Mrs. Wix and Maisie pay special attention to the "gold Virgin" of the church they can see from the ramparts. For Mrs. Wix, the

Virgin represents the purity of the "moral sense" she forces on Maisie, and this Virgin is also the old rigor of Catholic moral law that Mrs. Wix regrets she had not embraced as a young woman.[18] For some critics, the Virgin represents James's symbolic endorsement of Mrs. Wix's position and thus allows them to conclude that Maisie's rejection of Sir Claude and Mrs. Beale as stepparents means her embrace of Mrs. Wix's strict moral lessons.[19] It is generally assumed that the gold Virgin of Boulogne must represent symbolically a feminine ideal to which the "mothers" in the novel ought to aspire and thus of the general moral sense James wishes to inculcate in his proper readers.[20] But Sir Claude himself is an equally good avatar of that gold Virgin, and we have no need to insist that he emulate some latter-day Christ in the moment of his greatest sacrifice.[21] In giving up Maisie, he experiences as much the mother's as the father's sense of loss and satisfaction when the child becomes an independent adult.[22]

This moment of Sir Claude's apotheosis is admittedly very brief and by no means solves Maisie's numerous problems or those of the society to which he belongs. In the climactic scene of decision in the novel, he holds Maisie "in front of him, resting his hands very lightly on her shoulders" as he encourages her to face her "loud adversaries," Mrs. Beale and Mrs. Wix. James describes Sir Claude's position as symbolic of his salvatory function: "Sir Claude had rescued Maisie and kept hold of her" (*M*, 358). Sir Claude supports her as he grants her independence: "I only insist that she's free—she's free," and only the vicious imagination of Mrs. Beale is capable of viewing Sir Claude's relationship to Maisie in this moment as an erotic one. When Maisie asks Mrs. Beale again if that lady will give up Sir Claude so that he may become Maisie's father along with Mrs. Wix as her governess, Mrs. Beale shrieks: "To *you*, you abominable little horror?" Mrs. Beale's jealousy suggests that Maisie's love for Sir Claude—"I love Sir Claude—I love *him*"—entangles romantic and parent-child loves in dangerous ways (359).

Indeed, Sir Claude's intimate relationship with Maisie often verges on the erotic, especially as Maisie grows older. When in chapters 30 and 31 he takes Maisie away from the hotel to try to convince her to choose Mrs. Beale and him over Mrs. Wix, Sir Claude is dimly aware that there is something wrong about their privacy. At the train station, where Sir Claude has taken her to "meet the Paris papers" and also stall for time, Maisie brings the impropriety of their relationship into the open. This chapter begins with the narrator wondering about what Maisie once viewed as "the old safety": "They walked about, they dawdled, they looked in shop windows; they did all the old things exactly as if to try to get back all the old safety, to get something out of them that they had always got before" (*M*, 341). This "old safety" refers to the days when Sir Claude was able to accompany Maisie around London as her stepfather, with her proper mother, Ida, at home or abroad. But here, with both Sir Claude and Mrs. Beale free and Maisie older, his relation to Maisie is no longer so clearly parental. When at the station Maisie suggests to Sir Claude that the two of them simply take the next train to Paris, running away from the problems back at the hotel, she is responding to what she thinks she has read in Sir Claude's desperate glances all day long: "It was true that once or twice on the jetty, on the sands, he looked at her for a minute with eyes that seemed to propose to her to come straight off with him to Paris" (342). In Maisie's famous moment of urging Sir Claude to answer the porter in the affirmative about taking tickets on that train—"*Prenny, prenny. Oh prenny!*"— Sir Claude recognizes how romantic and parent-child loves would be hope-lessly entangled in any parental relations he might have with Maisie (345).[23]

In choosing to stay with Mrs. Beale, then, Sir Claude does more than simply succumb to his selfish passions; even in our postmodern world, the household of Sir Claude, Mrs. Wix, and Maisie would appear very improper indeed. Sir Claude not only enables Maisie to "be free" but does so at the sacrifice of his own freedom, for he knows well the doom of Mrs. Beale's manipulative love. It is nonetheless a sacrifice that further helps free Maisie from Mrs. Beale's use of her, and thus Sir Claude's final gestures—reinstating the incest taboo, letting go of his surrogate but very real child, and protecting that child from the Evil Stepmother—should be taken as part of his effort to earn his noble lineage.[24] In his ability to play various roles as Maisie's child-hood companion, stepfather, nurturing mother or "grandmother" or "nurse," and legal advisor, Sir Claude variously transgresses conventional gender, class, age, and family boundaries in showing his love for Maisie.

Sir Claude is not, however, an unproblematic hero. He helps Maisie in the diffident, distracted, and inconsistent ways that James conventionally associ-ates with the waning aristocracy. Sir Claude surrenders Maisie to Mrs. Wix not only because he knows Maisie must be free of the likes of her parents and stepparents; he is also hopelessly weak, afraid of dominating figures, both male and female, and lacks confidence in himself and the class he represents. In his "sacrifice" of Maisie, who represents the only ethical good in his experience, Sir Claude also imitates the rhetoric of sacrifice so typical of

James's fictional heroines from Claire de Cintré to Isabel Archer. For the reader hoping that James will engage the modern issues he raises in the novel, rather than yearning nostalgically for a bygone era, this is a far better way to view Sir Claude. For if Sir Claude could be taken as a heroic alternative to the obviously inadequate Beale Farange, Mrs. Beale, Ida, and Ida's long string of lovers, then James would be living vicariously through this charming but anachronistic aristocrat and implicitly restricting modern decadence to the middle class. James would thereby align himself with the conservative politics of the pseudonymous Brada, who had associated the feminization of culture with the decline of aristocratic power.

James does not identify with Sir Claude in any sustained manner, except perhaps in those moments Sir Claude approximates the "sacred" knowledge of others that James traditionally reserves for great artists. James identifies with his narrator and with Maisie, both of whom share the responsibility for telling the moral story in the novel—that is, for educating the reader about the ethical possibilities available in the modern age. Julie Rivkin points out that the narrator begins to vanish from the text as Maisie grows up and is increasingly capable of making her own moral choices. As Maisie becomes more difficult to represent, the narrator relies more on Maisie's own dialogue, thus allowing her own voice and identity to become central to the novel's later organization.[25] Merla Wolk argues that the narrator becomes Maisie's parent and teacher, leading her inevitably to the Jamesian sublime of the artistic imagination: "We must look to the narrator to find the only reliable guardian of her interests. He represents the beauty and stability of art, building a house of fiction for Maisie that offers permanence and form. . . . He can imagine for the vulnerable child security in the protective care of the narrator's world of language and form."[26] Both Rivkin's and Wolk's arguments depend in part on Juliet Mitchell's reading of how Maisie's aesthetic education approximates James's method of literary cognition: "James's description of Maisie's initiation at the deepest level is profoundly bound up with his method for the whole novel, her progress so much its progress, her art his art."[27]

Such interpretations pose various problems, chief among them the extent to which the reader must transgress the boundaries separating form and content, performing in effect what Maisie terms a "violent substitution" of one for the other (*M*, 301). The uncanny slippage of James's metafictional concerns into the very subject matter and even plot of his novels is often a distinguishing mark of his modernity; *The Aspern Papers* and *The Turn of the*

Screw are familiar examples. From the perspective of traditional literary realism, such play is decidedly improper, but it accomplishes some real work for the later Henry James. It is a commonplace to say that the contamination of the real by the imaginative reminds us of the fictional bases for social reality. The effect has yet further consequences in *What Maisie Knew* because to argue for the narrator as both surrogate of the author and parental role model for Maisie is to remind us of what is obvious yet often ignored in our reading experience: literary narrators need not tell their stories from subject positions that are gendered or sexually specific.

Even the most interesting feminist readings of *What Maisie Knew* never entertain the idea that the narrator might be a woman. Only a year later, James would publish *The Turn of the Screw,* narrated, at least internally, by a woman. I shall not make a case for the narrator of *What Maisie Knew* as feminine; I simply wish to make the theoretical point that she could be and that many literary narrators are falsely gendered not by what they say but by our reading assumptions about the genders of their authors. If modern social instabilities are reflected in Sir Claude's ambiguities about his gender role and even sexual identity, then the same may be said for all the characters, including the narrator.

Such an argument about the narrator as Maisie's surrogate parent and as capable of transcending the vicious struggles for domination—"violent substitutions"—among the characters in the novel is thoroughly compatible with the aestheticization of sexual relations by which James defends himself against the social transformations he experienced in the 1890s. No parent in the dramatic action of the novel is adequate to the real demands of Maisie's very modern education, but the narrator—and implicitly James and the proper reader—can fulfill that role by providing Maisie with examples of how to respond imaginatively to a world that is often indistinguishable from fiction. This interpretation can be supported by the fact that Maisie's dreadful education by Mrs. Wix actually consists of Mrs. Wix's ceaseless gossip regarding Maisie's shifting parents and stepparents. French, geography, and history are only fitfully treated as subjects by any of Maisie's teachers; the soap opera of her parents' amorous exploits is her real daily lesson.

There is considerable extrinsic evidence in James's *A Small Boy and Others* (1913) to support this idea of Maisie's aesthetic education if we are willing to entertain Maisie as an alter ego for Henry James, as critics such as Mitchell, Wolk, and Rivkin do. In a brief note, Wolk comments: "It is surely more than coincidental that James ends his novel about Maisie's childhood in Boulogne, the same location in which he ends the chronicle of his own early years, *A Small Boy and Others*. What is suggested is that James strongly identifies with his character."[28] The James family spent two periods at Boulogne in the summer and then winter of 1857 to spring of 1858, when Henry Jr. was fourteen. These visits are recalled in the concluding chapter (29) of *A Small Boy and Others*, but in ways that confuse the actual chronology of James's experiences.[29] During the summer visit, Henry was extremely ill with a typhus infection that caused him to run a high fever and slip occasionally into delirium. He was recovering when the family moved to Paris in October, only to discover that they had suffered financial reverses as a consequence of the September 1857 "stock market crash in New York." To save living expenses, Henry Sr. moved the family back to Boulogne in October, where they remained until "the end of May 1858."[30]

James concludes *A Small Boy and Others* with an account of the feverish delirium he experienced in September 1857, terming it "the gravest illness of my life," placing this significant episode at the *end* of his childhood experiences in Boulogne.[31] This reversal of chronology may only be for dramatic effect so that James may ironically mark his access to adulthood with a characteristic ambiguity, an uncanny "gap" separating the child from the adult:

> I might verily, on the spot, have seen, as in a fading of day and a change to something suddenly queer, the whole large extent of it. I must thus, much impressed but half scared, have wanted to appeal; to which end I tumbled, all too weakly, out of bed and wavered toward the bell just across the room. The question of whether I really reached and rang it was to remain lost afterwards in the strong sick whirl of everything about me, under which I fell into a lapse of consciousness that I shall here treat as a considerable gap.[32]

James's description of this illness recalls Henry Sr.'s and William James's moments of "spiritual vastation," and it is granted further significance by virtue of its placement at the very end of Henry Jr.'s childhood.[33] The child's illness thus serves symbolically to represent and then to repress James's shame regarding his father's aimlessness in these years—shame compounded by the specific financial reverses of September 1857, requiring "economies" of the sort practiced by Sir Claude in Folkestone and Boulogne and so baffling to the adolescent Maisie.[34]

The "gap" dividing James's childhood from adulthood is not unlike Maisie's final Channel crossing as she leaves behind Sir Claude and Mrs. Beale and, accompanied by Mrs. Wix, heads toward an unpredictable life back in England. Indeed, there is a great deal more that connects James's twentieth-century recollections of his childhood visits to Boulogne with Maisie's decisive visit there at the end of her childhood.[35] Because he was still recovering from typhus that winter, Henry did not enroll with William, Wilky, and Bob at the local Collège Communal; instead, he was tutored at home and allowed to spend much of his days wandering the charming streets of Boulogne, much as Maisie does with Mrs. Wix and later with Sir Claude.[36]

What Carol Holly identifies as James's "shame" in *A Small Boy and Others* regarding his father is complemented by Maisie's anxieties about her more obviously "rootless" and "aimless" parents and their surrogates, but I think the unnamed "shame" in James's first volume of his autobiography is in fact his profound sense of difference from other "small boys."[37] This difference is the focus of his recollections in the final chapter of *A Small Boy and Others* and is well represented by the passage used as an epigraph to my chapter. Like the more famous experience of fear and excitement in the Galerie d'Apollon in the Louvre, James's experiences of otherness in Boulogne are readable today as suggestive of sexual difference, but in his own account, James transforms them into variations on the Aesthetic Sublime.[38]

For the recuperating James in 1857 to 1858, Boulogne is a place primarily defined by fiction, especially Thackeray's, whose Colonel Newcome and Arthur Pendennis are both recalled in their associations with Boulogne (*SBO,* 400, 407–8), and James's fond recollections of borrowing books from "Merridew's English Library, solace of my vacuous hours and temple, in its degree too, of deep initiations" (406). Mocking the respectable British society Thackeray would also lampoon in *The Newcomes* (1855) and identifying with the artist-hero "Pen" from *The History of Arthur Pendennis* (1848–1850), James seems merely to emulate a conventional Victorian ideal of the artist as liminal figure, able to observe society's foibles from his aesthetic distance yet also capable of taking an active part in that social world, as Pendennis will eventually marry his true love, Laura.[39] James's avid reading must also have been part of his own effort to discover his own identity, independent from his family. As Habegger points out, James read so much that year that "his parents began to worry," and his father considered it necessary to distinguish the young James's "reading" from "study, properly so-called."[40]

It is "the frumpiest and civillest mid-Victorian" triple-decker novel that James recalls fondly from his days of recuperation and isolation in Boulogne, encouraging us to remember how Sir Claude at the train station purchases for Maisie and Mrs. Beale "three books, one yellow and two pink," telling her that "the pink were for herself and the yellow . . . for Mrs. Beale, implying in an interesting way that these were the natural divisions for the young and for the old" (*M*, 344). These books and Sir Claude's "eleven" newspapers are what Maisie proposes they use as "luggage" in the imagined flight to Paris. It is Henry James's recollection of how he would escape similar problems, albeit by way of Thackeray's Victorian novel, that James claims as his heritage. Reading those triple-decker novels in Boulogne, James associates them with a sense of purpose, a vocation, rather than the mere idleness popularly associated with reading fiction: "They fell, . . . every trio I ever touched, into the category of such prized phenomena . . . that something vague and sweet—if I shouldn't indeed rather say something of infinite future point and application—would come of it" (*SBO*, 414).

James's memories of his awakening to the vocation of novelist also evoke his tutor, the "mild M. Ansiot, 'under' whom I for some three hours each forenoon sat sole and underided" (*SBO*, 416). The "good M. Ansiot" appears at first a male version of the "frumpy" Mrs. Wix: "I see the good man as too helpless and unaggressive, too smothered in his poor facts of person and circumstance, of overgrown time of life alone, to incur with justness the harshness of classification" (417). The tutor also resembles Mrs. Wix in his adherence to the old ways, such that he "most literally smelt of the vieux temps" (416). Nevertheless, James distinguishes between M. Ansiot and Mrs. Wix by recalling the substance of what his tutor attempted to teach him, however arid the instruction and "drowsy" James's reception (417). Interestingly, M. Ansiot's principal subject matter is "literature . . . to my at once charmed and shamed apprehension of the several firm traditions, the pure proprieties, the discussabilities, in the oddest way both so many and so few, of that field as they prevailed to his pious view" (417). What M. Ansiot teaches the young James is "a saving as distinguished from a losing classicism," which is precisely what the novel-reading James has missed in his scattered education (418).

Pierre Walker has speculated that James's Ansiot was in fact Napoléon Ansieaux, who "was the professor of rhetoric at Boulogne's Lycée or Collège Communal, which the James boys attended, including Henry before the typhus attack."[41] Walker also explains that Napoléon Ansieaux was the "author of a series of articles that ran in the local newspaper *L'Impartial,* in July and August 1858, two months after the James family left Boulogne."[42] Those articles deal with M. Ansieaux's conviction that Boulogne needed a "literary society that would enrich" the culture of the city and that such a society "should be an umbrella organization for work in agriculture, science, the arts, and letters."[43] The significance of Walker's research is that the young James is called to the vocation of novelist in the international site of Boulogne and with the encouragement of a French rhetorician passionately committed to the importance of literature in the organization of social life. Yet both Boulogne's "cosmopolitanism" and Ansiot's (or Ansieaux's) literary idealism are ironized by James in his recollections: the former as a sort of English tourism and the latter as a sort of literary quixotism. The method is, however, typical of James's treatment of other important influences on his life and writings—those he had hoped most passionately to appropriate as his own.[44] James may describe Ansiot as an abler tutor than Mrs. Wix, but he is for all that still a "monster" in his own right, lost in the modern age: "I fairly think of him as a form of bland porpoise, violently blowing in an age not his own, as having had to exchange deep water for thin air" (*SBO,* 417). To be sure, Mrs. Wix never has sounded the "deep water" of either morality or education, but she shares M. Ansiot's air of anachronism.[45]

As I noted earlier, Maisie's only "education" is in the fictions and lies by which her parents and surrogates scrabble about, valuable perhaps only as they can be represented in literature as part of the larger social problems addressed by the serious novelist. What Maisie reads for most of the novel is merely the comic melodrama of a shabby everyday reality; what James and his narrator hope to encourage her to represent is the larger ethical significance that can be drawn from such negative lessons. Something of this sort is just what the author of *A Small Boy and Others* tries to carefully discriminate in his reconstruction of his childhood in Boulogne. M. Ansiot, the tutor, is just what the younger James fears he might become, as Maisie risks becoming the surrogate "daughter" to Mrs. Wix, substitute for the dead Clara Matilda and heiress of Mrs. Wix's ineluctable "moral sense." Just before the concluding delirium of his childhood, in which he will fall into "a lapse of consciousness," James reconstructs his work with his old tutor in metaphors of fertility overtly tied to gardening and peripherally connected with the young man's sexuality: "How can I allow then that we hadn't planted together, with a loose felicity, some of the seed of work?—even though the sprouting was so long put off. . . . The ministrations of M. Ansiot really wash themselves over with the weak mixture that had begun to spread for me, to immensity, during that summer day or two of our earlier residence when, betraying strange pains and apprehensions, I was with all decision put to bed" (*SBO,* 418). It would be wrong to conclude from these curious passages that James's "sickness," displaced from September to this climactic conclusion, now serves to represent by repressing homoerotic desires awakened by M. Ansiot. In his shabbiness and with his "greasily preserved" bits of classical learning, M. Ansiot is only marginally more alluring than Mrs. Wix.

Of course, this passage may be read exclusively in terms of the analogy between gardening and fictional creation that is quite conventional in James's late writings, especially his prefaces to the New York Edition. Such a reading ignores, however, the connotative richness that James himself considers indispensable to the literary imagination, which is the central topic of this suggestive memory. What remains attractive to the mature Henry James in his recollection is just what is so decisively charged with confused emotions of homoerotic and onanistic sexuality: the *being* of the novelist, who is always in one way or another "in love" with his characters, even if he or she hopes thereby to avoid the frightening sexuality of everyday life.[46] M. Ansiot (or Napoléon Ansieaux) is merely a negative version of the more passionate and higher ideals to which James aspires in his autobiographies and fiction: aesthetic ideals better represented by Thackeray, Victorian visitor to Boulogne, and Saint-Beuve, a native of the city and sometime model for James's own critical writings.[47]

James's use of the metaphors of gardening in other contexts, notably *The Aspern Papers* and the Prefaces, typifies his sublimation of such sexual energies as aesthetic powers. Whether it is the Bourdereaus' garden renewed by the narrator as part of his sneaky plot in *The Aspern Papers* or the "seeds" and "germs" of stories James grows within the garden of his imagination in the Prefaces, natural and imaginative fertility are rhetorically connected in James's writings in ways that are often erotically charged. In this respect, I want to keep in mind Eve Sedgwick's advice that "when we tune in to James's [sexual] language," we do so not "as superior, privileged eavesdroppers on a sexual narrative hidden from himself" but rather as readers "offered the privilege of sharing in his exhibitionistic enjoyment and performance of a sexuality organized around shame."[48] In both *What Maisie Knew* and *A Small Boy and Others,* James plays with rhetorical ambiguities involving literary production, sexual identity, and natural fertility. James's rhetoric is both defensive and expressive of instabilities in the categories of art, sexuality, and reality that are central to his thinking about modernity and his place in it.

Whether James's erotic rhetoric in the final pages of *A Small Boy and Others* speaks for the mature author or attempts to recapture the adolescent's confused sense of sexual repulsion and attraction, it should be taken neither as a frank engagement with homosexuality nor as a panicky repression of it.[49] The homoerotic and onanistic are just as much a part of heterosexual as homosexual identity; what matters in these crucial passages is James's apparent desire to detour such questions about his own sexuality into aesthetic concerns. There is thus a certain danger in reproducing just this defensive psychology in critical readings of *What Maisie Knew* (or other texts by James from the 1890s to the Major Phase) that stress Maisie's "aesthetic education" as an answer to the difficult social and moral problems she faces throughout the novel. Once we send Maisie back to England as acolyte of James's aesthetic ideals, we risk not only confusing social and metafictional dramas but using one as a "violent substitution" for the other. Thus when James's narrative ironies and strategies become too clever, we may abandon them for "practical" questions about Maisie's real life. When that "real" life of neglectful and abusive parents cannot be transcended, we are invited to substitute the *narrator* for such narcissists as Beale Farange, Mrs. Beale, and Ida.

All of this is very clever, but it has the appearance of a confidence game, even if it is handled with far greater elegance than any of the scams run by the adults in the novel. There are real social issues beyond the sheer melodrama of the waning aristocracy (Sir Claude) handing over its power and privilege to a grasping bourgeoisie composed variously of minor civil servants (Beale Farange), entrepreneurs (Mr. Perriam, Mr. Tischbein, and the "American Countess"), military officers (the Captain), and professional performers (Ida, the billiards champion). James constantly reminds us that modern social life takes place in an increasingly international context, and he does so not only by representing London as one of the new metropolitan centers but also by staging the climactic drama of the novel on the border between France and England, with crossings of the Channel serving symbolic as well as practical purposes. Interesting as it may be, then, to draw analogies between the young

Henry James and Maisie in terms of their aesthetic inclinations, it is important that we situate the biographical individual and the fictional character in the changing social, political, and economic circumstances of their times.

What Maisie Knew is rare among James's fiction for allowing working-class characters to challenge openly their so-called betters. Like other governesses, Mrs. Wix occupies the social limbo between the excluded working class and the privileged bourgeoisie. Her scant education suggests she is closer to the working class than Mrs. Beale, who as "Miss Overmore" was able to exceed her station as governess by marrying a gentleman with an income and then divorcing him to pursue her love of the aristocrat Sir Claude. The governess in *Turn of the Screw* and the unlettered Mrs. Grose come, of course, from an earlier generation than Mrs. Wix and Mrs. Beale, and they are maddeningly obedient to their social "betters" even in the most trying circumstances. Mrs. Wix, however, openly argues with Sir Claude, Ida, Beale Farange, and Mrs. Beale throughout the novel. Even the under-house maid, Susan Ash, challenges the authority of her employers, especially when she is not paid.[50]

There is, then, a certain democratic leveling that is dramatized in *What Maisie Knew* and anticipates the more explicit class conflict dramatized in *In the Cage* that I discuss in chapter 6. In both works, however, there are residual elements of older class and "national" identities, even though James goes to considerable lengths to argue that these conventions are also unstable. One of Ida's suitors, the "immensely rich," self-made man Mr. Perriam, is described as Mrs. Wix's "idea . . . of a heathen Jew" and as Maisie's "idea of a heathen Turk" (*M,* 91). Maisie assumes he must come "from the East," whereas Mrs. Wix knows his exotic origin to be merely "the City" (91).[51] Such Orientalism is quite typically applied to European Jews in the Victorian novel, as I note about Anthony Trollope's fiction in the preceding chapter, but the category of "peoples of color" is surprisingly large and diverse in *What Maisie Knew.* To the list of "heathen" Turks and Jews, James adds working-class characters such as Susan Ash, whose name suggests both color and victimization, and characters straddling class lines, such as the "fat dark little lady with a foreign name and dirty fingers" whom Beale Farange first hires "by the hour" to take care of Maisie (21). Miss Overmore is described as "the bright creature" who quickly replaces "this strange apparition," but this early nurse anticipates not only the infamous "American Countess" but also the working-class woman on the London omnibus who had once offered Maisie an orange and with whom Maisie compares the Countess: "The Countess brought back to her a dim remembrance of a strange woman with a horrid face who once, years before, in an omnibus, bending to her from an opposite seat, had suddenly produced an orange and murmured, 'Little dearie, won't you have it?' She had felt then, for some reason, a small silly terror, though afterwards conscious that her interlocutress, unfortunately hideous, had particularly meant to be kind" (194).

Since Toni Morrison wrote in *Playing in the Dark: Whiteness and the Literary Imagination* that the American Countess is one more character in the white literary imaginary's obsession with black-and-white racial divisions, critics have hastened to reinterpret *What Maisie Knew* in terms of its racial unconscious. Morrison quite cannily leaves it to the critics and scholars of James to evaluate what she means when she contends that this character is the "agency of moral choice in the novel": "It is possible . . . to read Henry James scholarship exhaustively and never arrive at a nodding mention, much less a satisfactory treatment, of the black woman who lubricates the turn of the plot and becomes the agency of moral choice and meaning in *What Maisie Knew*."[52] Morrison is wrong about the critical history, because Maxwell Geismar argued pointedly in *Henry James and the Jacobites* (1962) that "to this later James also, it almost appeared that Jews, Negroes and Lovers were the worst culprits in his *fin de siècle* scene of bohemian decadence. . . . The 'brown Countess' is described as 'a clever frizzled poodle in a frill, or a dreadful human monkey in a spangled petticoat.' (Is it possible that she is an *American Negro*?)"[53] Morrison is nevertheless right to challenge James scholars to address more explicitly James's attitudes on race, as critics such as Kenneth Warren, Sara Blair, Beverly Haviland, and Walter Michaels have done in recent years.[54] The apparent absence of racial representation in James's writings is in fact as much a consequence of critical repression as of James's own conflicted views, and these attentive scholars have shown us how contemporary nineteenth-century and early-twentieth-century conventions regarding race and nationality are as readable in Henry James as in most of his contemporaries.

Walter Michaels has offered the most interesting response to critics such as Morrison and Warren who contend that James's thinly repressed racial content was in keeping with the racist ideology of Jim Crow America.[55] Michaels neither condemns James in the manner of Morrison and Warren nor defends him; instead, Michaels interprets James's representation of race as fundamentally different from the ideology of Jim Crow racism in America. *What Maisie*

Knew is a crucial text for Michaels's argument not only because of its importance for Morrison but also for its non-American treatment of racial issues rendered as strict binaries of black and white in the America of *Plessy vs. Ferguson:*

> What's extraordinary about *Maisie* is not that it actually represents miscegenation but that it doesn't, that it fails to see the "mixed" social manifestation of Beale Farange's relation with the Countess as an instance of *racial* mixture. Indeed, it fails, by American criteria, to see either Beale or the Countess as properly belonging to races in the first place. Not only is Beale not white, the Countess, Morrison to the contrary notwithstanding, is not black—she is a "brown lady"; by which I mean not that, under the American system of racial classification, she wouldn't count as black but rather that, in the world of *What Maisie Knew* and *The American Scene,* the American system of racial classification is not in force.[56]

Michaels makes the important point that Jim Crow racism in the United States followed a different ideological logic than the classification and hierarchizing of different groups in England and Europe. James's "American Countess" is probably not an "American Negro," as Geismar speculates and Morrison hints, but merely one among several characters used by the modern English imaginary to mark the boundaries of "proper" English identity. Challenging Warren's criticism of Jamesian realism, Michaels may argue that "the point to be made about Jamesian realism is not that by identifying blacks with vulgarity, it contributed to Jim Crow racism but rather that, by failing to disarticulate blacks from vulgarity, it was unable to understand the kind of contribution Jim Crow racism was making to the reorganization of American social life."[57]

Described as a "brown lady," the American Countess may thus be linked with a wide range of other marginal peoples in the English imaginary— working-class, Orientalized "foreigners" and colonial subjects, Jews, prostitutes, children, and the elderly. In other words, the significant fact for Michaels that the Countess is "brown," rather than "black," by no means concludes the discussion of the status of racism in Jamesian realism; it merely shifts the question from American binaries of "black and white" to the confusions of race, nationality, class, gender, sexuality, and age often used to prop up otherwise unstable notions of English "national" identity in the late nineteenth century.[58] Like Miriam Rooth's supposed Jewish heritage, the American Countess's "color" is represented by James in radically ambiguous terms. The "brown" lady with Beale Farange whom Mrs. Beale and Maisie encounter accidentally at "the Exhibition" is always "colored" by the contexts in which the other characters place her. Maisie's claim that "she's almost black" follows Mrs. Beale's vilification of both Beale and his companion for their infidelity (*M*, 172). By this point in the narrative, the reader knows that social meaning is constituted only by the relations of the particular context in which words are spoken and acts performed, so the surrounding context of the American Countess's appearance is crucial to her racialized significance.

Just before Beale Farange and his lady appear, Mrs. Beale and Maisie have "paused" before one of the free exhibits: "The Flowers of the Forest, a large presentment of bright brown ladies—they were brown all over—in a medium suggestive of tropical luxuriance, and there Maisie dolorously expressed her belief that [Sir Claude] would never come at all" (*M*, 171). We are reminded that the infidelity for which Mrs. Beale will condemn her husband in the very next paragraph is precisely what she has planned to commit with Sir Claude, using her trip with Maisie to the exhibition as their cover. The exhibit has an immediate associative effect on the woman who appears with Beale Farange, identifying her with the "bright brown ladies" even to the extent that Maisie will later attribute to her the animal characteristics of the "tropical luxuriance" in which the ladies of this exhibit are displayed. If the original description of "the Flowers of the Forest" as "brown all over" suggests that they are scantily clad, then their representation of illicit and racialized sexuality is linked by rhetorical contiguity with the Countess's "character."[59]

In the American Countess's elegant salon with her father, Maisie characterizes "the brown lady": "She literally struck the child more as an animal than as a 'real' lady; she might have been a clever frizzled poodle in a frill or a dreadful human monkey in a spangled petticoat. She had a nose that was far too big and eyes that were far too small and a moustache that was, well, not so happy a feature as Sir Claude's" (*M*, 193). These animal images do not, however, quite fit the "tropical luxuriance" of the ladies in the exhibit, because the highly stylized French poodle and the monkey in a "spangled petticoat" are animals we associate with the urban domestication of animals, especially in European metropolitan centers. Indeed, what first appears to be the erotic and racial link between the Countess and "the Flowers of the Forest" results in a crucial rhetorical difference: the exhibit's spectacle of natural primitivism contrasts sharply with the Countess's cultivation, represented metaphorically by the poodle's stylized cut and the monkey's "spangled" dress. In fact, the Countess's representation as a monkey associates her explicitly with Maisie, who is described early in the novel as "Poor little monkey!"[60]

The strange process of racialization by association that occurs in these passages in chapters 18 and 19 occurs elsewhere in Henry James's writings, notably in the final chapter of *A Small Boy and Others.* James recalls the "few early weeks" he "suffered" at the Collège Communal with his brothers before he was unable to continue, "thanks to the interrupting illness that placed me so long, with its trail of after-effects, half complacently, half ruefully, fully apart" (*SBO,* 399–400). Among other schoolmates, James recalls "a brownish black-eyed youth, of about my own degree of youthfulness," who tells James "of an awful Mutiny in India, where his military parents, who had not so long before sent him over thence, . . . were in mortal danger of their lives; so that news of their having been killed would perhaps be already on the way" (402). This "Napier, or Nappié as he was called at the school," prompts a remarkable reflection by James:

> Why I should have thought him almost Indian of stamp and hue be-
> cause his English parents were of the so general Indian peril is more than
> I can say; yet I have his exotic and above all his bold, his imaginably even
> "bad," young face, finely unacquainted with the law, before me at this
> hour quite undimmed—announcing, as I conceived it, and quite as a
> shock, any awful adventure one would, as well as something I must even
> at the time have vaguely taken as the play of the "passions." He vanishes,
> and I dare say but I make him over, as I make everything. (*SBO,* 403–4)

Why, indeed, would the young James confuse the son of English parents in colonial service in India with the "stamp and hue" of East Indians, and why, above all, would James take the time more than fifty years later to "make him over" into what appears to be a little commentary on racism, even as James protests that the memory's meaning "is more than I can say"?[61] Certainly British colonial officials at risk of their lives in the 1857 Sepoy Mutiny in India would be at the furthest possible remove from the "stamp and hue" of their native antagonists, unless it were that these racialized Indians—those dark "wogs" exoticized and popularized by Kipling—are the *products* of the British imperial imaginary, rather than of any essential physical, psychological, moral, or cultural differences from Europeans.

James does not give the reader enough information to identify the family of his schoolmate, but the surname "Napier" was familiar to Victorians as that of the military hero, Robert Cornelius Napier (1810–1890), 1st Baron of Magdala, who played an important part in the suppression of the Indian Mutiny, commanded a British division in the suppression of the Taiping Rebellion in China, and won a baronetcy for his daring liberation in 1868 of Europeans held captive by Emperor Theodore of Abyssinia, whose troops were defeated by Napier's forces on April 13, 1868, at the Emperor's capital of Magdala.[62] A celebrated hero of the British Empire in India, China, and Abyssinia, Napier typifies the "dashing brilliance" he shares with contemporaries, like "Chinese" Gordon, in the Victorian imperial imagination. Whether Lord Napier of Magdala's genealogical or merely literary "son," the young Napier at the Collège in Boulogne expresses in his " 'bad,' young face, finely unacquainted with the law" James's commentary on the British Empire's reckless colonialism in India. Indeed, the Indian Mutiny marks the end of Indian colonial rule by the East India Company and the beginning of formal rule by the British government; it also marks the beginning of a very long and finally successful history of rebellion by Indians against British colonial rule, masked poorly by the heroism of such Victorian adventurers as Napier and Gordon.[63]

James's care in attributing the American Countess's "color" only to the characters, especially Mrs. Beale and Maisie, who observe her in these special circumstances suggests that a similar contextual racializing is at work in *What Maisie Knew*. Part of the ironic genius of the novel is achieved by way of Maisie's elementary misunderstandings of what she observes and hears, many of which turn out to have a certain ironic truth. Thus the lectures to which Mrs. Beale drags Maisie either at the University of London or at the British Museum—another cover for Mrs. Beale to meet Sir Claude—are for Maisie in "Glower," rather than "Gower Street." There is no Glower Street in London, but the significance of these episodes in education, as they comment both on Mrs. Beale's and Sir Claude's infidelities and on the likely tedium of the actual lectures, are aptly expressed in the "glower" we are encouraged to direct at them. Another possible misunderstanding is that the American Countess does not even appear to Maisie as an American: "There was something in the Countess that falsified everything, even the great interests in America. . . . Mamma had known an American who was not a bit like this one. She was not, however, of noble rank; her name was only Mrs. Tucker" (*M*, 196).

James plays on the apparent oxymoron of an "American Countess." From such early works as "The Last of the Valerii" and *The American,* James consistently challenges the popular cliché that America is a classless society. A new, modern aristocracy will certainly emerge from wealthy entrepreneurs such as Christopher Newman who conveniently forget and deny their aristocratic heritages for the sake of democratic pretensions. James also lampoons the myth of the "representative" American, either in its Emersonian or more popular late-nineteenth-century senses, by suggesting that neither Mrs. Tucker nor this "American Countess" can convey properly to Maisie what an American *is.* Perhaps the American in the modern age is precisely what *cannot* be precisely defined or "typified," much in the manner that Miriam Rooth in *The Tragic Muse* captures the temper of modern identity by remaining unclassifiable.

In more practical ways, of course, the American Countess, whom Beale Farange praises for her vast commercial enterprises, may be either an American once married to some European aristocrat, like Martha in "The Last of the Valerii," or a European aristocrat once married to an American entrepreneur, like Prince Amerigo in *The Golden Bowl.* In each case, the lady's "color" would have a different contextual significance, even if it would still speak clearly to the social psychology of racism James analyzes in his own experience in *A Small Boy and Others.* As I pointed out in chapter 3, the Victorian novel is full of "dark gentry" from other European countries, especially Italy, Poland, and Bohemia, suggesting miscegenation and thus "racial impurity" attributable to Jews, Gypsies, and Middle Eastern peoples. The ideological purpose of these "other" aristocrats is generally to reaffirm the purity of the English ruling class, especially as the Victorian bourgeoisie was claiming to replace such aristocracy and thus experiencing considerable anxieties regarding its own right to rule.

In keeping with this ideology, Beale Farange tells Maisie that the Countess's "isn't an English title. . . . nor French either. It's American" (*M,* 177). At one level, James merely ironizes the lady's social pretensions: such a title must be bogus. On another level, "American" could mean Central or South America and the Caribbean, rather than the United States.[64] What matters for James, however, is a certain strategic ambiguity with regard to the Countess's title, ethnicity, and national origin, as if James suggests thereby how these three factors determine social standing in the modern world. To be sure, James also signifies that such standards betray a certain decadence, which the

Countess exemplifies, no matter how we interpret her characterization and narrative function in the novel.

While Maisie waits with her father for his new lover to arrive at her elegant flat, Beale Farange tries halfheartedly to convince Maisie to "come away" with them to America, but when the American Countess arrives, this destination turns out to be Spa, the fashionable health resort and gambling destination in the late nineteenth century.[65] When Maisie asks, "It isn't to America, then?" her father can only mutter, "what the deuce it mattered" (*M*, 194). If this lady is indeed any kind of "American," she is certainly a cosmopolitan for whom Spa is as much a destination as New York or San Francisco. The same may be concluded of the Countess if we interpret her merely as a fashionable prostitute; her cosmopolitanism is a function not only of her adaptability to different places but also of her flexible "identity." Indeed, James's point seems to be that however the American Countess is "colored" by us, her identity is that of the new cosmopolitans for whom the world, rather than any particular nation, defines their particular identities.

Will these modern cosmopolitans be inevitably "brown" as a consequence of some terrified antimodern fantasy of cultural miscegenation, as in Shreve McCannon's mocking conclusion to Faulkner's *Absalom, Absalom!* that the Jim Bonds will inherit the earth, or is James suggesting rather that the issue of race is now an inevitable question for those growing up in the midst of the internationalizing forces of modernity?[66] By the second half of the nineteenth century, the consequences of European imperialism were evident everywhere in metropolitan centers such as London, Madrid, and Paris. Whereas the slave labor working colonial plantations and thereby supporting the leisurely lives of the English gentry in Jane Austen's *Mansfield Park* (1814) and Charlotte Brontë's *Jane Eyre* (1847) hardly cracks the surface of their perfect English scenery, the evidence of European imperialism is an ineluctable part of late-nineteenth-century urban experience.

James does not specify any particular exhibition that Mrs. Beale and Maisie visit on the fateful night they encounter Maisie's father with the American Countess, but "the Exhibition" is very likely a fictional rendering of the regular exhibitions, international expositions, and commemorative jubilees that celebrated both Victorian technological progress and the global reach of British imperialism. Among the most popular Victorian entertainments, "pay-as-you-enter exhibitions," featuring "performing animals, . . .

acts by fire-eaters or men who played turns by tapping their chins," were both condemned as vulgar and yet attended regularly by people of all classes, including "the Queen herself."[67] From the Crystal Palace Exhibition of 1851 to Queen Victoria's Golden Jubilee in 1887 and Diamond Jubilee in 1897, London helped invent itself as one of the great metropolitan centers of modernity by displaying the cultural diversity of the British Empire.[68] In *Victorian Things*, Asa Briggs refers to "a Colonial and Indian Exhibition held in South Kensington in 1886," which offered "lavish displays both of things and in retrospect most disturbingly of people—of cheap tickets and rich carpets, of New Zealand wool and Australian wines—and of Kaffirs and Bushmen from the Cape (*inter alia* they were shown washing diamonds)," all testifying to British imperial power.[69]

Maisie's visit to the American Countess's house is described in terms that recall the Orientalist fantasies often simulated at such international expositions. Whirled away in the confusion of the accidental encounter between Mrs. Beale and her husband, Maisie experiences her transport as something straight out of "the Arabian Nights" (*M*, 175). Recent scholarly interest in these American and European exhibitions has revolved around the ways such displays helped organize a new "global hierarchy of nations and races," often simulating in the very spatial organization of the expositions the explicit hierarchy of "civilization" presumed to govern the peoples and nations of the earth.[70] The appearance of the American Countess in the midst of such imperial display in London suggests how the United States played its own part in Western territorial and cultural expansion. Amid the patriotic British displays that were part of these exhibitions, imports such as "Buffalo Bill" Cody's Wild West Show announced the United States as a new competitor with Great Britain for imperial authority.[71]

There is one final connotation possible for the "color" of the American Countess, and it is suitably ironic. When she first appears at the exhibition with Beale Farange, she is mistaken by Mrs. Beale for "Mrs. Cuddon," in part because Mrs. Beale has already classified the woman as part of a group that dresses in a particularly vulgar manner. The mark of such dress is "an upright scarlet plume," which serves for this part of the narrative as the synecdoche for this woman's loose morals (*M*, 172). When Mrs. Beale comments, "They're always hideous," she must explain to Maisie, "Oh not his *wives*," thus strengthening the implication that she has misidentified the American Countess as a prostitute. Victorian prostitutes were often characterized as "dark" or "brown," in keeping both with the coloring of moral categories in the West and with the association of prostitutes with the working classes. As Sander Gilman writes: "The late nineteenth-century perception of the prostitute merged with that of the black" because both "were . . . seen as outsiders" and were associated with "primitive" sexuality beyond their "control."[72] The ambiguities of race, class, and national origin do cast an aura of the illicit around the Countess, and we are encouraged by more than just Ida's jealous remarks to view the Countess as some kind of prostitute, ranging from a sophisticated courtesan to a hunter of fortune or social status.

What, then, do all of these possible connotations for the American Countess's "brown" appearance tell us about what Maisie and Henry James respectively knew about race in 1897? The many different connotations and the deliberate ambiguity regarding the Countess's racial identity may well be James's play with a racialized character for the scandalous aura it lends the novel, thus making James part of the growing obsession in Euramerican cultures with "racial" and "national" purity at the very moment the old categories of race and nationality were changing with social and economic conditions. Certainly the "vulgarity" of the American Countess is primarily displayed through the phenomenology of Mrs. Beale and then that of Maisie, suggesting how what Maisie "knows" in the novel is often distorted by the jealousy and hatred of the adults around her. When linked with James's recollection of his own childish racialization of his schoolmate Napier in Boulogne, James's representation of how Maisie comes to "see" the American Countess as "brown" and "almost black" might well be interpreted as a brilliant understanding of how racial categories are screens for other aggressive interests in a vicious social hierarchy that includes racism, sexism, classism, and Eurocentrism, among many others. "Racism," then, is very often a projection of our own deepest anxieties and hatreds; the "darkness" of the American Countess is as much a reflection of Mrs. Beale's hatred of her husband as it is of her husband's immoral conduct toward both his wife and his daughter. If the Countess is in fact a courtesan, then she no more commodifies herself than do the other more socially acceptable characters in the narrative, including Maisie's parents. Such a reading may do nothing to dissociate color from morality—an association that has a long history in the West, but it nevertheless helps clarify that "color" has little to do with any kind of racial essence.

The American Countess is not, after all, vulgar, as her elegantly furnished house and her generosity to Maisie testify. When the Countess hurries her to take a cab home to Mrs. Beale, Maisie protests that she has no money. In response to Beale's crude command, "Make your stepmother pay," the Countess replies, "No stepmother ever paid in her life!" and promptly gives Maisie "a cluster of sovereigns" far in excess "even of a fee in a fairy-tale," much less for a London cab (*M*, 196–98). Previous critics have judged this gift of money confirmation of the Countess's association with the general prostitution of human relations in the novel, and her imperious " 'Here's money,' said the brown lady: 'go!' " seems to reinforce such an interpretation. But Henry James does not treat money in this novel with the aristocratic disdain he had in such earlier works as *The American* and *The Portrait of a Lady*. Maisie's parents and stepparents are always in desperate need of funds, and they rarely give her any tangible means to learn about the world outside their restricted and vicious domestic circles. Money can mean freedom, as Sir Claude will make clear at the end of the novel when he proposes to save Maisie's inheritance.

The American Countess is the least likely candidate for the title of "prostitute," regardless of her scarlet plume, in a novel in which every adult seems willing to "sell" himself or herself either for cash or for power. The "cluster of sovereigns" that makes Maisie believe that "there *must* then have been great interests in America" is still for her evidence that she has been transported into a tale from "the Arabian Nights," but back home at Mrs. Beale's, Maisie will awaken to the nightmare of everyday reality; Mrs. Beale will appropriate those sovereigns on the improbable grounds of honor: "We're to send them back on the spot!" (*M*, 197, 199). The real prostitutes in this novel are clearly Beale Farange and his two wives, Ida and Mrs. Beale, who will do anything for money.

We may conclude from such a reading of the American Countess that issues of race and their entanglement with those of class, gender, and nation are central to any young person's education in the modern world that James evokes in *What Maisie Knew*. To be sure, James is somewhat terrified of this brave new world, and he cannot be said to criticize calmly and dispassionately the fictions of racial stereotyping that are still very much a part of the social problems we struggle to overcome today. James's representations of the American Countess as a "poodle" and a "monkey," as well as his exhibit of the "Flowers of the Forest"—those "bright brown ladies"—still carry racist connotations no matter how effectively they may be said to serve James's critique of the racial imaginary of modern English society.[73] James's radically ambig-uous prose style, dependent as it is on relentless irony, might also be said to confuse readers at a time when clear statements were needed regarding the fictions of racial classification, including such pseudosciences as eugenics.

What does emerge as a crucial part of Maisie's education in the novel, however, is her encounter with the whole set of social ambiguities surround-ing the classification of human beings according to artificial categories such as race, class, gender, sexuality, nationality, and age. Few other protagonists in James's fiction either before or after *What Maisie Knew* are exposed to such a variety of human beings and such conflicts among their different means of identifying themselves as belonging to particular groups. Michaels's distinc-tion between the representation of race as part of everyday life in *What Maisie Knew* and as a segregated and specific race, "black," in Jim Crow America should remind us that Maisie's very exposure to different classes, races, and "loves" suggests that her social world is a more comprehensive one than those in James's earlier novels. Whatever the Countess's "proper" identity—African, African American, South Asian, Italian, Jew, Latin American—it is neverthe-less an identity that has social *visibility,* however scandalous, in London.

When Maisie leaves France with Mrs. Wix, she travels with a woman and governess whom she has trivialized only a few pages earlier—"Oh you're nobody"—and whom Maisie knows is woefully inadequate as a formal teacher, surrogate mother, or moral adviser (*M,* 309). Critics are fond of pointing out how James seems thereby to drop Maisie from the brink of adult knowledge into the abyss of Mrs. Wix's class-specific economic and intellec-tual poverty, signifying thereby Maisie's defeat: "The eponymous heroine of *What Maisie Knew* is ejected from all of her various family circles and left to the devices of Mrs. Wix at the end of the novel."[74] Yet Maisie travels back to England with Mrs. Wix for more than mere reasons of convenience; Maisie's return thus signifies far more than her surrender before such terrible knowl-edge. Mrs. Wix comes to represent the whole range of other people—all variously "nobodies" in the false society of her parents and stepparents—from whom Maisie has learned in the course of her education: Susan Ash, the American Countess, the "hideous" woman on the omnibus, the French fish-erwomen, the old ladies of Boulogne, the "bright brown" "Flowers of the Forest" at the exhibition. Scorned by Maisie's parents and stepparents as "nobodies," these same characters nevertheless make a collective difference in what Maisie knows.

These and many others constitute the wider world of a modernity that may permit the shabby immoralities of the Beales and their kind to shamble along but also brings their hypocrisy and pretension into stark relief. Taken by herself, Mrs. Wix represents an old moral code whose standards she repeatedly fails to meet; attractive as her ethical idealism may be to James, he also knows that she is an anachronism and thus a failure in this modern age. By the same token, "modern" characters such as Maisie's parents and step-parents represent for James the decadence of the present. Caught between Mrs. Wix's effort to recapture some premodern moral clarity and the immorality of her modern parents, Maisie seems doomed to the abyss separating two incompatible social orders. On the other hand, the inadequacies of both the premodern and the thoroughly modern might also offer Maisie certain emancipatory possibilities. To be "ejected" from such "family circles" may not be such a tragic fate for Maisie. In the 1890s, Henry James certainly did not have available to him the term that best describes what links the "nobodies" in the novel together, but we might find in the marginality of these characters a certain *postmodern* potential. There are other worlds, after all, and they lie all before Maisie as she makes her way home in the middle of the Channel, buoyed by the fluid medium that enables her to traverse, and symbolically to *know*, the gulf of our modernity (*M,* 363).

6 ✍ Spectral Mechanics: Gender, Sexuality,

and Work in *In the Cage*

> The cords of all link back, strandentwining cable of all
> flesh. . . . Put me on to Edenville. Aleph, alpha: nought,
> nought, one.
>
> —James Joyce, *Ulysses* (1922)

Justly celebrated as quintessentially modern, *The Turn of the Screw* is curiously devoid of modern trappings. Regarded in terms of contemporaries such as *What Maisie Knew* and *In the Cage,* it seems deliberately archaic and antimodern in its stubborn refusal to invoke the machinery of the new age. Ghost stories around the fire, faded old manuscripts, haunted country houses, and London rakes are the stuff of the romances the governess likely reads. The modern is present only in the absence of its material referents—an absence rationalized by the historical setting of the story within the frame. Only James's rendering of the action by way of psychic, hermeneutic, and sexual entanglements—figural weavings that produce quite literally the bodies of ghosts—tells us decisively that this is a modern narrative playing wickedly with our nostalgia for a premodern age that probably never existed. There is simply no evidence of modern technology in *The Turn of the Screw* beyond the mechanics of writing, the postal system, and that notorious metaphor in the title: "screw."

In *The Turn of the Screw,* we can hardly speak of "technologies of communication." James distinguishes the governess from Mrs. Grose by way of the former's literacy, and much of the dramatic action revolves around the governess's temptations to break the uncle's original taboo against any direct communication with him. The governess's abilities to read and write are integrally related to her authority at Bly and her class identification, however marginal, with those in power. Yet the "scenes of writing" that poststructuralist critics have convincingly shown to organize the narrative are decidedly old-fashioned, both in James's and in poststructuralists' treatments, because they are assumed to be structured by the private individual employing a stylus (pen or pencil) to make alphabetical marks on a page to be sent physically to another individual to be read and understood.

The deconstruction of this scene of discrete message sending was accomplished long before poststructuralists called attention to the *différance* by which language functions. Indeed, I would historicize poststructuralism by arguing that it follows technological developments in communication of this century that have utterly transformed the presumably discrete "sender" and "receiver," "writer" and "reader," as well as their relations to the putative message and its transmission. In *What Maisie Knew,* characters' messages are completely bound up with the ways they are received—often with hostility and suspicion, so that Maisie soon learns to take no statement as discrete or simply denotative. Communication in that novel floats among many different senders and receivers. *In the Cage* also addresses this transformation of the scene of writing from a premodern to a modern phenomenon for which the descriptive term "scene of writing" can only appear archaic and crude.[1]

In *In the Cage,* the traditional scene of writing is transferred from the domestic space of the governess's bedroom at Bly to the "obscure and barely adequate" corner of Cocker's Grocery, where Lady Bradeen is directed by "the gesture made by the counter-clerk in answer to her sharp question" about "the place to write" her telegraph forms. "There?" Lady Bradeen asks with "the light note of disgust" in "her clear voice" that suggests just how squalid she considers the "obscure" corner to which she is directed.[2] Of course, the telegraph, together with the social and technical practices it requires, have replaced the privacy of writing and its assorted rituals. At the center of Cocker's, there is the click of the "sounder," Samuel F. B. Morse's mechanism for transmission that James specifies quite carefully and accurately even as he keeps it teasingly hidden from the reader's view: "The sounder . . . being the innermost cell of captivity, a cage within the cage, fenced off from the rest by a frame of ground glass" (*Cage,* 376).

Yet why should this shift from writing to the telegraph change anything at all in the customary representation of class, gender, work, and culture—the categories of social life whose hierarchies dictate power, authority, and thus identity in the Victorian period? The bare plot, after all, of Lady Bradeen's affair with Captain Everard and its apparent discovery by her husband, Lord Bradeen, differs little from countless social melodramas out of which James spun finer designs. The telegraph appears to be a mere instrument of communication, whose technical command by the telegraphist gives her no more genuine power over social discourse than the governess has in her illusory reign at Bly. Further, if the telegraph is so important, then why did James wait so long to take into account an instrument of communication that by the end of the century already operated through a nationalized network in England with sending offices in local groceries?[3]

What Maisie Knew and *In the Cage* were two of the first works James dictated, and as several scholars have pointed out, there are remarkable similarities between James's practices of dictation and the scenes of telegraphy in *In the Cage*. As Kaplan notes, James had experienced problems of rheumatism in his right wrist for more than a year when he decided in 1897 to employ a "secretary, William MacAlpine, to take dictation," and James "practiced the new skill during the spring of 1897 with some delight."[4] James's third and last secretary, Theodora Bosanquet, describes James's response to dictation as considerably more enthusiastic. " 'It all seems,' he once explained, 'to be so much more effectively and unceasingly *pulled* out of me in speech than in writing.' "[5] Both Mary Weld, his second typist, and Bosanquet took dictation directly on the Remington typewriter to which James grew so accustomed that "the click of the Remington machine acted as a positive spur. He found it more difficult to compose to the music of any other make."[6] But when he began dictating, "he experimented with two procedures. Sometimes MacAlpine, an expert stenographer, made longhand copies of the dictation; other times MacAlpine typed his words as he spoke them directly on the new Remington machine he had bought. He soon preferred the latter."[7]

In *Bodies and Machines,* Mark Seltzer stresses that James wanted the practice of "dictation to the machine" to be "absolutely identical with the act of writing" as James put the matter. Both Bosanquet and Mary Weld stressed James's desire that each be simply "part of the machinery." Seltzer concludes that this was James's psychic defense against a new system of communication that threatened the essential mastery and authority he, like other writers, had spent a career developing: "Reducing technologies of writing to the 'only' material and the material to the 'illusory,' James thus insists on the transparency of writing in general and on its disembodiment (such that, for instance, the difference of bodily motions—the difference of walking up and down—makes no difference)."[8]

Yet MacAlpine's first efforts were taken down in stenographer's symbols, then transcribed at the end of the day on the new Remington. It is imaginable

that James experienced some of the same ignorance contemplating Mac-
Alpine's stenography as Maisie experiences with the coded adult conversation
that swirls about her. It was quite reasonable of James to have preferred the
method of direct dictation to the Remington, as any writer without knowledge of stenography would prefer the greater control over the ongoing dictation afforded by an always available transcript to the greater speed afforded by
shorthand transcription. There is yet another reason, however, why James
may have chosen direct dictation over MacAlpine's stenography. Bosanquet
observes: "The business of acting as a medium between the spoken and the
typewritten word was at first as alarming as it was fascinating," but she was
merely playing the amanuensis.[9] How much more "alarming and fascinating"
must it have been to both James and MacAlpine to have worked together in a
scene of communication in which the speech of James was transformed into
written symbols legible only to MacAlpine, who until the end of the day,
when he would type out a readable copy, would have virtual possession of the
great writer's thoughts?

In *The Turn of the Screw,* the absent uncle maintains his authority by
granting the governess the illusion that when she speaks and writes, her word
is law.[10] James's dictation to MacAlpine reverses the traditional ways in which
ideological control is effected through language; in this case, the author of a
discourse, not the reader, must depend crucially on an other, in this case a
hired technician, for the proper transcription and delivery of his words and
his work. It is precisely the situation of *In the Cage,* with the difference that
the Remington's click is replaced by the sounder's centralizing "tick" (the
machine itself remaining invisible) and the stenographer's shorthand replaced by the Morse code into which the senders' messages must be translated.[11] James's own desire for a "typist without a mind" parallels that of the
aristocrats in the novella, who hope for telegraphists who will simply translate
and transmit their messages without interference. But interference is the
constant threat posed by this new, decidedly public mode of communication
that has pushed an archaic writing into the grubby corner of Cocker's store.
(Writing, we should note parenthetically, has been doubly affected, both
marginalized and yet made public in the service it renders the telegraph.) In a
similar fashion, Maisie often serves to deliver messages between warring parents and stepparents, often misinterpreting both the original message and its
reception. Maisie's childish mediation and the telegraphist's interpretations at
the sounder serve as wild cards in the process of social communication.

James's own writing style is affected by the telegraphic mode, or at least by what James imagines is the paratactic mode both of telegrams and of the coded clicks by which they are transmitted. There are several marvelous conversations that are perfectly "telegraphic," especially at the end of chapter 18, when the telegraphist makes a pact not to "give up" Captain Everard and he blusters, "See here—see here," and the conversation with Mrs. Jordan in her flat in Maida Vale in the final three chapters (25–27), which I will discuss in more detail later in this chapter. A certain amount of James's imitation of a telegraphic style is part of his overall intention, but there is also a degree to which the telegraphic mode threatens to undermine James's customary control of discourse, especially the wonderfully complex and nuanced sentences that have become the hallmarks of his modernism. No two styles could be more opposite than the modernist long sentence with its implication of connotative complexity and the short and economical style of the telegram. Yet they are two styles that typify modernity.

James mediates between these opposing styles of modernity in a very interesting fashion in *In the Cage*. In general, he incorporates telegraphic messages into his narrative, and he then embeds them in a connotatively complex narrative. At one level, then, James defends his own style against the encroachments of modern technology (and its new modes of communication) by appropriating both the technology and its style.[12] For all their centrality to the plot and James's response to modernization in general, surprisingly little has been said about the telegraphic messages, except by Ralf Norrman and Janet Gabler-Hover.[13] The melodramatic plot turns on three telegrams included in the text, one of which (the second of the three) was sent by Lady Bradeen, corrected at the time by the telegraphist, apparently intercepted by Lady Bradeen's husband (or his representative), and concerning whose contents the putative lover of Lady Bradeen, Captain Everard, urgently inquires of the telegraphist, whose infatuation with him has encouraged her earlier to offer: "I'd do anything for you" (*Cage*, 225). This telegram apparently finalizes arrangements for a romantic meeting between Lady Bradeen and Captain Everard, who have used different signatures and disguised identities throughout the narrative. The text of the telegram is important: "Miss Dolman, Parade Lodge, Parade Terrace, Dover. Let him instantly know right one, Hôtel de France, Ostend. Make it seven nine four nine six one. Wire me alternative Burfield's" (425).

The dominant rhetorical mode of the telegram is *parataxis*, the practice of placing related clauses, words, and phrases in series without the use of connecting words. The paratactic mode has recently been used to characterize the dominant rhetoric of postmodern culture.[14] Beyond mere economy of expression, such parataxis in telegrams depersonalizes and even disguises the message, responding to the new public conditions of discourse required by the telegraph. Since the 1840s, the publicity with which the telegraph was associated had been cause of both grand optimism on the part of technophiles and apocalyptic warnings from confirmed Luddites. On January 3, 1845, for example, John Tawell, "dressed as a Quaker in a great brown coat reaching nearly to his feet, was arrested at a lodging house in London after murdering his mistress at Slough. The transmission of his description by telegraph to Paddington was largely responsible for his rapid arrest," and the newspapers celebrated the telegraph with the headline: "The cords that hung John Tawell."[15] The military advantages of the telegraph had been demonstrated in the U.S. Civil War, and the abuse of the telegraphic style was infamously recorded in Bismarck's infamous revision of the exchange between Kaiser Wilhelm I and the French ambassador Comte Vincente Benedetti in the Ems Dispatch of July 1870, which precipitated the Franco-Prussian War. As the police made more extensive use of telegraph networks following the celebrity of the Tawell arrest, they both increased their powers of surveillance and prompted public anxiety about the misuses of the telegraph by "the 'dangerous classes,' 'assassins and burglars' " who might use "the telegraph to decoy people from their homes. *The Detective,* a new weekly journal of 1858, urged companies to date stamp their telegrams only at the place where they were actually received, for telegrams written in London were dated 'Aberdeen' or 'Brighton' to deceive recipients."[16] In addition to the several ways James's fiction addresses and contributes to the modern arts of surveillance analyzed so well by Michel Foucault, we should add this connection between his writing and telegraphy.[17]

   The potential for surveillance built into the telegraph system frightens Lady Bradeen and Captain Everard, prompting them to communicate in code. Certainly the numbers in the telegram constitute some sort of cipher code, undoubtedly suggested to James by the fact that the Morse code is itself a cipher code.[18] Honorific or purely decorative as the good captain's military title undoubtedly is, it nonetheless gives some warrant for his use of a system of coding developed primarily for military secrecy. As Ralf Norrman points out, in an essay otherwise notable for its pathological effort to prove how the telegraphist "is wrong about everything," the crucial part of the telegram consists of "the series of numbers," since this is the information that the telegraphist remembers and apparently satisfies the anxious Captain Everard, who is himself transformed scenically by James into his own version of a telegraphic sender, but now of the luminous sort: "He shone at them all like a tall lighthouse, embracing even, for sympathy, the blinking young men. 'By all the powers—it's wrong!' " (*Cage,* 484). He is delighted, even as the "blinking young men" act as naval signals to his lighthouse, because the numbers remembered by the telegraphist and jotted on the back of his card—"He fairly glared at it. 'Seven, nine, four—' 'Nine, six, one'—she obligingly completed the number"—are wrong, and we remember with the telegraphist, "If it's wrong it's all right," which she quotes to the still uncomprehending signal corps of young male clerks after the captain has fled "without another look, without a word of thanks, without time for anything or anybody," like some embodied telegram darting through the wire.[19]

Is there a cipher code buried in *In the Cage,* as legible as the code cracked (complete with instructions) in Poe's "The Gold-Bug" (1843)?[20] If so, it is a "code" much like the message contained in the incriminating letter Christopher Newman so good-naturedly burns in *The American,* the "secret" of the ghosts in *The Turn of the Screw,* or the unmentionable object manufactured by the Newsomes in *The Ambassadors.* It is a code that carries another, literary message, a first step on James's path toward partial escape from the threats of the new technologies to his authority as a writer, as *the* writer of his turning century.[21] Whatever is coded means more than simply, "Meet me in Ostend, dear, Hotel de France, at 7:00, if you can, rooms 94 and 96, they connect, you know!" The usual Jamesian intimation of horrors is here, decorously disguised, but peeping through the flowers nonetheless.

Isn't it convenient that Lord Bradeen dies, "most sudden," just after "It all got about" to "a point at which Lord Bradeen had to act," as the telegraphist's friend, Mrs. Jordan explains (*Cage,* 504)? For just what social event is Lady Bradeen preparing, twenty-four chapters before the poor lord's sudden death, when she sends her first wire to "Marguerite, Regent Street, Try on at six. All Spanish lace. Pearls. The full length" (375)? "Spanish lace" normally meant "black silk in a floral pattern" for the Victorian lady, against which the pearls would undoubtedly show quite nicely, at a funeral. But then again, it might be the white lace of a wedding dress. A few pages later, the telegraphist reflects, "Pearls and Spanish lace . . . and also red velvet bows, which, disposed on the lace in a particular manner . . . were of course to adorn the front of a black brocade that would be like a dress in a picture" (378). In either case, the lady's anonymity—"[the telegram] had no signature"—would be understandable, as well as compatible rhetorically with the unsigned telegram she sends with the cipher code. Just hints, to be sure, but typical of Jamesian implications of horrors. "After you have poisoned the old brute, meet me in Ostend."[22]

If some such explicable mystery is hinted, then it is finally its figurative significance that matters for James and his readers. What does it matter, after all, if fictional characters murder each other? But if some ghost haunts this ghost story as definitely as the specters of Quint and Jessel trouble its companion for 1898, then the telegraphist has helped Lady Bradeen and Captain Everard produce it.[23] In short, the telegraphist would be no different from the governess, imagining her independence and yet still reproducing the distant authority of the dominant ideology. In this case, what Mark Seltzer argues is James's complicity in his early works with the arts of surveillance and the complementary effort to recover the old values of such an ideology in the face of new technologies could be extended to include later works such as *In the Cage* and *The Turn of the Screw:* "What is most evident, particularly in James's earlier writings such as *The American,* is the pressured *re*articulation of writing and self-expression: that is, the *recovery* of the relations of identity, self-possession, and self-recognition that define . . . the appeal of market culture and hence . . . one way in which the regressive appeal to market relations allays the becoming visible of the machinelikeness of persons and writing in machine culture."[24]

In what we may take as either an interesting coincidence or significant historical fact for James in his use of telegraphy in the novella, Morse was both a distinguished painter and inspired inventor, suggesting either art's potential complicity in modern systems of surveillance and control or a potential link between the aesthetic and technological imaginations. Connecting Morse's interests in the telegraph and painting, Paul Staiti concludes that Morse's technological and artistic abilities were complementary:

> The greatest material evidence for abstract congruency in Morse's imaginings in art and machine technology exist in small but revealing moments when Morse was on the cusp between his two careers. For instance, he did some of his most imaginative work on the telegraph

between 1835 and 1837, at precisely the same time and in the same building in which he painted his most imaginative pictures, *Allegorical Landscape of New York University* and *The Muse*. He drew faces rotating on gears, superimposed a troubled character on a design for the Atlantic cable, and wrote the word "signalization" on a sketch of macabre heads. There is a curiously Duchamp-like appearance to the receiver for his telegraph of 1837, built out of a canvas-stretcher, in the open space of which he invented—metaphorically "pictured"—the electromagnetic recording device.[25]

Staiti's late-twentieth-century view of the inherent compatibility of art and technology—an opinion shared by many classical aestheticians—is not, however, James's prevailing outlook in *In the Cage* or in his cautious responses to modern inventions such as the telegraph, typewriter, bicycle, and automobile. Always interested in new technologies, James nonetheless responds to them, especially at this time in his life and art, in a defensive manner, as if they were direct competitors with the novel's ability to represent life, consciousness, social relations, and reality.

James preferred the term "amanuensis," rather than "secretary," to describe the job done by MacAlpine, Weld, and Bosanquet, and we often think of it as simply his pedantic word. But the telegraphist and the amanuensis (from *manu,* "hand," and *ensis,* "relating to") are more than just technicians. They command a technology whose mere operation exceeds the author's. Scribes were hired in ancient times for precisely their competencies in a relatively unfamiliar technology of communication, a fact generally reflected in their social positions in ancient Egypt and Greece. Rosenheim points out that although cryptography is an ancient art of secreting messages, it developed rapidly into a host of different techniques with the introduction of the telegraph, which "expanded the cryptograph's imaginative possibilities, particularly regarding its users' predilection for subversive histories and conspiracies."[26] In short, the telegraph rapidly became a medium of communicative *power.* In his references to those who transcribed his dictation as "amanuenses," James reflects both his recognition of the special, potentially *secret* power they might have wielded over his art, just as he went to considerable lengths to establish his own aesthetic superiority to the new, threatening technologies.

James's fictional technician is a working-class woman, whose poverty, alcoholic mother at home, and modest prospects of marriage to the grocer Mr.

Mudge signify a class whose access to power has traditionally been foreclosed. This may be James's way of entertaining the power of modern technology without letting it actually exceed *his* artistic and imaginative controls. In the drawings by Morse to which Staiti refers, the artist and inventor come together in casual doodles in which technological and aesthetic images easily occupy the same space. For Henry James and other aesthetic moderns, machines and artworks are in more contestatory, troubled relations. Ralf Norrman is unfortunately right most of the time in claiming that the telegraphist is wrong most of the time, but this does not mean that James's novella simply repeats the usual message of his earlier work: "The rich are different from you and me; they have all the power." Without understanding the significance, Norrman points out how frightened Lady Bradeen is when she comes to Cocker's store for the second and last time to send her infamous and apparently incorrect telegram:

> Lady Bradeen next discovers that a word is wrong and must be altered. The telegraphist, overcome with the desire to show that she "knows," takes a jump and gives the "right" word. " 'Isn't it Cooper's?' It was as if she had boldly leaped—cleared the top of the cage and alighted on her interlocutress. 'Cooper's?'—the stare was heightened by a blush. Yes, she had made Juno blush. This was all the greater reason for going on. 'I mean instead of Burfield's.' " At this her ladyship becomes quite helpless, "not a bit haughty nor outraged. She was only mystified and scared. 'Oh you know—?' "[27]

From this Norrman concludes that Lady Bradeen "is just aghast at the little spying, meddling telegraphist."[28] He is right to identify both the fear in Lady Bradeen's response and the ambiguity of her "you know?"—that is, "You know—[the right word]" or "You know—[about my affair with Captain Everard. . . . You spy into my private life and meddle in my business]."

In this scene, the telegraphist has assumed a psyche, a face made possible for Lady Bradeen by the challenge she has offered to the customary expectation of the merely efficient servant—pouring tea, delivering cards on a silver tray, silently placing sealed postal deliveries on the hall table. Lady Bradeen is accessible now in the very essence of the power that represents and maintains her class—the power of a special discourse banned from those who have not learned to drop their "aitches" (on which James comments in this narrative and *What Maisie Knew*). They are now translators and transcoders of the secrets of power, and on this new class of technicians, the ruling class increasingly must rely.

If she is "wrong about everything," as Norrman insists, it is only because the telegraphist has been reading the wrong books. Her "ha'penny stories" are the stuff of the governess's world in *Turn of the Screw;* it is little wonder that the telegraphist should end up hating upper-class women and falling in love with upper-class men. She ought to be reading a code and cipher book, a treatise on the future of the telegraph system, opportunities for women in Marconi's new Wireless Telegraph and Signal Co., formed as a private corporation in July 1897, the very time James was writing his novella, while Marconi was completing tests on the new wireless telegraph in England.[29] After all, the "telegraph industry was a new area of female employment," which advertised the "light work," despite the long hours ("generally a nine or ten-hour day, six days a week"), and the skills involved.[30] For technophiles and liberal progressives, the telegraph industry was an opportunity for working-class women to improve their positions from unskilled laborers to skilled technicians.

I do not wish to take social effects for their causes; technological innovation tends to be the consequence of new social needs. The telegraph responds to the demands of industrial, urban, densely populated societies in which market forces drive values (from wages to ethics) and the privacy of the individual is increasingly a lost illusion. The telegraph responds to a world in which the old boundaries between public and private, the industrial economy and household economics, and "society" in the senses of the nation and culture have broken down. The secret world of the ruling class is increasingly open to view. The uncle can command the governess "never [to] trouble him . . . neither appeal nor complain nor write about anything" with some expectation that the class divisions of his world will support this taboo.[31] Servants such as Quint and Jessel are presumed to carry their secrets to their graves, however much they might embody the corruption of their masters. But the private world of the Bradeens, Captain Everard, and Lord Rye is full of traffic from the outside world. Not only are their messages open to the view of the counter clerks and telegraphists at Cocker's Grocery, but Mrs. Jordan arranges the flowers for their parties, in place of the invisible and discreet servants of the previous generation; the telegraphist thinks of her as "a friend who had invented a new career for women—that of being in and out of people's houses to look after the flowers" (*Cage,* 371). In earlier times, the servants gathered flowers from the vast gardens of the country estate; now Mrs. Jordan can imagine expanding her business to include the telegraphist, to whom she proposes taking over the accounts of all the "bachelors." Still dazzled by the upper classes, dreaming of a "match" out of a "ha'penny" romance, neither Mrs. Jordan nor the telegraphist understands what James makes explicit—the new powers of the working classes to understand and perhaps even seize what James had always understood as the primary mode of social production: discourse.

Jennifer Wicke points out that "the realm of language is not privileged, not exempt, and certainly not related to political economy in merely metaphorical ways" to encourage scholars of James to pay more attention to how textual questions are related to modes of socioeconomic production in his works and times.[32] Bauer and Lakritz have shown us how Taylorism rationalizes, systematizes, and mechanizes both the telegraphist's work and sexuality to the point where both she and the words she counts fail any longer to "count" in the sense of social significance or intellectual meaning.[33] While noting the material conditions of production in the late Victorian period, we must also remember that the telegraphist's "cage" differs importantly from the smoke-stack factories and the sweatshops where women and children had wasted their vision, minds, and lives in the earlier phases of industrialism. Shawn Rosenheim points out how "Morse's telegraph represented a watershed for mass culture" not only because it enabled news media—and thus national authority—to operate with such speed but also because "the Newtonian unities of being are replaced by the prosthetic extension of the self over a network of wires."[34] The telegraphist's work represents fundamental changes in the epistemology and ontology of modern experience, as well as in practical aspects of everyday life.

Just who owns the words and the flowers is less definite in this changing urban world than it was for the children, the governess, and Mrs. Grose at Bly. The telegraphist understands dimly what James knows with perfect clarity—that in this new age the values come not from accumulated possessions, not from hoarded wealth, but from the combinations and arrangements compatible with this exchange economy: "Combinations of flowers and greenstuff forsooth! What *she* could handle freely, she said to herself, was combinations of men and women" (*Cage*, 373). For someone who counts words every day in terms of their monetary value, she knows well enough that textual combinations are the new sources of value. At one point, prompted by

Mrs. Jordan's bragging about her ability to arrange a "thousand tulips" for her clients, the telegraphist reflects: "A thousand tulips at a shilling clearly took one further than a thousand words at a penny" (396). But the narrative suggests that there are other ways for words to be worth vastly more than the coppers she counts out at Cocker's.

In Regents Park with Captain Everard, she surprises, puzzles, and probably frightens him with her combination of independence, frankness, and familiarity. Above all, she disturbs him, like some uncanny ghost of his own worry, with her claim to knowledge. Whatever she thinks she knows and however wrong it may be, she nonetheless has touched the one region in which the ruling class is vulnerable—its control and command of language. It is when she says, "Yes, I know," that "She immediately felt him surprised and even a little puzzled at her frank assent; but for herself the trouble she had taken could only, in these fleeting minutes . . . be all there like a little hoard of gold in her lap" (*Cage,* 437). From the first chapter of *In the Cage* to the last, the telegraphist fitfully experiences the glimmers of a class consciousness that she mistakes most often for her own genius or for the love she imagines draws her to Captain Everard. Whatever class consciousness emerges, however, will not be of the traditional Marxian sort, nothing like what James had already ridiculed in Hyacinth's decorative labors in *The Princess Casamassima.* For James, such awareness must be integrally connected to the new productive value of language in the emerging economies of information and communication.

There are hints in the narrative that a new working-class solidarity might be built by service workers such as Mrs. Jordan, the telegraphist, and even the late arrival, Mr. Drake, butler to Lord Rye and then Lady Bradeen, affianced at the very last to Mrs. Jordan herself. The offer Mrs. Jordan makes to the telegraphist to join her business is an unusual one in James's fiction. It differs from Olive Chancellor's and Verena Tarrant's working relations in *The Bostonians,* even though Mrs. Jordan is "ten years older" than the telegraphist and inclined to brag shamelessly and domineer. Beyond the interest we should take in the idea of two working-class women starting their own business, we should also note how Mrs. Jordan flatters the telegraphist about her special qualifications for the job: "One wants an associate—of one's own kind, don't you know? You know the look they want it all to have?—of having come, not from a florist, but from one of themselves. Well, I'm sure *you* could give it—because you *are* one. Then we *should* win. Therefore just come in with me" (*Cage,* 392). To be sure, James informs us early in the narrative how the telegraphist, her elder sister, and their mother were "ladies, suddenly bereft, betrayed, overwhelmed," who "had slipped faster and faster down the steep slope," not entirely unlike Mrs. Jordan, the pastor's widow, who is dignified enough, except for her "extraordinarily protrusive teeth" (370, 394). On the other hand, both Mrs. Jordan and the telegraphist have learned most of what they know about the upper classes from their respective jobs. Mrs. Jordan claims that "in the practice of her fairy art . . . she more than peeped in—she penetrated"; the telegraphist is perhaps a bit behind her, "educated as she had rapidly been by her chances at Cocker's, there were still strange gaps in her learning" (393, 394).

The romance of a co-owned business by two women, anticipating the "pants' factory" begun by Sug Avery and Cele in Alice Walker's *Color Purple*, is unfortunately brought back to earth by Mrs. Jordan's proposal that the telegraphist take on the bachelors' accounts and the telegraphist's own obsession with Captain Everard. But the ideal of cooperative labor as an alternative to the alienation and thus victimization of workers under industrial capitalism seems more realizable in the service- and information-intensive economy of *In the Cage* than in traditional industrial labor. Mr. Buckton may be found most often at the "sounder," but the telegraphist and other counter clerks know how to use it. Labor at Cocker's Grocery and Post-Telegraph is not strictly divided, and thus the workers are not fundamentally alienated from the total process of production. Selling stamps, counting words on telegram forms, sending transmissions, and perhaps occasionally filling a grocery order may not amount to thrilling work, but the variety of tasks suggests also the new cooperative possibilities of the workplace.

In this regard, there is considerable evidence that some such symbolic resolution is what James offers and then withdraws from the telegraphist, whose education at the end remains distinguished by its "strange gaps." In the end, it is Mrs. Jordan's "Mr. Drake," Lord Rye's former butler, now "going to Lady Bradeen," who can fill those gaps in the reader's and telegraphist's knowledge regarding the fate of Lord and Lady Bradeen and Captain Everard (*Cage,* 493). We know that conclusion: how "something was lost—something was found" and "it all got about" to "a point at which Lord Bradeen had to act," were it not for his "most sudden death," giving "them a prompt chance," since "She just nailed him" for the "injury . . . he [had] done her," which is to say, "He *must* marry her, you know" (504–6). We feel a bit as the telegraphist does on leaving Mrs. Jordan's little flat in Maida Vale, on the Paddington canal: "It was strange such a matter should be at last settled for her by Mr. Drake" (507). Strange, indeed, unless what she has missed all along is just the cooperative work that Mrs. Jordan has clumsily proposed and for which each of them in turn—Mrs. Jordan (the clergyman's widow), the telegraphist (a "lady" fallen down the steep slope), and Mr. Drake (a butler in the service of the rich and powerful)—has part of the talent to solve the puzzle, a piece of the cipher code no one alone can read in the telegram the frightened Lady Bradeen sends and the anxious Captain Everard tries to check.

If the cooperative labor required by the new information technologies is an alternative James holds out to the telegraphist in *In the Cage*, then we must wonder why she has so much difficulty accepting Mrs. Jordan's proposal, working with her fellow workers at Cocker's, or accepting that the mystery has nominally been solved by Mr. Drake. In each case, strict distinctions between Victorian gender roles account for her reluctance to work with others. The persistence of such gender stereotypes is all the more noticeable in the new workplaces, in which men and women share many of the same tasks, unlike the common segregation of men and women according to the physical demands of heavy industrial labor. I have already mentioned how the telegraphist refuses Mrs. Jordan's offer of a share in her floral arranging business for two reasons relating to gender stereotypes: Mrs. Jordan's meretricious proposal that the telegraphist take the bachelors' accounts, thereby vaguely hinting at some sort of coquetry in the merchandising of services; and the telegraphist's infatuation with Captain Everard and vain hope that her continuance at the "PO," as Mrs. Jordan calls Cocker's, might lead to a genuine romance.

Gender stereotypes are also at the heart of her alienation from the other workers at Cocker's, and here we must grant James an extraordinary sensitivity to women's vulnerability to harassment in the late Victorian workplace. One reason she detests the "sounder," in its "ground-glass" cage within the cage, is that Mr. Buckton employs "devilish and successful subterfuges for keeping her at the sounder whenever it looked as if anything might amuse" (*Cage,* 376). The meaning here is deliberately ambiguous, suggesting either that Buckton assigns her to the sounder whenever interesting clients arrive or that he takes advantage of her in the privacy of the sounder room. In either case, she must endure his "devilish and successful subterfuges" as well as the counter clerk's "passion for her," whose "unpleasant conspicuity . . . she would never have consented to be obliged to him" (376–77).

It is little wonder, then, that the telegraphist finds no solidarity with the other workers at Cocker's; what interferes is just what prevents her from recognizing in Captain Everard their common poverty and dependence on others who can "nail" them. Of course, James renders ambiguous as well the precise "poverty" of the good captain. Mrs. Jordan tells the telegraphist that "he has nothing" but in reply to her "Isn't he rich?" reflects, "It depends upon what you call—! . . . What does he bring? Think what she has. And then, love, his debts" (*Cage,* 502). Of course, Captain Everard's real poverty is not so much financial as moral. Beyond his different identities on the telegrams—Everard, Captain Everard, Philip, Phil, "the Count," William, "the Pink 'Un," he has little to recommend him. Beyond his stylish smoking, there is a certain emptiness that is revealed all too tellingly in the telegraphist's meeting with him in Regents Park. Despite her boldness, she elicits little from him beyond, "See here—see here!" (449).[35]

By the time the telegraphist must write the crucial numbers of his telegraphed cipher code on the back of his calling card, well before Mrs. Jordan announces that he has been "nailed" by the compromised Lady Bradeen, Captain Everard has lost much of his military and masculine authority, at least as far as the conventions of Victorian gender roles are concerned. Whatever the "mistake" she has made in the telegram signifies, it at least contributes to Lady Bradeen's success in "nailing" him. But this is hardly the sort of collaboration that appeals to the telegraphist, even if it suggests that women working together might cross class lines to reverse the patriarchal authority of the dominant culture.

It is not, however, the reversal of conventional gender roles that James has in mind, although this seems nearly the point of the telegraphist's bold conversation with the shrinking Captain Everard—"See here—see here!"—in the park and her triumphant recollection of the crucial numbers in a scene that concludes with her not only explaining the mystery to the confused counter clerk but also answering Mr. Buckton's rude inquiry—"And what game is that, miss"—with the "reply that it was none of his business" (*Cage,* 485). Much as the novella revolves around a certain feminine empowerment at the expense of conventional masculine authority, this reversal seems finally to be a kind of illusion. After all, James must introduce Mrs. Jordan's Mr. Drake in the final chapters to explain it all.

Yet one of the consequences of the new working relations of men and women in worksites where the conventional physical differences between masculine and feminine labor power are no longer self-evident is that gender boundaries are transgressed, even if many of the same behaviors persist (as in the harassment the telegraphist must endure variously from Buckton and the moonstruck counter clerk). New media such as the telegraph are symptomatic of such social changes; as Rosenheim points out, "The telegraph ushered in a time in which bodies and information *can* be separated."[36] By this late date in our postmodernity, it has become something of a commonplace to stress the sociohistorical forces determining gender. As Judith Butler has written: "If the inner truth of gender is a fabrication and if a true gender is a fantasy instituted and inscribed on the surface of bodies, then it seems that genders can be neither true nor false but are only produced as the truth effects of a discourse of primary and stable identities."[37]

Beyond the veneer of conventional class and gender distinctions, James offers us peeks at an extraordinary diversity of new class and gender possibilities. Once again, the technology of the telegraph has not *caused* these new possibilities, not all of which are emancipatory, but it has some coincidence with the socioeconomic conditions informing such alternatives. Perhaps the most obvious example of such an alternative is Mr. Mudge, who is dismissed by critics almost as summarily as Napoleon was reputed to have defeated the English with the judgment, "A nation of shopkeepers." To be sure, Mr. Mudge's courtship of the telegraphist appears only slightly more agreeable to her than the counter clerk's idiotic passion, and Mudge's values seem to be utterly commercial. Nothing is valuable unless it pays a material return, and everything in their relationship is as managed as a Taylorized factory. Worst of all, perhaps, Mudge defends the class hierarchies in the manner of a classic petit bourgeois and what survivors of the Reagan-Bush years recognize as the tiresome rhetoric of "trickle-down" economics (*Cage*, 410). What benefits the upper classes is likely to be good for the shopkeeper's business, as far as Mr. Mudge is concerned. Selling tomatoes or telegrams is the same business to him: "Above all it hurt him somewhere . . . to see anything *but* money made out of his betters" (410).

Yet he does differ from caricatures of the Victorian bourgeois patriarch. When the telegraphist candidly tells him, "I went out the other night and sat in the Park with a gentleman," Mudge does not go to pieces as does the jealous husband in Trollope's *He Knew He Was Right* (1869) (*Cage*, 456). When she challenges his masculinity by telling him, "You're awfully inferior" to Captain Everard, Mudge can say with both humor and pride in her, "Well, my dear, you're not inferior to anybody. You've got a cheek!" (458). And when she tells him she hasn't seen "the gentleman" since, Mudge can judge him with little consideration for his own inferiority: "Oh what a cad!" (460). Showing no regard for "his honor," Mudge expresses a quiet "confidence in her" that "only gave her ease and space, as she felt, for telling him the whole truth that no one knew" (456). In what other fiction of the late Victorian period do we find a man giving a woman psychic space while she tells him of her meeting with another man?

Let me not overdo this idealization of Mr. Mudge, with his concern for order, his pocket full of chocolate creams, and his acceptance of upper-class rule as if it were a law of nature. Yet as the only male character with a name escaping the phallic aggressiveness of Buckton, Drake, and Everard, Mudge better approaches understanding of the telegraphist than any other character, including Mrs. Jordan. What he offers may be his petty ambitions, a move from fashionable Mayfair to the dreary suburb of Chalk Farm, and "savings" of "three shillings" a week on lodgings. Chalk Farm is the suburb where swells such as Captain Everard gamble at the races, but it is also the neighborhood of "clerks and railroad men and electrical workers."[38] What Mudge offers her is a community of other workers, especially those in the newer communications and transportation industries.[39] Of all the people she knows, Mr. Mudge is the only one who gives her mother any recognition, and he does so in an exchange that shows he is not without imagination: "The little home. . . . had been visited, in further talk she had had with him at Bournemouth, from garret to cellar, and they had especially lingered, with their respectively darkened brows, before the niche into which it was to be broached to her mother that she must find means to fit" (*Cage*, 473–74).

Hardly a revolutionary, Mr. Mudge nonetheless represents a different role for men in his times, reflecting perhaps necessary adjustments to the frank, independent, often bold behavior of the telegraphist. Perhaps James hesitates before Mr. Mudge in his usual caricature of the petit bourgeoisie. It may also be that what James treats with some wry affection in this characterization is, on closer examination, something like the regard Anthony Trollope accords his new bourgeois heroes such as Johnny Eames in *The Small House at Allington* (1864) or Phineas Phinn in the Palliser novels or others in a long list of good-natured, not particularly dashing, often clumsy, but steady and true young men. In Trollope's fiction, such heroes usually endure to win the women who have first declined their offers of marriage for the sake of someone finer. We should recognize this as a strategy of class and gender legitimation that works by demonizing an illusory aristocracy, so we must be cautious in identifying too readily with Mr. Mudge. The suburban Chalk Farm where he will settle with the telegraphist and her mother may turn out, after all, to be either a neighborhood of like-minded workers or an urban ghetto of exploited victims.

Suffice it to say that Mrs. Jordan is not Olive Chancellor or Henrietta Stackpole; James has changed the caricature of the professional woman to render her with some seriousness. Mr. Mudge is not, as the name at first suggests, simply the blot on the otherwise finely written page of Mayfair. Among his other noms de plume for his telegrams, Captain Everard once selects "Mudge," and the accident is not lost on us. Whereas the captain can only expose his lack of imagination, his imitation of the rake, when the telegraphist engages him in Regents Park—"See here—see here!"—Mr. Mudge offers a community, a place for her alcoholic mother, a two-career family, and occasional holidays with "sundries," like those chocolate creams.

I am suggesting that some aspects of Judith Butler's postmodern understanding of gender as a function of discourse are already present in James's text, even though these features are not entirely under his control. New representations of gender establish new relations of gender, and both are often enough the consequence of new working and living conditions. All these gender relations have been shaped even more determinately than in previous Jamesian works by the conditions of their discursive production, although these are by no means separable from the material conditions of production.[40] Throughout *In the Cage*, James makes it clear that telegraphic communication depends on the cooperative labor of sender, technician, and receiver—a triad that drastically changes the transactional, intersubjective model for writing and speech. Few if any of the characters understand this change, which is as radical as the conflation of public and private spheres performed in telegraphy, and the telegraphist herself remains convinced to the very end that "people didn't understand her" (*Cage*, 372), "the immensity of her difference," "not different only at one point, . . . different all round" (403). But such difference belongs not to the telegraphist alone, "the betrothed of Mr. Mudge," but to the relations of a complex, changing social reality. It is a new social reality in which customary gender roles are "mudged," and I turn in this regard to two final examples: the telegraphist as "mother" and the dubious Mr. Drake.

I have already discussed how the sounder aurally dominates Cocker's Grocery and Post-Telegraph, even though it is invisible in its cage within the cage (within the shop). It is like some postmodern fetus ticking away at the center of the new object relations that determine subjects' identities: "She had made out even from the cage that it was a charming golden day: a patch of hazy autumn sunlight lay across the sanded floor and also, higher up, quickened into brightness a row of ruddy bottled syrups" (*Cage,* 461). This may be the ironic negativity of a new, denaturalized world, but the positive side comes from the slippage of older names from their proper referents to a wider range of possible significations. Taking care of her alcoholic mother by working at Cocker's and by worrying in the meantime just where her mother manages to get her bottles, the telegraphist is already "mothering." And it is when Captain Everard arrives at Cocker's the most desperate for help that he appears to her "quite, now, as she said to herself, like a frightened child coming to its mother" (476–77). Even in her indulgence of the self-important fancies of her friend Mrs. Jordan, the telegraphist displays qualities of tenderness and care that are too often attributed by patriarchy to the mother and would thus seem inappropriate for the care shown by a woman ten years younger for an older, often deluded woman. There is also the diverse imagery of vaginal, womblike, maternal spaces throughout the text, beginning with the "cage" itself (derived as the word is from its Latin root, *cavea,* meaning "hollow or enclosed space") to the presumably pseudonymous Miss Dolman to whom telegrams are routed by Lady Bradeen and Captain Everard. A dolman is a Hussar's fur-lined coat, combining thus the captain's military and amorous exploits in a manner not unlike the uncle's "trophies of the hunt" in his London house in *The Turn of the Screw.*[41]

In the customary Jamesian narrative of feminine limitation, the young woman is incapable of becoming either Artist or Mother, especially those characters who pursue careers of their own. On one level, *In the Cage* follows just that rhetoric, so that the promise of the telegraphist's marriage to Mr. Mudge is merely a repetition of the pathetic genealogy of working-class families of which the alcoholic mother will remind the young couple. On another level, which I have characterized as one of "hints" and "peeks," as if James is not quite comfortable with its meanings, mothering is unmoored from its customary domesticity and its conflict with work and the public sphere. I have already suggested in chapter 5 how Sir Claude simulates maternal purpose in his care for Maisie and pride in her independence. The telegraphic sounder need not be merely a grotesque image of the automated mother of the new technology; it might also suggest how the proper transmission of generational value resides less in persons (and their fragile bodies) than in the means of communication. This, too, is often enough James's theme, even argument, as he thunders about the "historical consciousness" that can be achieved only through a proper interpretation of the semiotically dense texture of everyday reality. But now he offers an alternative to those otherwise barred from access to such means of communication.

In her extraordinary reading of "The Beast in the Jungle," Eve Sedgwick shows how Marcher refuses the homosexual plot of his story and becomes the "irredeemably self-ignorant man who embodies and enforces heterosexual compulsion" as he turns away from the "beast" and what it signifies.[42] Sedgwick reads Marcher's encounter in the cemetery with the male stranger—the stranger who is capable of mourning—as Marcher's reenactment of "a classic trajectory of male entitlement":

> Marcher begins with the possibility of *desire for* the man. . . . Deflecting that desire under a fear of profanation, he then replaces it with envy, with an *identification with* the man in that man's (baffled) desire for some other, presumably female dead object. . . . The loss by which a man *so bleeds and yet lives* is . . . supposed to be the castratory one of the phallus figured as mother, the inevitability of whose sacrifice ushers sons into the status of fathers and into the control (read both ways) of the Law.[43]

All of this presumes that the "woman" remains unchanged, the "figure" of "mother" as the one *without* the phallus, the image of the possibility of being unmanned and thus the motive for repression, not only of the castration feared in the Freudian family-romance but also of a fundamental lack of authority that provokes the entire cycle of masculine desire in the first place. Yet the telegraphist in *In the Cage* is not merely a negative image, the convenient "female, dead object" used (fetishized) for a masculine narrative. The "mother" is no longer just the medium of masculine transmission of genealogical authority from father to son. At a certain level, the telegraphist assumes the phallus of a newly empowered "mother," especially as she assumes *maternal* functions outside the conventional and literal roles of mother reserved for a young, affianced, working-class girl. As mother to Captain Everard, to her own mother, to Mr. Mudge, and even to her friend Mrs. Jordan, the telegraphist escapes the strict division of private and public, as well as the presumed naturalness of the mother's relation to her own child. "Mothering" has been refigured by association with the powers of communication, and the degree to which the telegraphist dons those powers is some measure of an authority that no longer is precisely that of mother or father, but of some authority for transmission that exceeds their outmoded and gender-specific roles. Such a redefinition of motherhood can encompass masculine agency, such as Sir Claude's in *What Maisie Knew* when he claims: "I think I've produced life," meaning thereby something radically different from phallic possession (*M,* 354).

Finally, there is Mr. Drake, whose introduction by Mrs. Jordan in the last three chapters (25–27) as her affianced seems merely a clumsy deus ex machina. Despite—or perhaps because of—his very masculine name, Mr. Drake is the occasion for what I shall term James's *rhetorical cross-dressing.* The novella concludes with a conversation between Mrs. Jordan and the telegraphist that is hilarious in its double entendres involving the "gentleman" Drake. The misunderstandings revolve overtly around Mrs. Jordan's habit of exaggerating her involvement with the aristocracy, so that we assume along with the telegraphist that Mr. Drake is the equal of Lord Rye, Lord and Lady Bradeen, and Captain Everard. The bathos appears to be in his revelation as simply the butler, but we do not know this until a certain rhetorical banter has accomplished a very different effect.

> "I think you must have heard me speak of Mr. Drake?" Mrs. Jordan had never looked so queer, nor her smile so suggestive of a large benevolent bite.
> ". . . Oh yes; isn't he a friend of Lord Rye?"
> "A great and trusted friend. Almost—I may say—a loved friend."
> Mrs. Jordan's "almost" had such an oddity that her companion was moved, rather flippantly perhaps, to take it up. "Don't people as good as love their friends when they 'trust' them?" (*Cage,* 491)

If James has allowed mothering to slip somewhat from its conventional referents of mother and biological child, he is here more daringly causing love to drift from the amours of men and women (those "ha'penny stories") to the trust and care between people of whatever gender.

The rhetoric is explicitly homoerotic in these passages and for that very reason seems to emphasize James's more general point about affection and care that transcend traditional boundaries of masculine and feminine identities. In chapter 4, I argued that James disguises homosexual desire in stories from the first half of the 1890s, such as "The Middle Years" and "The Death of the Lion," in part by demonizing lesbian sexuality (and thereby creating an apparent moral "choice" between male and female same-sex relations) and in part by sublimating sexual desire as *textual* passion. Although I argue that gender transgressions can be liberating in *What Maisie Knew,* they can also cause a child such as Maisie considerable anxiety and insecurity as she struggles to find her adolescent identity. In the final chapters of *In the Cage,* however, there seems to be little of this anxiety and much more of a certain delight in the comedy of gender and sexual varieties. If *In the Cage* represents a change in James's thinking, it is by no means consistently played out in James's writings from 1898 to the end of his life. *The Turn of the Screw* is strong evidence that James has not yet changed his mind completely. Even if we do not read *The Turn of the Screw* as an allegory of homosexual desire, enacted either in the imagined relations between Peter Quint and Miles or Miss Jessel and Flora, we must still read it as a narrative that focuses on forms of human possessiveness and control that are both perverse and sexual in their workings. *The Turn of the Screw* is organized as a tragedy, and the dark hints of sexuality's dangerous consequences encompass frequent hints of homosexuality as the horizon of such sinfulness.

The tone of *In the Cage* differs utterly from either the rhetorical dodges of the stories from the first half of the 1890s or the tragic and distinctly erotic gloom of *The Turn of the Screw;* it even seems to resolve the anxious play with gender instability at work in *What Maisie Knew.* As the conversation about Mr. Drake and Lord Rye's friendship increasingly becomes explicitly analogous to the telegraphist's friendship with Mrs. Jordan, the homoerotic rhetoric increases in frequency and explicitness: "Mr. Drake has rendered his lordship for several years services that his lordship has highly appreciated and that make it all the more—a—unexpected that they should, perhaps a little suddenly, separate." Still confused about the real identity of Mr. Drake as the butler, the telegraphist can only echo, " 'Separate?' Our young lady was mystified, . . . and she already saw that she had put the saddle on the wrong horse" (*Cage,* 491–92). The rhetoric of the conversation between Mrs. Jordan and the telegraphist is a Jamesian tour de force, operating as it does simultaneously on the following registers: confusion of "gentleman" as either aristocrat or servant; confusion of Mr. Drake's sexual preference as either straight or gay; and confusion of what amounts to a ménage à quatre of Drake, Lord Rye, Lady Bradeen, and Mrs. Jordan with the confused relations of the telegraphist, Captain Everard, Lady Bradeen, and Mrs. Jordan.

All of this is further entangled with the sheer plot function played by Mr. Drake in providing information about the fates of Lord and Lady Bradeen and Captain Everard following the scene of the undelivered telegram. For this purpose, Mr. Drake must leave Lord Rye for the "service" of Lady Bradeen, at which point the telegraphist, still uncertain just who Mr. Drake is (servant, lover, fiancé, gentleman) can only wonder, with the help of Mrs. Jordan, about how "immensely surrounded" Lady Bradeen will be with male admirers (*Cage,* 494). And when Mrs. Jordan tries to clarify what she has meant by Mr. Drake "going to Lady Bradeen" (493), she only seems to confuse things:

> "He's 'going,' you say, to her?"
> At this Mrs. Jordan really faltered. "She has engaged him."
> "Engaged him?" . . .
> "In the same capacity as Lord Rye."
> "And was Lord Rye engaged?" (*Cage,* 495)

The rhetorical effect of this cross-dressing lasts only a moment, and at the beginning of the next chapter, the telegraphist begins to see that "Mr. Drake then verily *was* a person who opened the door!" (496). (It is fair, however, to add parenthetically that it is James opening the door to our repressed fears of homoeroticism.)

As Mrs. Jordan brags that she and Mr. Drake, like the telegraphist and Mr. Mudge, "shall have our own" house "too," she explains just what caused the breakup of Lord Rye and Mr. Drake:

> "For, don't you know? he makes it a condition that he sleeps out."
> "A condition?"—the girl felt out of it.
> "For any new position. It was on that he parted with Lord Rye. His lordship can't meet it. So Mr. Drake has given him up."
> "And all for you?"—our young woman put it as cheerfully as possible.
> "For me and Lady Bradeen." (*Cage,* 500)

These are just bits and pieces from a sustained banter of confused gender and class roles that stretches across three chapters at the very end of the novella. Desperate to find solid ground amid this shifting rhetoric, the telegraphist clings to the "one" (Captain Everard, presumably) she knows in Lady Bradeen's set by answering Mrs. Jordan's question, "He's a gentleman?" with "Yes, he's not a lady" (494).

Neither Mrs. Jordan nor the telegraphist has intended such confusions of gender, sexuality, and class, but they have been produced nonetheless by the new circumstances of work, communication, and social relations. One of the venerable biographical anecdotes about the contemporary reception of *In the Cage* is André Raffalovich " 'once teasing' James 'to know what the Olympian young man in *In the Cage* had done wrong. He swore he did not know, he would rather not know.' "[44] Marc André Raffalovich (1864–1934) was the author of *L'Affaire d'Oscar Wilde* (1895) and *Uranisme et Unisexualité*, published in 1896, the year before James would write *In the Cage*, "in which he argued that homosexuality . . . and heterosexuality are two equally legitimate manifestations of human sexuality, rejected the current view that homosexuality was a disease, and advocated a life of chastity, supported by friendship, as the Christian ideal!"[45]

In his biographical account of James's "passionate friendships" with contemporaries such as Morton Fullerton, Howard Sturgis, and Hendrik Andersen, Fred Kaplan shows that what James most desired from male companions in his middle and later years was companionship. Without ignoring or diminishing James's capacity for sexual passion, however repressed or evaded, Kaplan understands that what James most desired was someone with whom he might talk, walk, bicycle, garden, and, perhaps above all *work*. When Sturgis "made his first visit early in 1900," James "read to him each evening from his work-in-progress, *The Ambassadors*. Sturgis was at work on a new novel, the details of which he shared with his host, who urged him on."[46]

At the furthest reach of the melodrama of *In the Cage,* the telegraphist may forget her dreary life in fantasies of the passionate loves, diabolical murders, and coded messages of the rich and famous. In the sad realism of late Victorian urban London, she is as trapped by her dead-end job as she will be by the hapless Mudge and the squall of children they will visit on the Malthusian nightmare of London. Mudge's chocolate creams will give way to silent screams.

But in the Jamesian text, the possibilities of the new workplace, the developing service industries, and the emancipatory potential of the new century begin to make a difference. To be sure, it is a difference of which the telegraphist herself is at best dimly aware, trapped as she must remain to the end in her stubborn insistence that no one understands her, that she is "different" from the other workers, especially those men whispering and insinuating as she tries to count the words and sell the stamps. Perhaps it is only possible for such changes in gender, class, and identity itself to be registered first in the textual space where a certain liberty has always been possible, where the constraints of convention, of consciousness, even of the unconscious, need not be taken as final. Certainly James found it safer to entertain the idea that the slippage of gender boundaries that he recognizes in this novella might accompany, for better or worse, the changing social and economic boundaries of the new age. He identifies far more consciously with the telegraphist, even down to her trip to Bournemouth, which recalls his first trip to the southern coast of England that would become his home until the very end at Lamb House, Rye. Whether he knows how much he shares the anxiety of Lady Bradeen, Captain Everard, and the others once in charge of the symbolic discourse of culture is difficult to determine from the surface of a novella with such depths. Sounding those depths, we find James's own unconscious betrayed, not only regarding his ambivalence about his own sexual preference, but also regarding his status as the master, the figure who had devoted his life to "coded" texts, not so much to prevent detection as to encourage, even provoke, it. In that, there is a great difference, all the difference, I would say, to distinguish Henry James from less worthy authorities.

ᴧᴫ Conclusion: Henry James and the Art of Teaching

> The order in which the drama simply says things gives it all its
> form, while the story told and the picture painted, as the novel
> at the pass we have brought it to embraces them, reports of an
> infinite diversity of matters, gathers together and gives out
> again a hundred sorts, and finds its order and its structure, its
> unity and its beauty, in the alternation of parts and the
> adjustment of differences.
>
> —Henry James, "The New Novel" (1914),
> *Notes on Novelists*

The other Henry James I have interpreted in this book requires a different
literary pedagogy from what has been customary for Henry James, the master
of realism and early modernism. In this regard, the study of Henry James has
followed more general changes in the uses of critical theories, which in the
past decade have been increasingly validated by their relevance to actual
classroom situations. What I have described elsewhere as a "new pedagogy"
has indeed transformed critical theory from an abstract, speculative discourse
into practices to be tested in interpretive situations such as classrooms, conferences, research groups, even everyday social interactions.[1] According to
these criteria, the traditional Henry James has often been excluded from all
but the most specialized and professional curricula. Henry James is rarely
taught in high school, in large part because teachers consider him too difficult
for students on both stylistic and conceptual grounds. He is also often judged
to be irrelevant or archaic, insofar as the traditional James is understood to
focus so exclusively on the vanished age in which an immensely wealthy
bourgeoisie challenged the waning aristocracy for social power. In this incar-
nation, Henry James may be taught as a literary "example" of his times, but
James's interests seem less relevant to introductory courses in the humanities
concerned with modern social values than more contemporary works dealing
with social problems of race, ethnicity, class, gender, and sexuality that students must address every day.

The value of my argument in this book should be its relevance for teaching Henry James in a wide range of educational situations, so it is fitting that I conclude this book with a consideration of just how the other Henry James helps us overcome the limits of James's traditional "difficulty," the relative narrowness of his focus on the upper classes, and thus his growing irrelevance for postmodern societies. One topic that arises quite predictably at conferences dedicated to Henry James and other modern writers is the readability of these authors by the next generation of students. If Henry James is to be read by that generation, then his teachers will have to address these problems of difficulty, narrowness, and irrelevance. Insofar as critical studies in the humanities are primarily guides to our interpretive practices in real classroom situations, no critical study claiming to transvalue a humanistic topic can afford to ignore its pedagogical consequences. For these reasons, then, I conclude this book with some sustained consideration of what it means to teach Henry James, both in his older dress as the modernist master and in the newer fashion of the writer struggling with changing social attitudes toward gender, sexuality, class, race, and nation.

Let me begin with the notorious problem of James's difficulty. Of course, James's writings require great concentration by the reader, careful attention to the dialectic of form and content, a special ear for shifts in tone, and a heightened awareness of how narrative perspective is often worked through multiple narratorial centers. For formalist critics, such technical and stylistic difficulty established James as one of the preeminent modern writers and made him a "major author" in most post–World War II college and university curricula in literature. For my teachers in the 1960s, when formalist methods still held sway, James's writings were virtual textbooks in the key aesthetic techniques and rhetorical devices used by great or classic literature. This emphasis on Jamesian technique has always impressed me as an odd, even perverse, strategy for *teaching* Henry James. Whatever the origins and reasons for the focus on technique in Henry James, as well as other major authors judged by such aesthetic criteria, this emphasis has caused contemporary students and their teachers to think of Henry James as a difficult writer. In short, James's admittedly complex aesthetic techniques, when separated from the ethical, psychological, semiotic, and social purposes to which they are put in his writings, are as bewildering and arcane to us as the Marquis de Bellegarde's support for the Bourbon pretender appears to Christopher Newman: "He felt as he should have felt if he had discovered in M. de Bellegarde a taste for certain oddities of diet; an appetite, for instance, of fishbones and nutshells" (*American,* 153).

In practical terms, this focus on aesthetic "fishbones and nutshells" is best suited to the specialized group of creative-writing students, who study literary texts to develop their own techniques, understand literary conventions, and otherwise reflect on literary craft. Graduate students and undergraduates preparing for graduate work in English and American literatures might also be reasonably expected to develop expertise in such aesthetic and technical areas of literature, even though such concerns should not be the primary areas of their training. Yet in too many graduate programs, just such an obsession with the rhetorical and stylistic techniques of literature, to the exclusion of other literary functions, remains central to the curriculum and professional training. One reason for this is that despite the waning of the New Criticism and formalist assumptions about literature, many graduate programs are still dominated by senior faculty trained in the critical age when formalism and modernism worked in complementary ways to justify themselves as critical and aesthetic movements. Because most graduate students first learn to teach in introductory English composition and literature courses, their freshman and sophomore students, many of whom do not have settled ideas about literature's purposes and values, learn the highly technical aspects of literature that these graduate students are studying in their own graduate seminars.

Add to this admittedly general scenario the fact that many high school and community college teachers of literature studied literature in the formalist era and have, in many cases, not had opportunities to read much literary criticism, other than what is obliquely folded into high school textbooks and teachers' manuals, since the formalists dominated the academic study of literature.[2] Such formalist assumptions often persist in the high school, community college, undergraduate college and university, and graduate curricula long after faculty and students have recognized to varying degrees that such interests are no longer central to the field. In my own department, our prerequisite for the English major is a yearlong series of genre courses, normally taken in the sophomore year, which attempts in turn to define "lyric," "comedy and tragedy," "romance and realism." Primarily taught by advanced graduate students under the supervision of a ladder-rank faculty member, our English 28 A-B-C series changes the literary texts it teaches with great frequency and has had over the years many different methodological emphases—New Criticism, phenomenology, deconstruction, cultural studies—but its primary generic structure remains unchanged since the mid-1960s, when the course was developed.³ As anyone involved in education for any length of time knows, the inertia established by approved curricula is tremendous; changes must always be argued and justified, whereas what is already in place is often accepted tacitly as educationally sound and proper, even when it is obvious that humanistic education is closely tied to specific historical circumstances. Nowhere is this more evident than in high school curricula, where the process of curricular development, approval, and implementation is even more formalized, time-consuming, and thus resistant to change than in colleges and universities.⁴

The formalist Henry James had his own special part to play, of course, in the development of the institutionalized study of literature in terms of aesthetic techniques. Percy Lubbock's *The Craft of Fiction* first appeared in 1921, and it established the image of the "great writer" as the model for the discriminating critic and reader, both of whom ought to avoid scrupulously the hasty judgments of evaluative critics writing for the popular press and intent on telling careless readers which books they should like: "If you ask Henry James whether he 'likes' some book under discussion, the roll and twinkle of his eye at the simplicity of the question is a lesson in itself, and one that a young critic will never forget. Where, he seems to say, on the loose fabric of a mere preference or distaste will be found the marks of the long wear and tear of discrimination that are the true critic's honourable and recognizable warrant?"⁵ What is the purpose of this "long wear and tear of discrimination" that identifies the true critic and aligns him or her with the spirit of genius that inspires a great writer, like Henry James? Lubbock has a ready answer: "A large unhurried mind, solitarily working and never ceasing to work, entirely indifferent to the changes and chances of the popular cry, it was this that gave its sonorous gravity to Henry James's opinion of the thing that he rated, when all was said, to be the vessel of the essence of life—a book."⁶

In Lubbock's terms, then, Jamesian difficulty is equated with the singular genius of the major author, possessed of a subjectivity that refuses "entirely" the "changes and chances of the popular cry," and thus is somehow exemplary of what the reader should aspire to become: "The reader of a novel—by which I mean the critical reader—is himself a novelist; he is the maker of a book which may or may not please his taste when it is finished, but of a book for which he must take his own share of responsibility."⁷ On the face of things, Lubbock's elevation of the reader from passive recipient to active participant in the fictional act is liberating. How many of us must have said something of this sort to our students over the years: "This work of literature appeals to *you* to bring it into existence, to elaborate its meanings, to solve its riddles. You, too, are a *writer.*"[8] The "novelist" constructed by the actual writer and the critical reader is a far cry, of course, from the novelist that creative-writing students aspire to become. We do not literally mean that every student in our classes should aspire to become a novelist when we make this appeal to the participatory role of critical reading.

What precisely do we mean when we make this offer to our students—an offer of compensation, in effect, for the very hard work of reading self-evidently complex texts such as those by Henry James? In his brief foreword to the 1957 edition of Lubbock's *Craft of Fiction,* Mark Schorer concludes: "Without Lubbock's respect for the artist in the novelist, the loose form of the novel would have floundered on for how many more years without the prestige that, as a form of art, it had always deserved? He gave the criticism of the novel not only terms by means of which it could begin to discuss the question of how novels are made ('the only question I shall ask'), but also a model of the way that the question might plausibly be put."[9] Schorer effectively explains that the critical reader *legitimates* the novel as a properly artistic genre, and thus Schorer clarifies why modern criticism of the novel focused so centrally on the aesthetic techniques of the novel. From Daniel Defoe and Fanny Burney to Henry James, novelists struggled to legitimate the genre according to the changing standards of aesthetic excellence. This is an understandable and interesting issue of literary history, but it can no longer be taken seriously as *the* task of critical reading; it is safe to say that formalist criticism from Lubbock to Krieger and Iser succeeded in legitimating the novel as a serious genre that draws variously on the sophisticated techniques, methods of allusion, and rhetorical devices evident in other, more established genres, such as epic, lyric, comedy, and tragedy.

In effect, when we make the familiar appeal to our students that as critical readers they will "help construct" the novel they are reading, we are implicitly saying that they are helping us justify the intellectual legitimacy of the novel within the academy. From this claim, it is but a step to the next contention that this work of teaching literature to *justify* such literature is merely one part of a pervasive aesthetic ideology that contributes to the construction of com-modified notions of "culture" and "artistic value" that have certain exchange values for tenured faculty, graduate students, and even undergraduates who take the acquisition of such culture seriously, even if they pursue completely different careers from our own. I dare say that every one of us has had an angry, cynical, or simply very acute student who has in one way or another suggested that his or her value to us as teachers depends centrally on that student's ability to validate our existences as professionals in a discipline as demonstrably *unprofessional* as literature.

My point is not that the notorious difficulty of Henry James—the often cited reason his work cannot be taught before achieving a certain educational level—is a complete illusion of the formalist critical tradition working in league with novelists anxious about the legitimacy of a genre frequently identified with other popular and mass media. I fully recognize the inherent difficulties of the Jamesian text, but I suggest that the difficulty that derives from an obsessive interest in Jamesian technique has the singular effect of *producing* those other two problems with James: his narrowness and his irrelevance. These side effects of the formalist Henry James are also reasons for not teaching Henry James, except at the "highest" levels of education, to say nothing of how these same side effects often keep the general reader from picking up a James novel (or a tape) for the fun of it. The notorious "narrowness" of James is generally meant as a code for his exclusive focus on the problems besetting the rising middle class and the waning aristocracy in the late nineteenth and early twentieth centuries. James's oeuvre is too narrow for many because it defends and bolsters bourgeois values in a historical struggle that is long past, won decisively by a powerful middle class that in our own age masquerades as a single class, when in fact we know it to be hierarchically divided in ways that reproduce an old, vanished aristocracy and render even more invisible the working class on whose labor these other groups depend.[10]

This elitist Henry James is, of course, directly connected with the aestheticist Henry James constructed by formalist critics. I need not quote again those passages from Percy Lubbock that I cited earlier to remind the reader that Lubbock's "critical reader" aspires to the solitary and singular genius of the great novelist, who distinguishes himself precisely as a consequence of his literary difficulty. Such technical complexity and subtlety constitute for Lubbock and other formalists an ontological category, no matter how often formalists have denied such connections.[11] The great writer thus appears to the imagination as some latter-day country gentleman, untouched by urban fashion and focused on timeless, natural verities.

Even if we leave aside the obvious implication in the Jamesian text that the fine consciences and supersubtle characters are generally delegates of the authorial presence, we may still understand why the casual reader of Henry James assumes that these characters generally represent the Jamesian ideal of cultivated behavior through the sophisticated use of language. The technique of Henry James, then, appears all too often to be the social utopia of James's characters—the best characters are those able to master the complexities of social rhetoric in ways isomorphic with the task set for the reader of wending his or her way through James's endless sentence. In the preceding chapters, I have treated this metafictional dimension in James as a problem, rather than an ideal, that virtually all of James's writings address. From Count Valerio's fetishizing of the writing hand and Newman's uncanny identification of himself with Mozart's Don Giovanni to Maisie's artistic inclinations and the postmodern scenes of writing in *In the Cage,* these reflections on representation are prompted by changing social conditions. Although few literary formalists would admit it, their concepts of metaliterariness and autotelicism helped legitimate, rather than challenge, middle-class culture.

The familiar conclusion that James's stylistic difficulty mirrors his social elitism is cause for the final reason James is often excluded from the reading list of curricula short of the English major and the graduate program, where his works remains universally required. Except for professionals, James's complexities strike many contemporary teachers and their students as irrelevant to the practical issues investigated in many literature classes. Such readers object to James's primary concern with the problems of the ruling classes, especially as this attention excludes serious treatment of the working classes. Insofar as James's plots revolve around fairly conventional problems of marriage, adultery, child rearing, divorce, financial security (or its lack), and social standing, the high drama James ascribes to just such normal aspects of middle-class life seems as excessive as his prose and thus as irrelevant as that prose to the problems of our contemporary postmodern society.

I have devoted this much space to the consequences of the formalist Henry James for the various resistances to teaching Henry James because I believe that such formalism continues to haunt James's reputation at the several levels of education where his works would be of considerable value in pursuing the goals of what I shall term *postmodern education*.[12] I want to devote the rest of this conclusion to a discussion of what ought to take the place of the aestheticist, elitist, and formalist Henry James because the value of this book depends on the contribution it makes to the work of teaching. First, if we do not deal primarily with James's aesthetic and rhetorical techniques, then what should be the center of our interest? The language-based critical approaches of the 1970s and 1980s that were avowedly antiformalist ought to provide us with some ways to answer this question. By "language-based criticism," I mean structuralist and semiotic approaches to literature, deconstruction, and other versions of poststructuralist and postmodern theories, virtually all of which have had specific impacts on the study and teaching of Henry James.

Critics of language-based or textualist theories have often pointed out how structuralist and poststructuralist approaches to literature reproduce many of the basic values of Anglo-American New Criticism and other formalist methods. Insofar as textualist theories ignored historical particulars and focused on the "deep structure" of language as a universal, they deserved such criticism. Nevertheless, structuralist and poststructuralist theories helped shift our attention from the uniqueness of literary language to the entanglement of literary discourse with other everyday discursive practices. For the textualist, the condition of textuality may be more marked in literary or other highly stylized uses of language, but it merely manifests what is always already operative in every act of communication. Thus the obsession with poetic technique in New Critical studies could be shifted to an even more encompassing fascination by textualists with the rhetorical devices and stylistic mechanisms of any discursive act. Because of their authors' intense self-consciousness about language use, literary texts became for such critics excellent opportunities to investigate the dialectic between convention and innovation, between regularity and change in the system of language.

By establishing literary study as a crucial part of linguistics, often insisting that *only* in literary language could the critic understand changes otherwise invisible in the essentially conservative dynamics of ordinary language use, structuralist and poststructuralist theories liberated the "difficulty" of great writers such as Henry James from their formalist association with "narrowness" and "irrelevance." Thus the great difficulty of Henry James became for critics such as Ruth Yeazell, Shlomith Rimmon, and Tzvetan Todorov (to mention only three of the most important of such critics of James from the 1970s) a function of his sustained reflection on how language works in the very course of using language in innovative ways.[13] Whether the arguments of such critics stressed the semiotic codes operative in human discourse and thus depended on the structuralist definition of the sign or emphasized the radical ambiguity and essential undecidability of a poststructuralist theory of language, such textualist approaches allowed teachers of the 1970s and 1980s to connect Henry James and other writers who focused on the problematic of language with linguistic theories that often touched the boundaries of disciplines such as psychoanalysis, philosophy, anthropology, and sociology.

I suspect that many of those critics share the experience of successfully teaching the dry subjects of Ferdinand de Saussure's concept of the "arbitrariness of the sign" or Noam Chomsky's theory of transformational grammar thanks to their use of Henry James as an example. I can recall numerous classroom situations in which an otherwise difficult Henry James text, such as *The Turn of the Screw* or *The Sacred Fount,* has helped clarify the even more difficult concepts in modern linguistics. Rather than constructing Henry James as a distinctive genius whose authorial identity students and teachers were encouraged to emulate, in the manner Lubbock recommends, such textualist teachers used James to exemplify and illustrate general problems in language. As the language model was broadened, as it inevitably had to be, to include a wider range of communicative practices than simply those identified with speech and writing, James and similarly complex writers were used to illustrate theoretical positions concerned with the general process of cultural self-representation.[14]

Nevertheless, the textualist approach to Henry James and to literature in general still relied on an implicit hierarchy that distinguished the "serious" literary work from popular literature by virtue of the former's higher degree of self-consciousness concerning its own language use. As a consequence, there was also an expectation on the part of teachers that such serious literary texts could not be readily taught until certain competencies had been achieved by students. Because such competency levels involved ever more demanding fields—a little philosophy, basic linguistics, at least *some* psychoanalysis, a history of critical and aesthetic theories, and so forth—access to Henry James and other so-called major authors remained the privilege of literature majors and graduate students.

The other textualist approach, informed more by the work of Michel Foucault than Jacques Derrida, still recognized the importance of the artist in bringing to self-consciousness certain rhetorical and representational strategies available to his or her cultural epoch but found in selected literary and artistic texts the capacity to interpret critically the hierarchy of such strategies. Not all discourse is equally powerful, the Foucauldian argues, and it is the historically specific ways certain representational strategies achieve ideological authority that should most interest us. Like other textualist positions, Foucauldian and other ideological interpretations shifted the "difficulty" of an author to the problem of articulating social reality in general once we understand truth and meaning to be socially constructed and thus effects of historically specific representations. Of course, major authors such as Henry James remained part of this extremely difficult intellectual task, but such an approach had the pedagogical advantage of imagining "critical thinking" about ideology, for example, to be the work of the entire liberal education. If in some quarters James could be made to represent just such critical intelligence in his literary comprehension of the complex and devious ways specific ideologies interpellate concrete subjects, then he could be placed at the end of a liberal educational curriculum, together with other exemplars, as a fitting model for the critically thinking citizen that has traditionally been the aim of humanistic education.

By the same token, Henry James's works could also be read as effects of a complex process of ideological legitimation, in which even his most conscious criticism of the dominant order could be shown merely to bolster the authority of ruling ideas.[15] In either case, the ideological study of Henry James not only shifted the problem of difficulty from James to ideology but answered the questions regarding James's "narrowness" and "irrelevance." By arguing that James focuses on the system of ideological power, such approaches explain why James would devote so much fictional space to the struggle between the rising bourgeoisie and the waning aristocracy. As to the "irrelevance" of a battle long concluded in favor of the middle class and its capitalist values, ideological readings of James could contend that the historical genealogy of bourgeois authority must be studied to demystify its claims to "natural" authority and that such history, however difficult to trace, is crucial to any critical reflection on contemporary social life. Whether Henry James (or any other major modern author) is part of the problem or the utopian solution, his or her study is crucial to understanding how ideology works and discovering thereby whatever limited freedom is available to the human subject. Once again, the pedagogical aim is not to train discrete subjects who emulate the artist's avant-garde disdain for social reality, as in Lubbock's caricature of the "critical reader," but to educate self-conscious subjects capable of assessing their responsibilities for the social community to which they belong. It is the difference, in short, between educating a ruling elite, appropriate perhaps to the accepted class divisions of British society in the 1920s, and thoughtful individuals appropriate to the democratic ideals of post–World War II education in the United States.

In my introduction to this book, I distinguish between two different Henry Jameses, one constructed primarily according to the prevailing Anglo-American confusion of "critical" with "literary" theory and another anticipating the critical theories we now commonly trace to the Frankfurt school: social theories intent on changing society for the better. When viewed in the latter way as a precursor to critical theorists intent on understanding the world in order to change it (to borrow Marx's famous slogan), Henry James may remain a difficult subject to teach, but he is for that very reason a crucial part of a liberal curriculum. With this change of attention in understanding Henry James comes a wide range of new topics that have previously been ignored by critics, making their blindnesses equally interesting subjects of investigation. Reading Henry James in terms of the ways the dominant ideology operates involves identifying just those topics in the early modern period that are the most ideologically contested. Traditionally, race, class, and gender have been the major issues of social conflict in Euramerican societies in the period of modernity, and it is just in these respects that newer, ideologically attentive approaches to Henry James have transformed him from an ivory-tower aesthete into an important subject and object of critical theory. More recently, considerations of gender conflict have been broadened to include questions of sexual preference, so that the somewhat restricted consideration of masculine and feminine gender roles must be expanded to include lesbian and homosexual preferences as important parts of the social construction of identities. In a similar fashion, discussions of race and ethnicity have expanded to include prevailing definitions of nation and empire, whose political functions have significantly determined most forms of social identification in the modern period.

What has amazed many readers of Henry James, both professional and casual, is that this shift in scholarly attention has uncovered so much in Henry James's writings that was previously invisible or at the best treated as a minor theme. Chief among those lapses in previous critical attention must be counted our consideration of gender as central to James's writings. Whether this attention has meant James's studied effort to control and constrain the modern woman within a complex rhetorical frame that permits her only limited freedom for the sake of reaffirming patriarchal power or means James's alliance of his own aesthetic consciousness with the more open, less phallocentric conception of representation that Hélène Cixous has termed "*écriture féminine*" does not diminish the obvious conclusion that Henry James's fiction foregrounds questions of gender far more than technical or stylistic issues.[16]

James's gender conflicts are not restricted simply to the polite negotiations of bourgeois and aristocratic characters. The marginalization of bourgeois women in James's fiction often brings them face-to-face with their potential affinities with women of other classes. By focusing on James's women characters, teachers and scholars not only raise long-deferred questions about gender construction in modern Western societies but also may challenge generalizations about a monolithic middle class. Liberal critics are fond of laying the blame for the sins of Western civilization at the feet of a vaguely defined middle class. Given the haziness of its definition, such a middle class may be said to encompass the majority of students we teach at the college and university levels. Those students know well enough, however, just how many differences exist in the spectrum that ranges from lower- and middle-management personnel through shopkeepers and small-business owners to the upper-middle-class managers, executives, and owners who control substantial wealth and social power. A greater distance separates the governess in *The Turn of the Screw* from the children's uncle than divides her from Mrs. Grose in Victorian class hierarchies, just as Isabel Archer's relative poverty before Ralph makes his bequest to her constitutes a social gulf between her and the Warburtons and Goodwoods. Feminist criticism of James has helped us understand not only how stubbornly persistent gender hierarchies were rhetorically and socially constructed in the early modern period but how these same hierarchies disguised social differences within the bourgeoisie. In short, feminist criticism has helped answer the charge that Henry James is too "narrow" in his focus on the loves and lives of an established middle class by showing how that middle class is itself riven with internal conflicts and differences. What I treat in this book as the instability of class definitions in James's writings, especially from the 1890s on, should be understood as part of both a changing social reality and James's conscious effort to comprehend the middle class as locus of cultural power.

Complicating traditional class hierarchies by taking account of gender relations is only one way to use Henry James in the classroom to offer students more nuanced accounts of the social conflicts shaping modern societies than what used to be offered by strict Marxian versions of class conflict between the bourgeoisie and proletariat. Recognizing that women and children also work at the construction of society, whether or not they are part of the acknowledged mode of production, should also be extended to include characters defined by their sexual preferences and their marginalization by the deeply homophobic cultures of early modern England and the United States. Recent approaches to James's fictional and personal considerations of homosexuality have demonstrated just how crucial Henry James is to our critical understanding of patriarchal cultures that are deeply homophobic at the same time that they function by means of crucial homosocial bonds.[17]

Nowhere is James's revaluation as a gay writer more important than in the high schools, where teachers struggle with the problem of teaching their students about gay literatures, histories, and cultures. On the one hand, these teachers know their students must learn the history of gay self-expression and activism that has for so long been excluded from the curriculum of higher education. Not only does such education have historical importance, but it is immediately relevant to adolescents coming to terms with their own sexualities. As we develop even better definitions to describe the wide range of experiences an individual may have with a member of the same sex, we have an obligation to teach students the social and psychological significance of such sexual and personal diversity. What is the distinction between homosocial relations supporting patriarchy and male friendship? What are the differences between "romantic friendship" and lesbian or gay sexuality? How have gays and lesbians related to each other as distinct groups in different historical situations? Such questions are crucial to the historical recovery and *uncovering* that teachers normally do. Yet the homophobia of the dominant culture is such that teachers attempting to include gay materials in their classes often face vigorous criticism from individual parents, parent-teacher associations, and school boards and administrations. In this regard, James's canonical status is an advantage in addressing issues in his writings and life immediately relevant to our understanding of gay sexual identities.

Whether we approach James from the standpoint of a writer deeply conflicted regarding his own sexual identity or as a writer who increasingly came to terms with his homosexuality, especially as evidenced by his writings of the 1890s, we can no longer ignore how frequently the themes and images of homosexuality inform his writings. Because he wrote at a time when homosexuality was legally and ideologically demonized, James provides an excellent opportunity to investigate a history that is still of the greatest importance in our understanding of modern Western cultures. Still another advantage of teaching the history of homosexuality, gay studies, and queer theory by way of Henry James is that such pedagogy involves us in the biographical and historical study of Henry James and such contemporaries as Oscar Wilde. Formalist critics stressed the "critical reader's" emulation of a purely textual author function, which in its bloodless and fleshless construction lost much of the relevance and vitality of actual writers and their human struggles. The gay and feminist revisions of that remote, aloof, and finally irrelevant "Henry James" have substituted a vital, engaged, interested, and often conflicted human being who can never be separated from the times in which he lived and wrote.

It should not surprise us that even as recent scholars and critics have brought into view James's reflections on gender hierarchies, class distinctions, and sexual identities, so has the virtual invisibility of race in Henry James's writings come to be recognized as a certain critical blindness. In chapters 3 and 5 in particular, I try to respond to the challenges from Toni Morrison, Kenneth Warren, Walter Benn Michaels, and Sara Blair that James be reconsidered in terms of the racial conflicts shaping his times. Whether this means criticizing James for his relative neglect of racial issues, as Warren has done, or for his racist representations of peoples of color, as Morrison has, teachers of James must reconsider his writings in relation to one of the central social and political questions of his generation, in both the United States and Europe. Just as Edward Said has found in the margins of Jane Austen's *Mansfield Park* how significantly her casual references to Sir Thomas's "Antigua plantations," supported by slavery, structure the visible world of social life at his English country estate, so recent critical approaches to James have situated his writings and thought in the contexts of modern Euramerican imperialism.[18] Until they had read Jean Rhys's rewriting of Bertha Mason's story in *Wide Sargasso Sea* (1962), few readers understood that the madwoman in Rochester's attic in Charlotte Brontë's *Jane Eyre* represents a significant number of Creole white women married by English gentry for their fortunes and then socially marginalized in the metropolitan colonial centers.[19] By the same token, few readers remember how Miles and Flora's parents' ventures in colonial India are obliquely linked with the governess's and the children's fates in that haunted English country house.

Critics who have focused on issues of race and colonialism in James's writings have helped change the stereotype of him as a difficult writer with little to say to the contemporary age, and they have also helped us broaden our critical attention to include James' nonfictional writings. As I argue in chapter 5, what becomes visible in this way in James's fiction helps redirect our attention to the many passages in his autobiographies and travel writings where James reflects on the ways nationalism and imperialism shape categories of race, ethnicity, and even personal identity in the modern period.[20] *The American Scene,* for example, is an important supplement to James's fiction because it connects gender hierarchies with racism in the United States toward African Americans, Native Americans, and new European immigrants.[21] To be sure, there is not yet a critical consensus about James's at times diverse, if not conflicted, views of the groups he decisively recognizes as socially marginalized in early modern America. As I argue in this book, this critical debate should also consider different conceptions of race and ethnicity in the United States and England in the modern period. One of the interesting consequences of James's identity as both an American and English citizen is that he had the opportunity to reflect on the *differences* of race, ethnicity, gender, class, sexuality, nation, and empire in the two dominant political powers of his generation.

Teaching the new Henry James in terms of his conscious and unconscious responses to the debates regarding race, class, gender, and sexual preferences at the turn of the century certainly transforms him from a writer with an excessively narrow focus on bourgeois social life into a precursor of our own postmodern condition. Certainly, this is the aim of Jane Campion's film adaptation of *The Portrait of a Lady* (1996), which includes twentieth-century scenes (such as the opening shots of women's contemporary diversity) and techniques (the "home movies" taken of Isabel's tour of Greece, Turkey, and Egypt) while retaining the nineteenth-century setting of the novel to emphasize its relevance for current debates about gender and sexuality.[22] Less daring in its revision of James, Agnieszka Holland's *Washington Square* (1997) gives substance to Catherine Sloper's rebellion against the patriarchy of her father and Morris Townsend in the day-care center she happily conducts in the once gloomy parlor of number 21, Washington Square. Catherine's diffident smiles, both to herself and the young girl whose mother is late to pick her up, in the closing shots of this film are certainly more satisfying to the contemporary viewer than James's concluding image of Catherine "in the parlor, picking up her morsel of fancywork, . . . for life, as it were," exemplifying the truculent and powerless rebellion of other spinsters in James's writings.[23] As a teacher of James who has appealed, usually in vain, to students to recognize the importance of sexual favors, bargains, and illicit liaisons in his writings, I especially appreciate the sexually explicit scenes in Iain Softley's *The Wings of the Dove* (1997). All of these films bring to the surface erotic subtexts in James's fiction, even when these postmodern interpretations reach beyond the logic of James's text, in which sexual *secrecy* is crucial to social power. The reader of James can hardly accept such scenes as Isabel's passionate caresses of the bedridden Ralph in Campion's *Portrait,* Catherine's knee-buckling kisses with Morris in Holland's *Washington Square,* and Kate's and Merton's public sex in Venice as true either to the original novels or to the time and social classes they represent. Nevertheless, such scenes bring into sharp relief an erotic power in James's fiction that is deeply entangled with both his analysis of ideology and his own passionate use of language. "Hot sex" in recent film adaptations and other modernizations of James, such as the production of Dominick Argento's *The Aspern Papers* by the Dallas Opera—are not simply ways of *marketing* James to contemporary audiences; they often help fore-ground hitherto neglected aspects of his art.[24]

These recent film adaptations of James's fiction are part of a Henry James's "revival" that has been under way in a wide range of feature films in the past two decades, including the several Merchant-Ivory productions, and the adaptation of James's novels into film is a traditional focus of liberal pedagogy.[25] But do such revisions of Henry James in the postmodern classroom and multiplex theater overcome the notorious problem of his difficulty? Are we not simply creating another version of the complex, multilayered great writer by expanding James's scope and that of modernism in general to include all that the previous generation of critics had neglected? To be sure, the other Henry James becomes a much more difficult literary figure to teach because as teachers we must command so much more knowledge of him and his times. No longer can we substitute a fantastic "author" for a man; biographical knowledge of James is today crucial to responsible instruction. No longer can we focus exclusively on textual evidence to the exclusion of historical materials that tell us so much about the formation of modern social attitudes and prejudices. In addition, we must have at least some familiarity with the contemporary debates regarding race, class, gender, and sexuality if we are to understand the ways Henry James continues to circulate or is simply forgotten as a consequence of his "elitism" and archaic values.

Nevertheless, the difficulty involved in teaching Henry James is of a different order than those proposed by formalists from Percy Lubbock to Laurence Holland. The social, ideological, and cultural problems James investigates and at times helps reproduce are the real sources of that difficulty. Our attention in James's fiction is less focused on technical issues of little interest to all but creative writers or professional scholars; instead our attention is seized by James's plot and characters, his general themes and fictional aims, even as we acknowledge the importance of his style in realizing these literary purposes. In effect, we are making Henry James *readable* once again, even for the casual reader. It should come as no revelation to us, then, if we can turn to the Jamesian oeuvre and find a vast number of writings, both fictional and nonfictional, that are suddenly suitable for teaching at every level of higher education. There is nothing lexically inaccessible in *The Turn of the Screw* or *In the Cage* for high school students, even if *The Golden Bowl* remains a stretch for even our best undergraduates. With its concern for the effects of new technologies on personal identity and social relations, *In the Cage* is a remarkably relevant text for our students. In its flexible, often comic, discussion of new gender and sexual relations, it also helps defuse heated contemporary debates on such topics. Both Mr. Mudge and Mr. Drake suggest possibilities for the New Man, as Mrs. Jordan and the telegraphist do for the New Woman. Although I do not address it centrally in this book, "The Beast in the Jungle" might well become an exciting investigation of the conflicted emotions of a man unable to accept his own sexuality or about the Orientalizing of the Western unconscious, rather than an overlong story about "nothing" and the "wait" for that "nothing." Like *The Turn of the Screw* and *In the Cage,* "The Beast in the Jungle" is neither complexly allusive nor extraordinarily difficult at the purely lexical and stylistic levels. What has always been the greatest challenge in reading Henry James is to figure from the bare and often simple elements of his plot and dramatic actions just what intellectual conclusions we are to draw.

I do not wish to conclude without pointing out what high school and community college teachers often insist on as a criterion for adopting new literary texts or teaching old literary texts in new ways. Less concerned with the often micropolitical debates in which research scholars engage, these teachers want to know how these new texts or new approaches are configured in a curricular design with others texts. However radically we may teach Henry James, Ezra Pound, T. S. Eliot, Wallace Stevens, and William Faulkner, for example, we are likely to reproduce, even when we are the most critical of, the key terms of an aesthetic modernism that helped prompt the critical traditions that legitimated such high modernism. If we consciously acknowledge the need to change not just the texts but also the orders in which they are taught, then we should look for new configurations in which Henry James may profitably be taught with W. E. B. Du Bois, Kate Chopin, Charlotte Perkins Gilman, Zora Neale Hurston, *Black Elk Speaks,* John Dos Passos, John Steinbeck, Tillie Olsen, Jean Rhys, Chinua Achebe, Margaret Atwood, Maxine Hong Kingston, Louise Erdrich, José Donoso, Jorge Luis Borges, Kazuo Ishiguro, Salman Rushdie, and a host of other Euramerican, Asian-American, African American, Native American, African, postcolonial, gay and lesbian, and women writers who have contributed to the several other "modernisms" available to us in our postmodern condition. In other words, as I have proposed in the preceding chapters, it is not enough simply to reread Henry James as an American *and* English writer. If we are to connect his modernity with our postmodern condition, then his influence, reception, and limitations must be considered in our understanding of globally diverse literatures. Viewed in this way, the scholarly revival of Henry James should be part of the curricular reforms under way throughout higher education that have as their long-term goal a more inclusive representation of nationality, ethnicity, gender, and sexual preference in the literatures and cultures we teach our students.

Notes ૐ

Preface

1 The Henry James Sesquicentennial Conferences were held at New York University and several other sites in New York from June 1 to June 6, 1993. Sponsored by the Henry James Society, New York University, and Louisiana State University, the conferences were the idea of Daniel Mark Fogel, who realized the weeklong celebration of James's 150th birthday with the help of Leon Edel, Julie Rivkin, James Tuttleton, William Veeder, Carren Kaston, and Anthony Mazella.

2 Fred Kaplan, *Henry James: The Imagination of Genius* (New York: William Morrow, 1992), p. 503.

3 Maxwell Geismar, *Henry James and the Jacobites* (Boston: Houghton Mifflin, 1963), p. 4. I am grateful to Eric Haralson of the State University of New York—Stony Brook for pointing out Geismar's reference to "the other Henry James."

4 Ibid.

5 Henry James, "The Deathbed Dictation," in *The Complete Notebooks of Henry James,* ed. Leon Edel and Lyall H. Powers (New York: Oxford University Press, 1987), pp. 581–84.

Introduction: Henry James and Critical Theory

1 John Carlos Rowe, *The Theoretical Dimensions of Henry James* (Madison: University of Wisconsin Press, 1984), esp. pp. 3–28.

2 Richard A. Hocks, *Henry James and Pragmatistic Thought: A Study in the Relationship between the Philosophy of William James and the Literary Art of Henry James* (Chapel Hill: University of North Carolina Press, 1974), p. 16, argues that Henry came to understand how "William's thought identifies his [Henry's] own idiom—his prose," glossing thereby Henry's 1907 letter to William in which he confesses to having "all my life . . . unconsciously pragmatised" (Henry James to William James, 17 October 1907, in *Letters,* vol. 4, ed. Leon Edel, 4 vols. [Cambridge, Mass.: Harvard University Press, 1984], p. 466).

3 Mark Bauerlein, *The Pragmatic Mind: Explorations in the Psychology of Belief* (Durham, N.C.: Duke University Press, 1997), argues that neopragmatists such as Rorty, Fish, Knapp, and Michaels are not properly heirs to a more precisely defined philosophical pragmatism that begins with Emerson and includes William James, Charles Sanders Peirce, and John Dewey.

4 Alfred Habegger Jr., *Henry James and the "Woman Business"* (Cambridge: Cambridge University Press, 1989), and Eve Kosofsky Sedgwick, *Epistemology of the Closet* (Berkeley: University of California Press, 1990), play crucial parts in the rest

of this study as models for revisionary interpretation of Henry James in relation to the approaches of feminism and gay studies.

5 For a discussion of the interrelation of critical theory and cultural studies in the past decade, see John Carlos Rowe, ed., *"Culture" and the Problem of the Disciplines* (New York: Columbia University Press, 1998), esp. my introduction.

6 Ross Posnock treats both Henry and William James as "critical theorists" in the Frankfurt school sense of the term in *The Trial of Curiosity: Henry James, William James, and the Challenge of Modernity* (New York: Oxford University Press, 1991).

7 This is one of the arguments I make in *Henry Adams and Henry James: The Emergence of a Modern Consciousness* (Ithaca, N.Y.: Cornell University Press, 1976), and it is the central argument of Carol Holly's *Intensely Family: The Inheritance of Family Shame and the Autobiographies of Henry James* (Madison: University of Wisconsin Press, 1995).

8 I mean "modest" only in this relative sense because Henry James's literary criticism is a substantial body of work in its own right, deserving the careful critical attention shown to it by critics such as Sarah B. Daughtery in *The Literary Criticism of Henry James* (Columbus: Ohio State University Press, 1981).

9 For a more detailed discussion of James's various roles in the critique or legitimation of modern bourgeois values, see chapters 2 and 6 in this volume.

10 Fredric Jameson, *The Political Unconscious: Narrative as a Socially Symbolic Act* (Ithaca, N.Y.: Cornell University Press, 1981), pp. 221–22.

11 David Lloyd, "Arnold, Ferguson, Schiller: Aesthetic Culture and the Politics of Aesthetics," *Cultural Critique* 2 (1977): p. 2.

12 Wallace Martin, introduction to *The Yale Critics: Deconstruction in America,* ed. Jonathan Arac, Wlad Godzich, and Wallace Martin (Minneapolis: University of Minnesota Press, 1983), pp. xviii–xix, cogently describes the American reception of both deconstruction and the Yale school in the 1970s:

> Although many American critics thought that the theoretical revisionism of Miller, de Man, and Bloom in the early 1970s resulted from their acceptance of ideas current in Continental criticism, others interpreted it as an essentially defensive maneuver, intended to ward off the threat of a more radical critique of literature (Riddel, "A Miller's Tale"). From one point of view, de Man's and Miller's argument that literature demystifies or deconstructs all attempts to accord it a special status can be seen as an attack on the Anglo-American critical tradition and on literature itself. From another point of view, this argument may be intended to save literature from irremediable deconstruction: it acknowledges the validity of anti-idealistic theories and claims that literature has already anticipated them.

It is in this latter regard that the deconstructive James has had the widest appeal, and it is a version of deconstruction that recently has been significantly challenged by feminist, postcolonial, cultural criticism, and queer theory.

13 In *The Ethics of Reading: Kant, de Man, Eliot, Trollope, James, and Benjamin* (New York: Columbia University Press, 1987), J. Hillis Miller interprets James in terms of Miller's general argument for the ethical values of literature's deconstructive function.

14 A full bibliography of such deconstructive readings of James would be a scholarly project in its own right. Good examples include my own *Henry Adams and Henry James: The Emergence of a Modern Consciousness* (Ithaca, N.Y.: Cornell University Press, 1976), Susanne Kappeler's *Writing and Reading in Henry James* (London: Macmillan, 1980), Henry Sussman's *The Hegelian Aftermath: Readings in Hegel, Kierkegaard, Freud, Proust, and James* (Baltimore, Md.: Johns Hopkins University Press, 1982), and Miller's work on Henry James mentioned in the previous note.

15 Jane Tompkins, ed., *Twentieth-Century Interpretations of "The Turn of the Screw"* (Englewood Cliffs, N.J.: Prentice-Hall, 1970), and *Sensational Designs: The Cultural Work of American Fiction, 1790–1860* (New York: Oxford University Press, 1985).

16 Tompkins, *Sensational Designs*, p. 185.

17 Susanne Kappeler, *Writing and Reading in Henry James* and *The Pornography of Representation* (Minneapolis: University of Minnesota Press, 1986).

18 Juliet Mitchell, "*What Maisie Knew:* The Portrait of the Artist as a Young Girl," in *The Air of Reality: New Essays on Henry James,* ed. John Goode (London: Methuen, 1972), pp. 168–89.

19 Sandra Gilbert and Susan Gubar, *The Madwoman in the Attic: The Woman Writer and the Nineteenth-Century Literary Imagination* (New Haven, Conn.: Yale University Press, 1979).

20 In her reading of Olive Chancellor as "tragic lesbian" in *The Apparitional Lesbian: Female Homosexuality and Modern Culture* (New York: Columbia University Press, 1993), pp. 150–83, Terry Castle stresses how such a reading "lifts *The Bostonians* itself up and out of the tainted realm of antilesbian burlesque into the authentic space of tragedy." Nevertheless, such "tragedy" merely allows Olive to join a host of feminine characters in James's fiction who never achieve the sublimity of aesthetic or social transformation that James will claim for his own art.

21 In regard to Henry James's judgments of Margaret Fuller's literary value, see chapter 1 of this volume. In *French Poets and Novelists* (1878; New York: Grosset and Dunlap, 1964), James cites George Sand's claim that "she could write for an extraordinary length of time without weariness" to make an apparent pun on her "labored" writing and difficult life: "From the time she made the discovery to the day of her death her life was an extremely laborious one" (165). Later, James will conclude that Sand, unlike Balzac, lacked "form," even with plenty of "style" (180).

22 William Veeder, *Henry James—The Lessons of the Master: Popular Fiction and Personal Style in the Nineteenth Century* (Chicago: University of Chicago Press, 1975), esp. chap. 1.

23 In *The War of Words,* vol. 1 of *No Man's Land: The Place of the Woman Writer in the Twentieth Century* (New Haven, Conn.: Yale University Press, 1988), pp. 214–16, Sandra Gilbert and Susan Gubar use Vernon Lee's caricature of Henry James, in the character of Marion in Lee's novella "Lady Tal," to explain quite precisely the ambivalence women writers—both his contemporaries and many of his subsequent critics—feel toward James's authority.

24 Mark Seltzer, *Henry James and the Art of Power* (Ithaca, N.Y.: Cornell University Press, 1984).

25 Henry James, *The Letters of Henry James,* ed. Leon Edel, 4 vols. (Cambridge, Mass.: Harvard University Press, 1974–1984), vol. 4, p. 770; hereafter cited in the text as *Letters.*

26 As Greenblatt puts the case in "Shakespeare and the Exorcists," in *Contemporary Literary Criticism,* ed. Robert Con Davis and Ronald Schleifer, 2d ed. (New York: Longman, 1989), pp. 444–45: "There are, of course, further institutional strategies that lie beyond a love for the theater. In a move that Ben Jonson rather than Shakespeare seems to have anticipated, the theater itself comes to be emptied out in the interests of reading. In the argument made famous by Charles Lamb and Coleridge, and reiterated by Bradley, theatricality must be discarded to achieve absorption, and Shakespeare's imagination yields forth its sublime power not to a spectator but to one who, like Keats, sits down to reread *King Lear.* Where institutions like King's Men had been thought to generate their texts, now texts like *King Lear* appear to generate their institutions. The commercial contingency of the theater gives way to the philosophical necessity of literature." As Shakespeare goes, so goes James. It is in this dialectic between textuality and institutional practices that I find New Historicism's politics (which its critics insist are nowhere to be found) to have the greatest cogency and relevance for our postmodern condition.

27 Shoshana Felman, "Turning the Screw of Interpretation," in *Literature and Psychoanalysis: The Question of Reading: Otherwise,* ed. Shoshana Felman (Baltimore, Md.: Johns Hopkins University Press, 1982), pp. 94–207.

28 Frank Kermode, *The Classic* (Cambridge, Mass.: Harvard University Press, 1983), p. 114.

29 Max Horkheimer, "Traditional and Critical Theory," in *Critical Theory: Selected Essays,* trans. Matthew J. O'Connell et al. (New York: Seabury Press, 1982).

30 Ibid., p. 210.

31 Henry James, *The Art of the Novel: Critical Prefaces by Henry James,* ed. Richard P. Blackmur (New York: Scribner's, 1934), p. 5.

32 Henry James, *The Ambassadors,* vol. 21 of *The Novels and Tales of Henry James,* the New York Edition, 26 vols. (New York: Charles Scribner's Sons, 1907–1917), p. 218.

33 Horkheimer, "Traditional and Critical Theory," p. 210.

34 For a more detailed discussion of the interrelation of U.S. imperialism and early modern American thought and rhetoric, see my "Henry Adams' *Education* in the

Age of Imperialism," in *New Essays on "The Education of Henry Adams,"* ed. John Carlos Rowe (New York: Cambridge University Press, 1996), pp. 87–114.

35 Horkheimer, "Traditional and Critical Theory," pp. 210–11.

36 Dorothea Krook, *The Ordeal of Consciousness in Henry James* (Cambridge: Cambridge University Press, 1962); Hocks, *Henry James and Pragmatistic Thought;* Paul Armstrong, *The Phenomenology of Henry James* (Chapel Hill: University of North Carolina, 1983), and *The Challenge of Bewilderment: Understanding and Representation in James, Conrad, and Ford* (Ithaca, N.Y.: Cornell University Press, 1987); Sharon Cameron, *Thinking in Henry James* (Chicago: University of Chicago Press, 1989).

37 Horkheimer, "Traditional and Critical Theory," p. 244.

38 Ibid.

39 Ibid., p. 245.

40 Ibid.

41 Nowhere is this feminist revaluation of traditional ideas of class more significant than in recent reinterpretations of the American Left in the 1930s that include the protest of women intellectuals who often found leftist orthodoxy unsympathetic to women's rights. In particular, see Constance Coiner, *Better Red: The Writing and Resistance of Tillie Olsen and Meridel Le Sueur* (New York: Oxford University Press, 1995), and Paul Rabinowitz, *Labor and Desire: Women's Revolutionary Fiction in Depression America* (Chapel Hill: University of North Carolina Press, 1991).

42 Bruce Robbins, *The Servant's Hand: English Fiction from Below* (New York: Columbia University Press, 1986), takes this approach as the basis for rereading the tradition of English fiction, and I am suggesting that we adapt this approach to the study of Henry James's fiction.

43 Pansy's situation in the convent recalls, of course, Claire's "decision" to enter the Carmelite convent at the end of *The American.* See chapter 2 of this volume.

44 Henry James, *What Maisie Knew,* the New York Edition, vol. 11, p. 157.

45 Henry James, "The Pupil," the New York Edition, vol. 11, p. 577.

46 Ibid., p. 545.

47 Henry James, *The Wings of the Dove,* the New York Edition, vol. 11, p. 247.

48 Ibid., p. 250.

49 Ibid., p. 248.

50 Ibid., p. 249.

51 Ibid., p. 250.

52 See chapter 4 of this volume.

53 See Eve Sedgwick, *Between Men: English Literature and Male Homosocial Desire* (New York: Columbia University Press, 1985), p. 89: "So-called 'homosexual panic' is the most private, psychologized form in which many twentieth-century men experience their vulnerability to the social pressure of homophobic blackmail. . . . For a man to be a man's man is separated only by an invisible, carefully blurred, always-already-crossed line from being 'interested in men.'"

54 Sedgwick, *Epistemology of the Closet* (Berkeley: University of California Press, 1990), p. 206.

55 Joseph Bristow, *Effeminate England: Homoerotic Writing after 1885* (Buckingham: Open University Press, 1995), p. 129.

56 Kaja Silverman, *Male Subjectivity at the Margins* (New York: Routledge, 1992), pp. 161–62.

57 Ibid., p. 165.

58 Ibid., p. 179: "Sodomitical identification also permits the subject to participate at an imaginary level in the 'father's' phallic sexuality—to penetrate by identifying with the one-who-penetrates. It is thereby a mechanism through which a subject who is profoundly marked by passivity and lack can lay temporary claim to an *active* sexual aim."

59 Ibid., p. 180.

60 Ibid., p. 162, where Silverman notes that in James's fiction knowledge and power are "often placed in stark opposition" but then goes on to show how "knowledge" in James's fiction often means a certain powerlessness and thus passivity. But these are generally the negative consequences of previous narrative actions in which characters have missed opportunities, avoided responsibilities, or intentionally damaged passionate relations. Silverman is right that an "intractably Foucauldian reading" of James's fiction misses a great deal, but she too fails to recognize that James equates "knowledge" with a compassionate negative capability, moral righteousness with love or care for those who have failed to live up to the text's ethical standard. This "fuzzy" knowledge is what Silverman's revisionary Freudianism fails to understand.

61 Posnock, *The Trial of Curiosity*, p. 276, emphasizes James's sympathies and even identification with immigrants to the United States, especially in his discussions in *The American Scene*. I agree, but I also find that every effort by James to identify with immigrants is complicated by his repugnance for them. Such contradictory emotions are also present in James's responses to same-sex relations, as I argue at various points in this book.

62 Henry James, *The Question of Our Speech*, in *The Question of Our Speech and the Lesson of Balzac* (Boston: Houghton, Mifflin, 1905), p. 49; hereafter cited in the text as *QS*.

63 No matter how much we expand James's understanding of American nationalism in *The Question of Our Speech*, it remains what we would term today a version of "American exceptionalism" that distinguishes the American social experiment from previous social orders, all of which are European for Henry James. Latin America is generally an exotic and backward "place" about which James can generalize, as in the "little hot hole" of a Central American country to which Peter Sherringham is posted by the British Foreign Office in *The Tragic Muse*. India is an outpost of the British Empire, as it is for Miles's and Flora's parents, who die there in *The Turn of the Screw*, or a place of "escape" from the pressures of

civilization, as it is for John Marcher, who travels there after May Bartram dies. In short, James leaves unquestioned the Euramerican model for civilization that is central to the enlightenment project of modernity.

64 Eliot's "Tradition and the Individual Talent" is very clearly shaped by the sort of Jamesian historical consciousness that also organizes Eliot's reactions to modernity in poems such as "Gerontion" and *The Waste Land*.

65 Elsewhere in this book, I will refer to my essay "The Writing Class," in *Politics, Theory, and Contemporary Culture*, ed. Mark Poster (New York: Columbia University Press, 1993), pp. 41–82, as a theory of postmodern class distinctions based on relative communicative access and discursive power. I think in certain respects Henry James anticipates this theory in his writings.

66 Miller, *The Ethics of Reading*, p. 121.

1 Swept Away: Henry James, Margaret Fuller, and "The Last of the Valerii"

1 Austin Warren, *The Elder Henry James* (New York: Macmillan, 1934), p. 48.

2 Habegger, *Henry James and the "Woman Business,"* p. 32.

3 Margaret Fuller, *Woman in the Nineteenth Century* (New York: W. W. Norton, 1971), p. 116; hereafter cited in the text as *Woman*.

4 Emerson, "Woman," in *The Works of Ralph Waldo Emerson*, the Riverside Edition, vol. 11 (Boston: Houghton, Mifflin, 1883), p. 356. See my more extended discussion of Emerson's "Woman" in *At Emerson's Tomb: The Politics of Classic American Literature* (New York: Columbia University Press, 1997), pp. 37–40.

5 Habegger, *Henry James and the "Woman Business,"* p. 32.

6 Ibid., p. 36.

7 Ibid., pp. 27–62.

8 Ibid., p. 37.

9 Henry James, *The American Essays of Henry James*, ed. Leon Edel (New York: Random House, 1956), p. 64; hereafter cited in the text as *American Essays*.

10 Henry James, *Hawthorne*, English Men of Letters Series (New York: Harper and Brothers, 1879), pp. 76–77; hereafter cited in the text as *Hawthorne*.

11 Habegger, *Henry James and the "Woman Business,"* p. 223, argues not only that James reinforces nineteenth-century conventions of feminine domesticity but that feminine heroines such as Verena Tarrant in *The Bostonians* exemplify the elder James's "fervent convictions" that "it is not in female nature to care about personal freedom."

12 William Ellery Channing, J. F. Clarke, and Ralph Waldo Emerson, eds., *Memoirs of Margaret Fuller Ossoli*, vol. 1 (Boston: Phillips, Sampson, 1852), pp. 214, 324.

13 Carl Maves, *Sensuous Pessimism: Italy in the Work of Henry James* (Bloomington: Indiana University Press, 1973), pp. 3–8.

14 Throughout the nineteenth century, the portrait of Beatrice Cenci at the Palazzo

Barberini was considered the work of Guido Reni. Twentieth-century art historians have argued that the portrait is probably not his work. It now hangs in the Galleria Nazionale d'Arte Antica in Rome, housed in the Palazzo Barberini.

15 Henry James, *William Wetmore Story and His Friends,* vol. 1 (reprint, London: Thames and Hudson, 1903), p. 126; hereafter cited in the text as *Story.*

16 Shelley, preface to *The Cenci,* in *Poetical Works,* ed. Thomas Hutchinson, rev. G. M. Matthews, Oxford Standard Authors (Oxford: Oxford University Press, 1970), p. 276.

17 Earl Wasserman, *Shelley: A Critical Reading* (Baltimore, Md.: Johns Hopkins University Press, 1971), p. 95.

18 Nina Auerbach, *Woman and the Demon: The Life of a Victorian Myth* (Cambridge, Mass.: Harvard University Press, 1982), p. 94.

19 Francesco Domenico Guerrazzi was a follower of Mazzini and was jailed several times for his politics. The political allegory of his romance *Beatrice Cenci* is directed at the abuse of power by hereditary aristocrats, such as Count Cenci, unconstrained by just laws or due process. Money purchases all things in Guerrazzi's romance. Although Guerrazzi focuses his narrative on the destruction of the Cenci family by the mad count, he emphasizes how such patriarchal rule grows irrational when it is not controlled by civil or religious laws. The themes of incest and parricide so obsessively associated with the Cenci in the nineteenth-century imagination are transformed by Guerrazzi into metaphors for tyrannical power, rather than used for episodes of romantic titillation. Even so, Guerrazzi manages to sentimentalize his subject by turning the actual violation of Beatrice by her father into a merely perverse desire and by assigning Beatrice's lover, Guido, the task of dispatching the count. Happening on the count looking lustfully at his sleeping daughter, Guido stabs him in a rage of jealousy and offended honor. Guerrazzi thus trivializes his political themes by resorting to the melodrama of family conflict.

20 Nathaniel Hawthorne, *Passages from the French and Italian Notebooks,* vol. 10 of *The Complete Works of Nathaniel Hawthorne,* ed. George Parsons Lathrop, Riverside Edition, 13 vols. (Boston: Houghton, Mifflin, 1899), pp. 504–5; hereafter cited in the text as *French and Italian Notebooks.*

21 Nathaniel Hawthorne, *The Marble Faun,* vol. 6 of *The Complete Works of Nathaniel Hawthorne,* p. 85.

22 In *Hawthorne,* pp. 81–82, James writes of the Concord and Boston transcendentalists: "The compiler of these pages, though his recollections date only from a later period, has a memory of a certain number of persons who had been intimately connected, as Hawthorne was not, with the agitations of that interesting time. . . . They appeared unstained by the world, unfamiliar with worldly desires and standards, and with those various forms of human depravity which flourish in some high phases of civilization. . . . This little epoch . . . has three or four drawbacks for the critics. . . . It bore, intellectually, the stamp of provincialism; it was a beginning without fruition, a dawn without a noon; and it produced, with a single exception, no great talents." Although the "single exception" in this context

is Emerson, James uses the same rhetoric of innocence, provincialism, and intellectual "colorlessness" to characterize Emerson's life and work in "Emerson," in *Partial Portraits* (London: Macmillan, 1888), pp. 2–3.

23 Cornelia Kelley, *The Early Development of Henry James* (Urbana: University of Illinois Press, 1965), pp. 156–59.

24 Henry James, "The Last of the Valerii," in *The Tales of Henry James,* ed. Maqbool Aziz, vol. 2 (Oxford: Oxford University Press, 1978), p. 259; hereafter cited in the text as *V.*

25 Henry James, "From a Roman Notebook" (1873), in *Italian Hours* (New York: Horizon Press, 1968), p. 295; hereafter cited in the text as *Italian Hours.*

26 D. Mack Smith, *Victor Emmanuel, Cavour, and the Risorgimento* (London: Oxford University Press, 1971), p. 93.

27 The count's fetish anticipates the narrator's secret possession of the miniature portrait of Jeffrey Aspern, which he hangs above his writing desk, in *The Aspern Papers* (1888). By the late 1880s, James begins to include disguised male-male relations in his fiction, anticipating the more open consideration of gay and lesbian sexuality in the fiction of the 1890s.

28 Henry James, "The Jolly Corner," the New York Edition, vol. 18, p. 476.

29 Henry James, *The Other House* (New York: Arno Press, 1976), p. 175.

30 Priscilla Walton, " 'The Tie of a Common Aversion': Sexual Tensions in Henry James's *The Other House,*" *The Henry James Review* 17 (winter 1996): pp. 14, 20. Walton points out how Rose Armiger's threatening sexuality is represented in the late-nineteenth-century rhetoric reserved for lesbians, and how this nominally dangerous sexuality enables James to play with homoerotic bonds between two of the central male characters, Tony Bream and Dennis Vidal, in *The Other House* (19). Walton's analysis here complements my reading of "The Middle Years" and "The Death of the Lion" in chapter 4 of this volume.

2 A Phantom of the Opera: Christopher Newman's Unconscious in *The American*

1 Henry James, *The American,* ed. James W. Tuttleton, Norton Critical Edition (New York: W. W. Norton, 1978), p. 309; hereafter cited in the text.

2 See my "The Politics of Innocence in Henry James's *The American,*" in *At Emerson's Tomb: The Politics of Classic American Literature* (New York: Columbia University Press, 1997), pp. 179–99.

3 Gustav Kobbé and George Harewood, *The New Kobbé's Complete Opera Book,* ed. and rev. the earl of Harewood (New York: G. P. Putnam's Sons, 1976), p. 103: "*Don Giovanni* owes part of its success to the almost unique blending of the irresistibly comic and the tragically serious as much as to the speed of its dramatic and musical action."

4 For a fuller discussion of the significance of Valentin's military service, see Rowe, *At Emerson's Tomb,* pp. 188–89.

5 See my discussion of *The Sacred Fount* in *Through the Custom-House: Nineteenth-Century American Fiction and Modern Theory* (Baltimore, Md.: Johns Hopkins University Press, 1982), pp. 168–89, and of *The Aspern Papers* and *The Turn of the Screw* in *The Theoretical Dimensions of Henry James* (Madison: University of Wisconsin Press, 1984), pp. 85–146.

6 Sigmund Freud, "The Uncanny," in *On Creativity and the Unconscious: Papers on the Psychology of Art, Literature, Love, and Religion,* ed. Benjamin Nelson (New York: Harper and Row, 1958), p. 148; hereafter cited in the text.

7 R. W. Butterfield, "*The American,*" in *The Air of Reality: New Essays on Henry James,* ed. John Goode (London: Methuen and Co., Ltd., 1972), p. 10. In *Beyond the Pleasure Principle,* trans. and ed. James Strachey (New York: W. W. Norton, 1961), p. 30, Freud claims that the function of the repetition-compulsion, which itself seems to contradict so profoundly the psyche's instinctive drives for pleasure, is part of an equally profound "*urge inherent in organic life to restore an earlier state of things* which the living entity has been obliged to abandon under the pressure of external disturbing forces; that is, it is a kind of organic elasticity, or, to put it another way, the expression of the inertia inherent in organic life." Whatever functions "beyond the pleasure principle" is, for Freud, profoundly involved with the instinct for repetition as a defense against threats to the coherent ego.

8 Henry James, *The American Scene,* ed. Leon Edel (Bloomington: Indiana University Press, 1968), p. 347; hereafter cited in the text as *AS.*

9 Carolyn Porter argues in "Gender and Value in *The American,*" in *New Essays on "The American,"* ed. Martha Banta (New York: Cambridge University Press, 1987), p. 110, that Madame de Bellegarde "does not . . . apparently bargain for . . . her precious possession" Claire to retreat "to a convent" to "preserve her status as undegradable, as without a price." It is possible that the money-hungry Madame de Bellegarde is surprised by Claire's "decision," but the choice of going into a convent as a way for unmarried Catholic women in the nineteenth century to solve a host of problems is so common in fiction and in life as to trivialize any idea that Claire is acting courageously or independently.

10 Ibid., p. 103.

11 Ibid., p. 112.

12 Ibid., p. 113.

13 Ibid., p. 104.

14 When M. Nioche "portentously" worries about anything "happening" to the morality of Noémie, he clenches "his two fists" and jerks "back his head," declaring with violence, "I believe I should shoot her!" (*American,* p. 58). But once again this is the violent rhetoric of an otherwise utterly timid and thoroughly compromised man, like Valentin in his duel with Kapp.

15 Murillo's *Marriage of St. Catherine* and Rubens's *Marriage of Marie de Médicis.* Just after his initial meeting with the Nioches in the Louvre, Newman returns to the divan in the Salon de Carré and contemplates Veronese's *The Marriage at Cana* (*American,* pp. 25–26).

16 Porter, "Gender and Value," p. 110.

17 Russell J. Reising, "Condensing the James Novel: *The American* in *Hugh Selwyn Mauberley,*" *Journal of Modern Literature* 15, no. 1 (summer 1988): pp. 17–34, draws many helpful connections between James's Newman and Pound's Mauberley, including the aspects of both characters that James and Pound used to satirize the superficial commercialism of the modern age.

18 It is fictionally appropriate that Tom Tristram and Newman met in St. Louis "during the war," where Newman played poker with Tom and "cleaned [him] out" (*American*, p. 33).

19 Robert Penn Warren, *All the King's Men* (New York: Bantam Books, 1974), p. 270.

3 Acting Lessons: Racial, Sexual, and Aesthetic Politics in *The Tragic Muse*

1 Dorothea Krook, *The Ordeal of Consciousness in Henry James* (Cambridge: Cambridge University Press, 1962), p. 62.

2 Maxwell Geismar, *Henry James and the Jacobites* (Boston: Houghton Mifflin, 1963), pp. 103–4: "This was really an upper class romance, . . . and laid on thick for the tourist trade. Nick Dormer and Peter Sherringham ('old boy,' 'old fellow') are cousins" and "[Nick] is in fact a bore, and his conflict between politics and fame, and art and solitude, is tedious."

3 Richard Salmon, *Henry James and the Culture of Publicity* (Cambridge: Cambridge University Press, 1997), pp. 39–43, argues convincingly that James changed his mind about women in the public sphere between *The Bostonians* and *The Tragic Muse,* thus explaining why "Miriam breaks through the medium of her objectification, and is able to exercise a subjectivity which is denied to Verena" (41). The comparison and contrast of Verena and Miriam makes eminently clear the differences between Verena as a passive, infantile, and subjugated character and Miriam as active, mature, and able to make her own decisions.

4 Geismar, *Henry James and the Jacobites,* p. 104, stresses her "partly Jewish" background as crucial to James's patronizing tone in regard to her: "She is a lower class type who is struggling toward a career on the stage. That is to say, she is of dubious middle class parentage; and perhaps her Jewish strain was in accordance with a certain vulgarity which James also associated with the '*nature d'actrice.*'" Fred Kaplan, *Henry James: The Imagination of Genius* (New York: William Morrow, 1992), p. 334, concludes: "If she is ruthless, she must be so to accomplish her artistic ends." Krook, *Ordeal of Consciousness,* p. 87, even in her praise condemns Miriam as "a very handsome, very crude and gauche young girl, who is possessed by the single purpose of becoming a great actress" and is characterized by her "ruthlessness" and "utterly unscrupulous" exploitation of her "power" (92–93). It is part of James's brilliance in this novel to have selected the name "Rooth" to provoke different critics to conclude that she is "ruthless," Jewish, or a mere imitation of the famous nineteenth-century French tragedian Ruth, thereby re-

peating the snobbish judgments of her by her British admirers, whom James satirizes so thoroughly in this novel.

5 Geismar, *Henry James and the Jacobites,* pp. 105–6: "The second half of *The Tragic Muse* simply fell apart . . . or was dissipated into idle chatter and 'fine' writing' to conceal the lack of fictional development. . . . Maybe the real failure in the novel was the author's own betrayal of his gifted and entertaining heroine." Sara Blair, *Henry James and the Writing of Race and Nation* (New York: Cambridge University Press, 1996), p. 129.

6 Henry James, *The Art of the Novel,* p. 89. Two paragraphs later, James repeats this point: "I never 'go behind' Miriam; only poor Sherringham goes, a great deal, and Nick Dormer goes a little, and the author, while they so waste wonderment, go behind *them:* but none the less she is as thoroughly symbolic, as functional, for illustration of the idea, as either of them, while her image had seemed susceptible of a livelier and 'prettier' concretion" (91).

7 Ibid., p. 90.

8 In his introduction to *The Tempest,* in *Selected Literary Criticism,* ed. Morris Shapira (Harmondsworth: Penguin Books, 1968), p. 357, James claim that such a sublimation of life into art is Shakespeare's greatest triumph: "The secret that baffles us being the secret of the Man, we know, . . . that we shall never touch the Man *directly* in the Artist. We stake our hopes thus on indirectness. . . . The figured tapestry, the long arras that hides him, is always there, with its immensity of surface and its proportionate underside." James repeatedly offers us stories of artists whose personal secrets are indistinguishable from, or at least interestingly entangled with, their creative works, especially in *The Aspern Papers,* "The Middle Years," "The Death of the Lion," "The Author of Beltraffio," and "The Figure in the Carpet." To be sure, this would become a critical standard of literary formalism.

9 Salmon, *Culture of Publicity,* pp. 38–39.

10 *The Art of the Novel,* p. 91. James develops a curious extended metaphor between eating and art in this paragraph of the preface to *The Tragic Muse,* ranging from his interest in "the personal consequences of the art-appetite raised to intensity, swollen to voracity" to the final metaphor of the artist's "free plunge of the social fork into the contemporary salad." James seems to have in mind the process of social appropriation whereby what is external and other is either rejected or internalized and made society's own through a process of conventionalization. It is this latter process that generally interests James in his fiction. In this regard, James's preface seems to reflect the extraordinary rhetoric of orality that James uses throughout *The Tragic Muse.*

11 Blair, *Race and Nation,* p. 134.

12 Ibid., p. 136.

13 Ibid., p. 156.

14 In Anthony Trollope, *Nina Balatka,* in *Nina Balatka and Linda Tressel,* ed. Robert Tracy, World's Classics (Oxford: Oxford University Press, 1991), p. 69, Nina

Balatka's Jewish fiancé, Anton Trendellsohn, dreams of escaping the Jewish ghetto of Prague: "He had heard of Jews in Vienna, in Paris, and in London, who were as true to their religion as any Jew of Prague, but who did not live immured in a Jews' quarter, like lepers separate and alone in some loathed corner of a city otherwise clean. These men went abroad into the world as men, using the wealth with which their industry had been blessed, openly as the Christians used it. And they lived among Christians as one man should live with his fellow-men—on equal terms, giving and taking, honouring and honoured."

15 Anthony Trollope, *The Landleaguers*, ed. R. H. Super (Ann Arbor: University of Michigan Press, 1992), p. 124. Trollope's Rachel O'Mahony is based on Trollope's friend, the American actress Kate Field, assuring the reader that Trollope endorses the anti-Semitism of the ladylike Rachel O'Mahony. Trollope seems clearly to intend O'Mahony to be an Irish American version of the French acting sensation Rachel, after whom Miriam Rooth is also modeled. Once again the difference between Trollope's and James's views of Jews is epitomized in the ways these two fictional "Rachels" behave. Trollope's Irish American Rachel thoroughly appropriates the historical Rachel's talent while vilifying Jews; Miriam Rooth acknowledges her Jewish heritage but seems to identify more with Rachel in terms of her theatrical talents.

16 Ibid., p. 295.

17 Trollope did not finish *The Landleaguers* before his death, but his son, Henry Trollope, notes that his father "had intended . . . that Frank Jones should marry Rachel O'Mahony" (*The Landleaguers*, p. 333).

18 Ross Posnock, *The Trial of Curiosity: Henry James, William James, and the Challenge of Modernity* (New York: Oxford University Press, 1991), p. 156.

19 Ibid., p. 276. Posnock specifically identifies "James's sympathy for the alien and the marginal, particularly the perennially wandering Jew, for the latter is the emblem of democracy conceived as the 'uncontrollable adventure' of 'radical indetermination.' . . . James, Veblen, and Adorno had all nominated the Jew as being most resistant to American homogeneity. Certainly the exiled, deracinated status of each man helped foster their sympathy for and identification with the Jew."

20 Élisa Félix (1820?–1858), who took the stage name Rachel, was born in Switzerland; her father, an Alsatian Jew, was an impoverished peddler who wandered about Europe and eventually established his family at Lyon. Miriam Rooth's theatrical models are, of course, quite diverse. At various times, she is compared to Fanny Kemble, Rachel, Sarah Bernhardt, Ellen Terry, and other famous nineteenth-century actresses.

21 Henry James, *The Tragic Muse*, vols. 7–8, of the New York Edition of the Novels and Tales of Henry James, 26 vols. (New York: Charles Scribner's Sons, 1908), vol. 1, p. 61; hereafter cited in the text as *TM*.

22 In her enthusiasm for the tragic acting of Rachel, Margaret Fuller, *Memoirs of Margaret Fuller Ossoli*, vol. 2, pp. 200–201, nonetheless concludes: "She has no

beauty, except in the intellectual severity of her outline, and she bears marks of race, that will grow stronger every year, and make her ugly at last."

23 Queen Victoria's parents came from the Franconia region of South-Central Germany (roughly the contemporary Franken region), and Prince Albert was the prince of Saxe-Coburg-Gotha. Both rulers helped legitimate the German heritage of the English throne.

24 Blair, *Race and Nation*, p. 130.

25 Adeline R. Tintner, *Henry James and the Lust of the Eyes: Thirteen Artists in His Work* (Baton Rouge: Louisiana State University Press, 1993), pp. 56–69, traces the many connections between Miriam and Rachel in the novel, as well as less frequent references connecting Miriam with the actress Fanny Kemble. Tintner's discussion of James's allusions to Jean-Léon Gérôme's portrait *Rachel as the Tragic Muse*, which hangs in the greenroom of the Théâtre Français, where chapter 21 of the novel is set, reinforces Miriam's own idea here that her "identification" with the "race" of Rachel (and Fanny Kemble and Mrs. Siddons) refers to the tradition of great actresses, not her Jewish heritage.

26 Posnock, *Trial of Curiosity*, p. 146, interprets James's modernity as complementary with "the younger generation of self-conscious modernists," such as Randolph Bourne in America and Walter Benjamin in Europe, and distinct from the "genteel tradition," represented for Posnock by Henry Adams, E. L. Godkin (editor of the *Nation*), and Charles Eliot Norton, who railed against the vulgarity of the modern age. From a postmodern perspective, of course, these "self-conscious modernists" often universalized the alienation, heterogeneity, and transnationalism so characteristic of modernity as part of a universal cosmopolitanism.

27 Blair, *Race and Nation*, p. 138.

28 In the first edition of *The Tragic Muse* (London: Macmillan, 1890), James would write "you must live upon the country you *occupy*" (emphasis mine) to stress the extended metaphor equating Miriam with an invading army.

29 Salmon, *Culture of Publicity*, p. 41.

30 Ibid., p. 40.

31 Blair, *Race and Nation*, p. 136.

32 Ibid., p. 137.

33 In Charles Brockden Brown's *Wieland; or, the Transformation*, published in 1798 (Garden City, N.Y.: Doubleday, 1962), p. 144, the diabolical Carwin tries to flatter Clara Wieland by praising the "rectitude" and "firmness" of her "principles" in her rejection of "that specious seducer Dashwood." This Dashwood plays no other role in the narrative except to exemplify the "specious seducer."

34 Blair, *Race and Nation*, 156.

35 Geismar, *Henry James and the Jacobites*, p. 105.

36 Tintner, *Lust of the Eyes*, p. 66, argues convincingly that "Nick, an English painter, creates a contemporary version of the Tragic Muse very different from the French Gérôme portrait of Rachel. The master to whom Nick harks back is Sir Joshua Reynolds (his Tragic Muse was a portrait of Mrs. Siddons, the great

English actress who is mentioned once in the novel), even though it is only in the New York Edition version that James adds Sir Joshua's name." Nevertheless, Miriam's appearance in James's description of Nick's first portrait of her recalls much more the classical angularity and formality, as well as the forbidding look, of Gérôme's Rachel. The latter portrait (see figure 20 in Tintner) clearly resembles the classical style James had in mind in his description of the unearthed Juno in "The Last of the Valerii."

37 Silverman, *Male Subjectivity at the Margins,* p. 173.

38 Eric Haralson, "The Elusive Queerness of Henry James's 'Queer Comrade': Reading Gabriel Nash of *The Tragic Muse,*" in *Victorian Sexual Dissidence,* ed. Richard Dellamora (Chicago: University of Chicago Press, forthcoming). Oscar Cargill first observed in "Mr. James's Aesthetic Mr. Nash," *Nineteenth-Century Fiction* 13, no. 3 (December 1957): pp. 177–87, that Nash is based on Oscar Wilde. Dorothea Krook, *Ordeal of Consciousness,* pp. 83–84 n, takes account of Cargill's comparison but adds to it what we know of James's criticism of Oscar Wilde, arguing that Nash is "not merely a destructive critique of the current aestheticism but . . . an imaginative rendering of the ideal possibility (with all its limitations) of the phenomenon."

39 Richard Ellmann, *Oscar Wilde* (New York: Random House, 1984), pp. 117, 178–79.

40 Kaplan, *Imagination of Genius,* pp. 333–34.

41 Eric Haralson, "'Thinking about Homosex' in Forster and James," in *Queer Forster,* ed. Robert K. Martin and George Piggford (Chicago: University of Chicago Press, 1997), p. 60.

42 This "truth" of "fiction" is characteristic of aestheticist iconoclasm in this period, as Wilde's "The Decay of Lying" (1889) and Friedrich Nietzsche's "Truth and Falsity in the Ultramoral Sense" (1873) both indicate. See both works in *Critical Theory since Plato,* ed. Hazard Adams, rev. ed. (New York: Harcourt Brace Jovanovich, 1992), pp. 658–70 and 634–39, respectively.

43 The 1890 first edition reads: "I like him, therefore, because in intercourse with him you know what you've got hold of."

44 Blair, *Race and Nation,* p. 154, argues that "the novel must make Gabriel Nash disappear . . . because his unstable alterity contests James's version of racial theater." Blair's point is that Nash is a surrogate of James's authorial voice, which James must reclaim once Nash has done his work of ironizing "genteel cultural politics" (155).

45 Ibid., p. 157.

46 Christopher Lane, "The Impossibility of Seduction of James's *Roderick Hudson* and *The Tragic Muse,*" *American Literature* 68, no. 4 (December 1996): p. 755.

47 I agree with Terry Castle, *The Apparitional Lesbian,* p. 15, that the term "lesbian" should be used in "the 'ordinary' or 'dictionary' or 'vernacular' sense (a lesbian . . . is a woman 'characterized by a tendency to direct sexual desire toward another of the same sex')." Nevertheless, there is considerable flexibility in the application of

this definition to Victorian relations between women. In such a deeply repressive culture, how are the borders among "companions," "romantic friends," and "Boston marriages," for example, to be drawn?

4 Textual Preference: James's Literary Defenses against Sexuality in "The Middle Years" and "The Death of the Lion"

1 Eve Kosofsky Sedgwick, "The Beast in the Closet: James and the Writing of Homosexual Panic," first appeared in *Sex, Politics, and Science in the Nineteenth-Century Novel,* ed. Ruth Bernard Yeazell, Selected Papers from the English Institute, 1983–1984, n.s., no. 10 (Baltimore, Md.: Johns Hopkins University Press, 1986). It is reprinted in Sedgwick's *Epistemology of the Closet*, pp. 182–212.

2 For the biographical account, see Fred Kaplan, *Henry James: The Imagination of Genius* (New York: William Morrow, 1992), esp. chap. 12, "Passionate Friendships: 1894–1900," pp. 386–429. Michael A. Cooper, "Discipl(in)ing the Master, Mastering the Discipl(in)e in James' Tales of Literary Life," in *Engendering Men: The Question of Male Feminist Criticism,* ed. Joseph A. Boone and Michael Cadden (New York: Routledge, 1990), p. 68, points out how James manipulated this myth of the "master" in his personal male friendships, especially those in the 1890s noted for the eroticism of James's letters: "But however much he describes himself as submitting to the initiated, he always retains the titular power in these erotonomies."

3 An interesting history of twentieth-century literary criticism might be organized around the erotics of the rhetoric employed to represent literary creativity. A certain repugnance for the material, physical, and biological pervades discourses from very different schools. The New Critics' contempt for the body and their celebration of "poetic" ecstasies in the rhetoric of Christian "passion" (literature as communion, for example) constitute one example. Another is the deconstructionists' revulsion before the physical, ranging from Derrida's early borrowing of Rousseau's romantic figuration of poetic expression as onanistic in *Of Grammatology* to later figurations of disseminative excess as regurgitation in "White Mythology" and *Disseminations* and Derrida's recent meditations on the philosophemes of friendship and internalization by way of the rhetoric of cannibalism in his lectures at the University of California–Irvine.

4 See, for example, Nancy Hartsock, *Money, Sex, and Power: Toward a Feminist Historical Materialism* (New York: Longman, 1983); Judith Newton, Mary Ryan, and Judith Walkowitz, eds., *Sex and Class in Women's History* (London: Routledge and Kegan Paul, 1983); Joan Scott, *Gender and the Politics of History* (New York: Columbia University Press, 1988); Louise A. Tilly and Joan W. Scott, *Women, Work, and Family* (New York: Routledge, 1987).

5 Richard Dellamora, *Masculine Desire: The Sexual Politics of Victorian Aestheticism* (Chapel Hill: University of North Carolina Press, 1990), p. 9.

6 The problem is exemplified by the debate surrounding Luce Irigaray's use of the

term "hommosexuality" (which Irigaray uses in many variations) to refer to the homosociality that has defined women as secondary in patriarchal Western societies. Dellamora, *Masculine Desire*, p. 223, notes that "gay critics like Craig Owens and Simon Watney have noted the homophobia, albeit inadvertent, of Irigaray's term, which, in constituting the male sex as 'fundamentally homosexual,' erases the distinctions that gay men live. Nonetheless, the challenge that her stance poses to gay men, namely that they articulate their difference, is one that they continually remeet." My point is that this difference within the term "homosexuality"—homosociality and male same-sex desire—must also include that of female same-sex desire, and all three terms must be understood in terms of their relative historical determinations of each other.

7 Sedgwick, *Epistemology of the Closet*, p. 36.

8 Ibid., p. 37.

9 There are, of course, important exceptions, including Lillian Faderman's *Surpassing the Love of Men: Romantic Friendship and Love between Women from the Renaissance to the Present* (New York: William Morrow, 1981), pp. 190–96, which considers James to be sympathetic to the "Boston marriage" of Olive and Verena, and Terry Castle's *The Apparitional Lesbian*, pp. 150–85, which interprets Olive Chancellor in *The Bostonians* as a "tragic lesbian" heroine, thereby countering generations of critics who have treated her as perverse in her own rights or indicative of James's profound homophobia.

10 Castle, *Apparitional Lesbian*, pp. 150–51, offers a good historical summary of the critical treatment of lesbianism in *The Bostonians* by traditional scholars such as Oscar Cargill, Walter Wright, Lionel Trilling, F. W. Dupee, William McMurray, Irving Howe, and Edmund Wilson. As Castle points out, Judith Fetterley's more recent feminist reading of the novel in *The Resisting Reader: A Feminist Approach to American Fiction* (Bloomington: Indiana University Press, 1978), pp. 101–53, avoids discussing Olive Chancellor's sexual preference. The same is true of Alfred Habegger's analysis in *Henry James and the "Woman Business"* of how James incorporated his father's antifeminist views into the novel. Without commenting on Olive's possible lesbianism, Habegger refers merely to Olive as "a brilliant creation . . . an extraordinary study in pathology" (p. 218).

11 Wendy Graham, "Henry James's Subterranean Blues: A Rereading of *The Princess Casamassima*," *Modern Fiction Studies* 40, vol. 1 (spring 1994): pp. 35–68.

12 Kaplan, *Imagination of Genius*, pp. 401–2.

13 Leon Edel and Lyall H. Powers, eds., *The Complete Notebooks of Henry James* (New York: Oxford University Press, 1987), p. 87 n. 2. This footnote occurs in reference to James's long entry for February 3, 1894, describing his idea for "The Death of the Lion" (pp. 86–87).

14 Silverman, *Male Subjectivity at the Margins*, p. 179.

15 Ibid.

16 Henry James, "The Middle Years," the New York Edition, vol. 16, p. 86; hereafter cited in the text as "Middle."

17 Sedgwick, *Epistemology of the Closet,* p. 208 n. 33.

18 For an excellent study of the gender and sexual implications of symbolist poetics and its imagery, see Bram Dijkstra, *Idols of Perversity: Fantasies of Feminine Evil in Fin-de-Siècle Culture* (New York: Oxford University Press, 1986).

19 Carroll Smith-Rosenberg, *Disorderly Conduct: Visions of Gender in Victorian America* (New York: Alfred Knopf, 1985), pp. 271–72. See also Faderman, *Surpassing the Love of Men,* pp. 241–53, for a good discussion of Krafft-Ebing and Havelock Ellis's pathologizing of lesbianism: "Both writers cast love between women in a morbid light and associated it with behavior which had nothing to do with same-sex love but did have a great deal to do with the insanity of some of the patients they examined" (241).

20 Sander L. Gilman, *Difference and Pathology: Stereotypes of Sexuality, Race, and Madness* (Ithaca, N.Y.: Cornell University Press, 1985), p. 89, gives several examples, including: "H. Hildebrandt links [Hottentot genitalia] with the overdevelopment of the clitoris, which he sees as leading to those 'excesses' which are called 'lesbian love.' The concupiscence of the black is thus associated with the sexuality of the lesbian." Martha Vicinus, " 'They Wonder to Which Sex I Belong': The Historical Roots of Modern Lesbian Identity," in *The Lesbian and Gay Studies Reader,* ed. Henry Abelove, Michèle Aina Barale, and David M. Halperin (New York: Routledge, 1993), p. 443. The confusion of lesbianism and prostitution as aspects of a related sexual "deviance" persisted well into the twentieth century, as Vern Bullough and Bonnie Bullough, *Women and Prostitution: A Social History* (Buffalo, N.Y.: Prometheus Books, 1987), p. 306, point out in their survey of psychoanalytical attitudes toward prostitution and lesbianism in the 1950s.

21 James, *The Complete Notebooks,* p. 86.

22 "The Death of the Lion," the New York Edition, vol. 15, p. 99; hereafter cited in the text as "Lion."

23 This curious combination of youth and age in the narrator is characteristic also of Doctor Hugh, who is closer to Dencombe's age than he thinks. Clearly, James wanted the proximity in age to cover any suggestion of "man-boy" love often cited in Victorian culture as the reason for legally regulating homosexuality. Although James frequently pits aesthetic seriousness against superficial journalism, in "The Middle Years" and "The Death of the Lion," he seems to recognize that art's celebration of "genius" is often difficult to distinguish from the press's trade in "celebrities." On this topic, see Richard Salmon, *Henry James and the Culture of Publicity,* pp. 107–15.

24 Passages such as the following are typical: "He hadn't told me he was ill again— that he had had a warning; but I hadn't needed this, for I found his reticence his worst symptom" ("Lion," 137).

25 Cooper, *Discipl(in)ing the Master,* pp. 69–70, reads sexual and textual relations in the tales of artists as following the structure of René Girard's "triangular desire," which in the case of these plots by James "generally figures women, however

triumphant, in negative terms. . . . Only the young male disciple strives to protect the enfeebled and misunderstood author from . . . the threat of objectification by predatory women" (70).

26 In *The Complete Notebooks,* p. 87, James writes: "Shouldn't it, the little drama, take, in part, the form of this narrator's defending, attempting to defend—and attempting vainly—his precious friend against this invasion of the interviews, the portraitists and such; to defend him in particular against the appropriation of some arch and ferocious lion-huntress?"

27 James, *The Complete Notebooks,* p. 77. The notebook entry is dated August 26, 1893, antedating his notes for "The Death of the Lion" in February 1894 (pp. 86–87).

28 Cooper, *Discipl(in)ing the Master,* p. 79.

29 Ibid., p. 69. "The tales of the literary life all center on the conceit of the author's having two incarnations, one physical and one textual, each separately capable of being known, interacted with, and mistreated."

30 Joseph Bristow, *Effeminate England: Homoerotic Writing after 1885,* p. 128. James certainly had Symonds in mind in his "The Author of Beltraffio" (1884), and there are traces of Symonds, at least as James interpreted him, in the four male characters in "The Middle Years" and "The Death of the Lion."

5 The Portrait of a Small Boy as a Young Girl: Gender Trouble in *What Maisie Knew*

1 The Jamesian aura that so strikingly haunts high moderns such as Pound, Eliot, and Stevens—both in their critical discussions of, and frequent allusions to, James—is also one of the guiding spirits of the Anglo-American New Criticism that would perversely rename this antimodernism as *modernism.* For a fuller discussion of this paradox of high modernism, see my "Modern Art and the Invention of Postmodern Capital," in *Modernist Culture in America,* ed. Daniel Joseph Singal (Belmont, Calif.: Wadsworth Publishing, 1991), pp. 203–28.

2 *The Complete Notebooks of Henry James,* p. 117.

3 Ibid., p. 119. Alfred Habegger, *Henry James and the "Woman Business,"* pp. 6–7, notes that James had made a similar mistake about the source of antifeminist sentiments when in "1868 he ridiculed a sensational attack on modern women," *Modern Women.* Habegger points out in his note (239 n. 4) that "HJ believed the papers composing *Modern Women* were written by 'three or four sapient connoisseurs,' . . . presumably male. In fact, the author was Eliza Lynn Linton, a journalist." Of course, in this 1868 context, James criticizes the antifeminist sentiments, giving credibility to Habegger's general thesis that James was inconsistent throughout his career with respect to the women's movement, women authors, and the New Woman in general. I am grateful to Alfred Habegger for pointing out the analogy between James's comments on Brada and on *Modern Women.*

4 Ibid., p. 120.

5 *What Maisie Knew,* the New York Edition, vol. 11, p. 8; hereafter cited in the text as *M.*

6 Juliet Mitchell, "*What Maisie Knew:* Portrait of the Artist as a Young Girl," in *The Air of Reality: New Essays on Henry James,* ed. John Goode (London: Methuen, 1972), pp. 187–88, argues in favor of Mrs. Wix not only as an object of the reader's sympathy but also as representative of James's viewpoint. Marjorie Kaufman, "Beside Maisie on That Bench in Boulogne," *Henry James Review* 15, no. 3 (fall 1994): p. 263, concludes that Maisie's "genuine place is beside Mrs. Wix; she can care for that really awful, ugly, limited, convention-bound creature—the only *mother* Maisie . . . has ever known."

7 *The Complete Notebooks,* pp. 151, 166.

8 James deliberately renders Maisie's age ambiguous but gives hints and clues that make proper chronology possible. Her age in chapter 1 is specified by the narrator as six, and her custody is legally divided by her parents at six-month intervals (*M,* 11). James teases the reader by confusing these six-month visits, sometimes extending her stay with one parent (as when she stays longer with her father so that her mother can extend her tour on the Continent). Such play with actual dating follows the pattern in the manner of other works, notably *The Aspern Papers* and *The Turn of the Screw,* in which the reader's reconstruction of history is crucial to the moral meaning of the novel. By my own calculations of specific references to the passage of time, I can only make Maisie *eleven* or *twelve* by the end of the novel, but I tend to agree with Barbara Everett, "Henry James's Children," in *Children and Their Books: A Celebration of the Work of Iona and Peter Opie,* ed. Gillian Avery and Julia Briggs (Oxford: Oxford University Press, 1989), p. 318, that on the evidence of "the child's progression to emotional puberty," she is "at the novel's end" "nearer to fourteen or fifteen than to Edel's 'seven or eight, or perhaps a bit older.'"

9 James's extended notebook entries for *The Spoils of Poynton,* then entitled variously *The House Beautiful* or *The Old Things,* begin around May 1895 and continue until March 30, 1896, overlapping with his substantial notebook entries for *What Maisie Knew,* which extend from December 22, 1895, to December 21, 1896. See *The Complete Notebooks of Henry James,* pp. 121–22, 131–36, 147–51, 155–67.

10 Carren Kaston, *Imagination and Desire in the Novels of Henry James* (New Brunswick, N.J.: Rutgers University Press, 1984), was one of the first feminist critics to recognize this range of love in James's fiction, thus granting Mrs. Gereth due credit for the care she shows Fleda at the end of the novel: "And despite her incomprehension of Fleda's nature and motives for betraying her, she keeps Fleda with her and cannot help but care for her, even if waspishly" (p. 79).

11 Habegger, *Henry James and the "Woman Business,"* p. 39.

12 Harris W. Wilson, "What *Did* Maisie Know?" *College English* 17 (1955–1956): p. 281, argues for Maisie's incestuous sexual desires for Sir Claude, and Edward Wasiolek, "Maisie: Pure or Corrupt?" *College English* 22 (1960–1961): pp. 167–72, considers Maisie's relationship with Sir Claude to be increasingly sexual.

13 Many of the names in the novel either follow this pattern of the homophone or are literal tags, usually with the purpose of satirizing certain traits of the characters, as in the tag names used by Dickens and Trollope. Among the more obvious of these names used by James: Mr. Perriam (Pear I am; he is described as fat), one of Ida's suitors; Mr. Tischbein (German for "table leg" or necessary, phallic support), another of Ida's suitors; Miss Overmore (exceeding her class or social position), Mrs. Beale's maiden name; Mrs. Wix (wicks, as in candlewicks, indicating either older times, when candles were the principal means of illumination, or her "burned-out" condition, as in a wick that has burned out).

14 The narrator refers to Sir Claude as a "poor plastic and dependent male" and "brought back . . . in bondage" to Mrs. Beale; Mrs. Wix describes him as a "poor sunk slave. . . . to his passions"; Sir Claude even refers to himself as "a poor devil" (*M*, 263, 328, 313, 319).

15 Merla Wolk, "Narration and Nurture in *What Maisie Knew*," *Henry James Review* 4, no. 3 (spring 1983): p. 199, and Juliet Mitchell, "Artist as a Young Girl," p. 181.

16 Scott Derrick, "A Small Boy and the Ease of Others: The Structure of Masculinity and the Autobiography of Henry James," *Arizona Quarterly* 45, no. 4 (winter 1989): pp. 51–52, interprets James as an excellent example of the Victorian male in whom homoerotic desires are confused and thus conflict with the "homosexual panic" basic to homosocial norms for Victorian masculinity.

17 I discuss at greater length James's critique of primogeniture in English society and its legal and economic consequences in chapter 4 of *The Theoretical Dimensions of Henry James* (Madison: University of Wisconsin Press, 1984), pp. 132–37.

18 In their tours, Maisie and Mrs. Wix "looked down on the little new town which seemed to them quite as old, and across at the great dome and the high gilt Virgin of the church that, as they gathered, was famous. . . . They wandered in this temple afterwards and Mrs. Wix confessed that for herself she had probably made a fatal mistake early in life in not being a Catholic. Her confession in its turn caused Maisie to wonder rather interestedly what degree of lateness it was that shut the door against an escape from such an error" (*M*, 267).

19 See Mitchell, "Artist as a Young Girl," pp. 185–86, and Wolk, "Narration and Nurture," p. 199.

20 I think it is more likely that James is merely borrowing religious symbolism and rejecting specific religious orthodoxies, as he would do in early novels such as *The American* (see chapter 2 of this volume), and the novels and tales of the Major Phase, especially *The Wings of the Dove, The Golden Bowl,* and "The Altar of the Dead." Mrs. Wix's nostalgia for the stability of Catholic moral categories is countered by Mrs. Beale's recollection of her early travels—"at eighteen"—with a "distinguished Dutch family," her stay "on Lake Geneva," and a consequent knowledge of French culture from the perspective of Huguenot history—presumably, a history of victimization (*M*, 304). As he does in *The American,* James seems to argue in *What Maisie Knew* that the customary moral solecisms of either

Catholicism or Protestantism are inadequate to address the complex ethical problems of the modern age.

21 The gold Virgin of Boulogne is associated both with the golden dome of the
church and with the "whiteness" of its stone, both colors representing the glory
and purity of the Virgin Mary. The motifs of gold and white are ironically
repeated in the little salon that Sir Claude provides for Mrs. Wix and Maisie in
the hotel, ostensibly as a place for all three of them to meet privately and yet
respectably. It is this "white and gold" salon where Mrs. Beale will suddenly
appear and then usurp as her own space. The original association of the salon
with Sir Claude's kindness and the Virgin's grace is not intended, I think, to be
ironic. Traditional studies of the use of "color imagery" in this novel such as
James Lowe's "Color in *What Maisie Knew*," *Henry James Review* 9, no. 3 (fall
1988): pp. 188–98, miss not only this sort of subtlety but the much more important uses of racially marked colors such as brown, black, red, and white, which I
discuss later in this chapter.

22 Wolk, "Narration and Nurture," p. 199, also argues that Sir Claude serves as a
surrogate mother to Maisie: "The best mothering . . . Maisie receives from her
parent figures is from Sir Claude."

23 Some critics such as Randall Craig, " 'Read[ing] the Unspoken in the Spoken':
Interpreting *What Maisie Knew*," *Henry James Review* 2, no. 3 (spring 1981):
p. 207, think Maisie understands French, but he is tricked by James's attribution
to Maisie of a certain "knowledge" of French culture in her first, enthusiastic
response to Boulogne at the opening of chapter 22. There she lords it over the
poor Cockney maid, Susan Ash, and the narrator supports her knowledge: "She
recognised, she understood, she adored and took possession," but the narrator's
hint that "the place and the people were all a picture together" suggests that
Maisie's knowledge may be limited to the tourist's sensory impressions (*M*, 232).
By the end of chapter 29, when Sir Claude orders breakfast for Mrs. Wix, the
narrator notes how it was "a charm to hear his easy brilliant French; even [Mai-
sie's] ignorance could measure the perfection of it" (*M*, 322). James's intention
seems to be deliberately to confuse the reader, so that Maisie's "maturity," as
measured by her knowledge of French culture and language, fluctuates with the
context and the company. In strictly factual terms, it is very unlikely that Maisie
has learned any useful French beyond a few phrases in the scattered education she
has received from Mrs. Wix, Mrs. Beale, Sir Claude, and a host of other teachers.

24 Julie Rivkin, *False Positions: The Representational Logic of Henry James's Fiction*
(Stanford, Calif.: Stanford University Press, 1996), p. 158, also reads the novel as
addressing explicitly the incest taboo of the modern Euramerican family to raise
questions about the family's legitimacy as a social structure: "Maisie's desire to go
with Sir Claude . . . also removes the prospects of familial propriety forever. . . .
She meets his offer of an adulterous family with an offer of an incestuous one."

25 Ibid., pp. 159–60.

26 Wolk, "Narration and Nurture," p. 204.

27 Mitchell, "Artist as a Young Girl," p. 177.

28 Wolk, "Narration and Nurture," pp. 204–5 n. 3.

29 Alfred Habegger, *The Father: A Life of Henry James, Sr.* (New York: Farrar, Straus and Giroux, 1994), pp. 392–93, provides the most accurate chronology of the family's travels in these months of 1857 to 1858.

30 Kaplan, *Imagination of Genius*, p. 31; Habegger, *The Father*, p. 393.

31 Leon Edel, *Henry James: The Untried Years, 1843–1870* (London: Rupert Hart-Davis, 1953), p. 136.

32 James, *A Small Boy and Others* (New York: Charles Scribner's Sons, 1913), p. 419; hereafter cited in the text as *SBO*.

33 For interesting comparisons of Henry James's traumatic experiences with the nervous breakdowns of his brother, William, and father, Henry Sr., see Howard Feinstein, *Becoming William James* (Ithaca, N.Y.: Cornell University Press, 1984), pp. 182–205. Habegger, *Henry James and the "Woman Business,"* pp. 40–41, reads Henry James Sr.'s "breakdown in Windsor, England, in 1844" in terms of his "shame" regarding his psychological "combination of . . . carnality with a kind of wild ego."

34 Carol Holly, *Intensely Family: The Inheritance of Family Shame and the Autobiographies of Henry James* (Madison: University of Wisconsin Press, 1995), pp. 103–4, argues that *A Small Boy and Others* encrypts "something shameful" that is "connected . . . with the history of his family, . . . something . . . too amorphous and deeply buried to be named" that Holly associates primarily with "James's anxious memories about his father."

35 Kaufman, "Beside Maisie," pp. 260–61, also compares Maisie's and James's experiences in Boulogne but concludes that James's self-discovery is in sharp contrast with Maisie's disillusionment.

36 Kaplan, *Imagination of Genius*, p. 31.

37 Holly, *Intensely Family*, pp. 103–4.

38 Scott Derrick, "Structure of Masculinity," p. 51, reads the Galerie d'Apollon episode (quoted as the epigraph to this book) as a "homoerotic" dream that "works to contain" such desires: "Rather than allow a consummation of erotic desire, the dream displaces it through the homosociality of a kind of sporting competition . . . in which James put his opponent to flight."

39 For an early version of James's admiration for Thackeray, yet his clear intention to supersede Thackeray's importance as a Victorian novelist, see his review, "Thackerayana," *The Nation*, 9 December 1875, collected in Henry James, *Literary Reviews and Essays on American, English, and French Literature*, ed. Albert Mordell (New York: Grove Press, 1979), pp. 333–36. James would later write an extended reflection on Thackeray's unfinished *Denis Duval* in "Winchelsea, Rye, and 'Denis Duval,'" first published in *Scribner's Magazine* 25 (January 1901), then reprinted in *English Hours* (London: William Heinemann, 1905), pp. 275–301. In this latter essay, James makes much of Winchelsea and Rye as border regions, where refugees, like "Huguenot fugitives too firm in their faith to have bent their

necks to the dire rigours with which the revocation of the Edict of Nantes was followed up," fled and left the "colour" of their foreign names and cultures (p. 278). Again, James appears to identify with the literary Denis Duval, especially as he typifies a certain foreignness, and James's impressions of Thackeray's unfinished novel and its associations with James's own adopted region of Sussex suggest James's vague appropriation of the "foreignness" that strikes him in his classmate Napier.

40 Habegger, *The Father*, p. 394.

41 Pierre A. Walker, "From France in James to James in France," paper delivered at the Henry James Society panel on "Internationalizing Henry James," Modern Language Association Convention (1996), p. 2. I am grateful to Pierre for sharing with me his current research on the original for James's tutor. As Pierre points out in a letter to me, his postulation of a connection between James's "Ansiot" and the Lycée teacher, Napoléon Ansieaux, remains as of this writing a speculation, but it strikes me as a very good and informed scholarly guess.

42 Ibid.

43 Ibid., p. 5.

44 Such is my treatment of James's response to his biographical father and literary fathers in chapter 1, as well as in my fuller account of the psychopoetics of Hawthorne's and Trollope's influence on James in *The Theoretical Dimensions of Henry James*, pp. 29–83.

45 Novick, *Henry James: The Young Master*, p. 58, stresses the "sinister note in Harry's remembrance of M. Ansiot," as well as the repulsiveness of his "immensely fat," "unwashed person" "from another, older time."

46 Derrick, "Structure of Masculinity," pp. 51–52, observes that "James's general suppression of his homoeroticism was probably a powerful cause of his persistent unease in relation to other men. . . . An impermissible 'vulgarity' would have to be projected outward, and other men would have to be critically scrutinized and distanced, even as such criticism simultaneously serves as a kind of mediated contact." Derrick's general analysis of James's psychology applies quite well to James's "vulgarization" of M. Ansiot both in these passages from his autobiography and in James's youthful reaction to the tutor, described by Alfred Habegger in *The Father: A Life of Henry James, Sr.*, p. 394, as a "pathetic old man . . . who smelled so strong the boy wanted to open the windows after their sessions together." If Walker is right that Napoléon Ansieaux was the historical model for James's "M. Ansiot," then his sense of the tutor's shabbiness might also have been tangled up with the fact the Ansieaux "at one time was supporting an invalid wife" and may thus have typified an intellectual and *sexual* desiccation that the younger James feared he might repeat in his own life (Walker, "France in James," p. 3).

47 Walker, "France in James," p. 7, makes the point that Saint-Beuve was a native of Boulogne. Sara B. Daughtery, *The Literary Criticism of Henry James* (Columbus: Ohio University Press, 1981), p. 124, notes how James changed his mind about

Saint-Beuve, a critic James had criticized in his early writings but whom he had in his "Saint-Beuve" in the *North American Review* essay (January 1880) "come to regard as a defender of 'liberty of appreciation' in 'a society that swarmed with camps and coteries.'"

48 Eve Kosofsky Sedgwick, "Shame and Performativity: Henry James's New York Edition Prefaces," in *Henry James's New York Edition: The Construction of Authorship,* ed. David McWhirter (Stanford, Calif.: Stanford University Press, 1995), p. 229.

49 John R. Bradley, "Henry James's Permanent Adolescence," *Essays in Criticism* 47:4 (October 1997), 287–314, gives a fine account of the entanglement of James's nostalgia for his adolescence, his conflicted homoerotic desires, and his avoidance and deferral of heterosexual relations in his autobiographies and fiction. There is, however, some danger, which Bradley generally avoids, in equating homoerotic, adolescent, and gay sexualities. Gay sexuality is not, for example, a "reversion" to adolescent homoerosis nor are homoerotic desires exclusively expressions of gay sexuality.

50 When Maisie is given far too much money by the American Countess for her cab ride home to her father and Mrs. Beale's house, Susan Ash appropriates some of the extra money, only to be "scolded" by Mrs. Beale, who insists that the excess must be returned to Beale's new lover. Susan Ash makes it clear that she doesn't believe Mrs. Beale and suspects her of pocketing the loose change (*M,* 198–200). When the servants accuse the employers of being thieves, the customary hierarchies of master and servant have certainly been overturned.

51 The "City" capitalized usually means London's financial district, where Mr. Perriam will later be "smashed" and "exposed," presumably for fraudulent speculations, as Sir Claude explains Perriam's fate to Maisie (*M,* 141).

52 Toni Morrison, *Playing in the Dark: Whiteness and the Literary Imagination* (New York: Random House, 1992), p. 13. See also my discussion of Morrison's challenge to James scholars in the conclusion to this volume.

53 Maxwell Geismar, *Henry James and the Jacobites,* p. 154.

54 Warren, Blair, and Michaels are discussed and cited elsewhere in this book. Beverly Haviland, *Henry James's Last Romance: Making Sense of the Past and the American Scene* (New York: Cambridge University Press, 1997).

55 Kenneth Warren, *Black and White Strangers: Race and American Literary Realism* (Chicago: University of Chicago Press, 1993), p. 41. For example: "By the late 1890s laws mandating segregation in public places were widely seen as reasonable measures to promote public morals, and the attitudes expressed by James and some of his characters were in accord."

56 Walter Benn Michaels, "Jim Crow Henry James?" *Henry James Review* 16, no. 3 (fall 1995): p. 289.

57 Ibid.

58 As Michaels points out, in Jim Crow America ethnic and religious minorities "are all made white by not being black" (289), but as I argue out in chapter 3,

Englishmen such as Peter Sherringham construct "peoples of color" precisely for the purpose of defining themselves as English. Both modes are obviously racist; each works differently in its specific ideological context.

59 I am indebted to Alfred Habegger, who commented extensively on an earlier draft of this chapter, for the observation that "brown all over" suggests "scantily clad" as an "eroticized use of race" in James's description of "the Flowers of the Forest."

60 The "good lady . . . distantly related to Mrs. Farange" who offers to take Maisie into her home, where she has "children and nurseries wound up and going," calls Maisie "Poor little monkey!" when she learns that Ida will not give her up but instead use her as a bargaining chip in her ongoing fights with her ex-husband: "The words were an epitaph for the tomb of Maisie's childhood" (*M*, 5).

61 As Alfred Habegger suggests to me in his comments on a draft of this chapter, it's possible that James is condensing in his memories the vague East Indian aura of such Thackeray triple-decker novels as *The Newcomes* (1855), a relatively recent novel in the winter of 1857 to 1858, whose lovable Colonel Newcome served in India. Thackeray is one of the younger James's models of the successful novelist, and Thackeray was born in India, where his father was a merchant. Interesting as is this possible connection of what I might term an "Indian aura" with James's memories of his youthful discovery of a literary vocation in Boulogne, it seems to me far too remote and implicit in James's recollections in *A Small Boy and Others* to have a direct bearing on this curious passage. If any conclusion can be drawn, it must be a speculation about how James aspires, like Thackeray, to succeed as a novelist in such a thoroughly "English" manner that he will transcend his background: James's America, Thackeray's India, both of which may carry the unconscious elements of young Napier's racialized identity and social marginality.

62 Henry Dundas Napier, *Field Marshal Lord Napier of Magdala, G. C. B., G. C. S. I., a Memoir by His Son, Lieutenant-Colonel Honorable H. D. Napier* (London: E. Arnold and Co., 1927). This son does not qualify as Henry James's schoolmate in Boulogne, because Henry Dundas Napier was born in 1864, but twin sons were born to Lord Napier's first wife, Annie, in 1845, who died in childbirth (a third son) in December of 1849 (pp. 66–67). Lord Napier then married Mary Scott, daughter of Major-General Edward Scott, on April 2, 1861, mother of Henry Dundas Napier (p. 159). Among the Europeans held by Emperor Theodore during four years of unsuccessful negotiations with the British was the British Consul, Captain Charles Duncan Cameron. Gordon tried to volunteer for Napier's Abyssinian campaign, but he was turned down on the grounds that the force was being assembled exclusively from Indian units. See John H. Waller, *Gordon of Khartoum: The Saga of a Victorian Hero* (New York: Atheneum, 1988), pp. 125–27.

63 The celebrated Henry Morton Stanley (1841–1904) helped shape such Victorian myths of his own exploits in Africa and his advertisements for himself and other adventurers, including in this case *Coomassie and Magdala: The Story of Two British Campaigns in Africa,* 2d ed. (London: Sampson Low, Marston, Low & Searle, 1874). As a journalist for the *New York Herald*, Stanley accompanied the

Anglo-Indian force Napier assembled to march on Magdala. Stanley concludes that Napier executed a military campaign "to be numbered . . . among the most wonderfully successful . . . ever conducted in history" (p. 505). Lytton Strachey famously satirizes this sort of Victorian hero worship in his closing portrait in *Eminent Victorians* (1918), The Illustrated Edition (New York: Weidenfeld and Nicholson, 1988), "The End of General Gordon," pp. 135–92, which is also Strachey's way of bidding farewell to the Victorian era.

64 The Countess in "The Middle Years," discussed in chapter 4, is not American, of course, but "an Englishwoman by birth" and "the widow of a French nobleman" ("The Middle Years," p. 88). There are, however, a number of interesting similarities between this Countess and the American Countess. The former, for example, is "the daughter of a celebrated baritone, whose taste *minus* his talent she had inherited," thus anticipating the apparent meretriciousness of the American Countess. James also uses the foreign title and "mixed" nationalities of the Countess in "The Middle Years" to suggest something dangerous and sinister about her, including hints of her lesbianism and dislike of men.

65 Gambling was outlawed at Spa in 1902, but it seems clear that James uses Spa to suggest someplace where Beale Farange's immorality may become even more explicit. And "gambling" either with Maisie's money or with her future is Beale Farange's worst vice in the novel.

66 Shreve is, of course, merely articulating the racist unconscious of southern whites in the postbellum South when he taunts Quentin in the final scene of *Absalom, Absalom!* (New York: Random House, 1936), p. 378: "I think that in time the Jim Bonds are going to inherit the western hemisphere. Of course it won't quite be in our time and of course as they spread toward the poles they will bleach out again like the rabbits and the birds do, so they won't show up so sharp against the snow. But it will still be Jim Bond; and so in a few thousand years, I who regard you will also have sprung from the loins of African kings. Now I want you to tell me just one thing more. Why do you hate the South?"

67 Robert Altick, *The Presence of the Present: Topics of the Day in the Victorian Novel* (Columbus: Ohio State University Press, 1991), p. 493.

68 During the Golden Jubilee of 1887, celebrating Victoria's fifty years of rule, a children's exhibition was staged in Hyde Park where thirty thousand London children assembled to greet the queen and receive gifts of "a meat pie, a piece of cake, a bun, and an orange, besides being presented with a Jubilee mug made for the occasion by Doulton," as Jeremy Maas points out in *"This Brilliant Year": Queen Victoria's Jubilee, 1887* (London: Royal Academy of Arts, 1977), p. 13.

69 Asa Briggs, *Victorian Things* (London: B. T. Batsford, 1988), p. 91. Briggs stresses that the ostensible emphasis on "free trade" in these exhibitions, pioneered by the French, was usually a mere pretense for celebrating national and imperial powers.

70 Zeynep Çelik and Leila Kinney, "Ethnography and Exhibitionism at the Expositions Universelles," *Assemblage* (December 1990): p. 35. For another example of how these international expositions shaped cultural values at the turn of the

century, see my "Henry Adams's *Education* in the Age of Imperialism," in *New Essays on "The Education of Henry Adams,"* ed. John Carlos Rowe (New York: Cambridge University Press, 1996), pp. 101, 114.

71 James's description in *The American Scene,* pp. 363–64, of the "Indian braves" he encounters on the steps of the nation's capitol—"braves dispossessed of forest and prairie, but as free of the builded labyrinth as they had ever been of these,"—has been frequently discussed by critics; but none has commented on James's comparison of the Native Americans with "Japanese celebrities"—"circumstances all that quickened their resemblance, on the much bigger scale, to Japanese celebrities"—by which he must be referring to the role of the United States in 1905 in arranging the Portsmouth Treaty ending the Russo-Japanese War. Although nominally signed in Portsmouth, New Hampshire, the full treaty negotiations must have required the presence of high-ranking Japanese politicians in Washington, D.C., at the same time as James's visit to the city. James's comparison of Native Americans and Japanese calls attention to the relationship between internal and external modes of colonialism by the United States. Both Native Americans and Japanese are "specimens, on show, of what the Government can do with people with whom it is supposed able to do nothing" (363–64).

72 Gilman, *Difference and Pathology,* p. 99.

73 Elsewhere in the novel, the "brightness" of Mrs. Beale is contrasted with the "darkness" of the first governess, that "strange lady" discussed earlier in this chapter. The alliteration of "bright brown ladies" creates a near oxymoron even as it effectively refutes the popular opposition of "bright" and "brown."

74 Silverman, *Male Subjectivity at the Margins,* p. 170.

6   Spectral Mechanics: Gender, Sexuality, and Work in *In the Cage*

1 I discuss at greater length the ways postmodern economic and social conditions have shaped poststructuralism in "Structure," in *Critical Terms for Literary Study,* ed. Frank Lentricchia and Thomas McLaughlin, 2d ed. (Chicago: University of Chicago Press, 1995), pp. 23–38, and "Postmodernist Studies," in *Redrawing the Boundaries: The Transformation of English and American Literary Studies,* ed. Stephen Greenblatt and Giles Gunn (New York: Modern Language Association of America, 1992), pp. 179–208.

2 Henry James, *In the Cage,* the New York Edition, vol. 11, p. 423; hereafter cited in the text as *Cage.*

3 Jeffrey Kieve, *The Electric Telegraph: A Social and Economic History* (London: Newton Abbot, David and Charles, 1973), p. 44.

4 Fred Kaplan, *Henry James: The Imagination of Genius,* p. 423.

5 Theodora Bosanquet, *Henry James at Work* (London: Hogarth Press, 1924), p. 248.

6 Ibid.

7 Kaplan, *Imagination of Genius,* pp. 423–24.

8 Mark Seltzer, *Bodies and Machines* (New York: Routledge, 1992), p. 195.

9 Bosanquet, *Henry James at Work,* p. 247.

10 In referring to *The Turn of the Screw* throughout this chapter, I have in mind my own interpretation of the legal implications of the narrative in *The Theoretical Dimensions of Henry James* (Madison: University of Wisconsin Press, 1984), pp. 119–46.

11 The telegraphic sounder inspires imaginative associations for the telegraphist, as if James wants to evoke ironically the traditionally constitutive powers of literary writing. Thinking of Captain Everard, for example, the telegraphist imagines: "She could almost hear him, through the tick of the sounder, scatter with his stick, in his impatience, the fallen leaves of October" (*Cage,* 463).

12 The technique is typical of the high modernists. Extravagant metaphorization of otherwise functional technology, such as Hart Crane's representation of airplanes as "easters of speeding light" in *The Bridge,* were typical of several movements of modernism, especially symbolism and futurism.

13 Ralf Norrman, "The Intercepted Telegraph Plot in Henry James' *In the Cage,*" *Notes and Queries* 24 (October 1977): n.s., p. 425–27, and Janet Gabler-Hover in "The Ethics of Determinism in Henry James's *In the Cage,*" *The Henry James Review* 13, no. 3 (fall 1992): pp. 253–75.

14 N. Katherine Hayles, "The Paratactic Style of Postmodern Culture," *American Literary History* 2, no. 3 (fall 1990): p. 398: "Parataxis does not necessarily mean that there is no relation between the terms put into juxtaposition. Rather, the relation, unspecified except for proximity, is polysemous and unstable. Lacking a coordinating structure, it is subject to appropriation, interpretation, and re-inscription into different modalities. This aspect of parataxis makes it into a cultural seismograph, extraordinarily sensitive to rifts, tremors, and realignments in bodies of discourse, as well as in bodies constituted through discourse and cultural practices."

15 Kieve, *Electric Telegraph,* p. 39.

16 Ibid., p. 245.

17 The best application of Foucault to this aspect of Henry James's writings is Mark Seltzer, *Henry James and the Art of Power* (Ithaca, N.Y.: Cornell University Press, 1984).

18 Shawn Rosenheim, *The Cryptographic Imagination: Secret Writing from Edgar Poe to the Internet* (Baltimore, Md.: Johns Hopkins University Press, 1997), p. 88: "Because the telegraph depends on Morse's code for its utility, there exists a natural affinity between telegraphy and cryptography."

19 *In the Cage* is an interesting anticipation of postmodern narratives in many different respects, especially in its subtle insistence on the subordination of nature and the body to the technologies of urban modernity. The determination of people's identities by urban spaces and technologies and the virtual complete containment of any sort of "nature" (physical or human) shapes the prevailing atmosphere of *In the Cage.*

20 Poe's elementary code assigns numbers to the alphabet in order from 1 = a. Poe's deciphering tool yields these letters, "G-I-D-I-F-A" from James's code, which is of little help. Morse's original plan for his telegraphic code was to assign numbers to words, substituting later a system of numbers for letters, and finally evolving into the dot-and-dash code assigned to letters that is the present Morse Code. See *Samuel F. B. Morse: His Letters and Journals,* ed. Edward Lind Morse, vol. 2 (Boston: Houghton Mifflin, 1914), pp. 7–12, 62–68, and Carleton Mabee, *The American Leonardo: A Life of Samuel F. B. Morse* (New York: Octagon Books, 1969), pp. 151–54.

21 The field of cryptography was complex and included many different kinds of codes by the end of the nineteenth century. If James is using an actual code, he could have selected from a long list of different genres, from simple cipher codes to "dictionary codes" and the like. For a good account of the varieties available, see Alexander d'Agapeyeff, *Codes and Ciphers* (London: Oxford University Press, 1939).

22 The word "poison" appears with some frequency in *In the Cage,* even though it is not used in the specific context of murdering someone else.

23 See Gabler-Hover, *Ethics of Determinism,* pp. 265–66, for a good discussion of *In the Cage* as one of James's ghost stories.

24 Seltzer, *Bodies and Machines,* p. 197.

25 Paul J. Staiti, *Samuel F. B. Morse* (Cambridge: Cambridge University Press, 1989), pp. 225–26.

26 Rosenheim, *Cryptographic Imagination,* p. 95.

27 Norrman, "Telegraph Plot," p. 426.

28 Ibid.

29 Kieve, *Electric Telegraph,* pp. 243–44.

30 Ibid., p. 85.

31 Henry James, *The Turn of the Screw,* the New York Edition, vol. 12, p. 156.

32 Jennifer Wicke, "Henry James's Second Wave," *The Henry James Review* 10, no. 2 (spring 1989): pp. 150–51.

33 Dale Bauer and Andrew Lakritz, "Language, Class, and Sexuality in Henry James's *In the Cage,*" *New Orleans Review* 14 (1987): p. 64.

34 Rosenheim, *Cryptographic Imagination,* p. 91.

35 Norrman, "Telegraph Plot," p. 427, thus concludes that "perhaps Captain Everard did not deserve to be saved, penniless and deglorified as he turns out to be at the end," as if only the wealthy and glorious ought to be saved!

36 Rosenheim, *Cryptographic Imagination,* p. 93.

37 Judith Butler, "Gender Trouble, Feminist Theory, and Psychoanalytic Discourse," in *Feminism/Postmodernism,* ed. Linda J. Nicholson (New York: Routledge, 1990), p. 337.

38 John Kimmey, *Henry James and London: The City in His Fiction,* American University Studies, series 4, vol. 121 (New York: Peter Lang, 1991), p. 117.

39 Jeffrey Kieve, *Electric Telegraph,* p. 35, points out that the telegraph lines were first laid out along the railroad lines and that the first major telegraphic system was developed in the 1840s and 1850s by the Great Western Railroad Company.

40 Wicke, "Henry James's Second Wave," p. 150.

41 For a psychoanalytic approach to maternal imagery in *In the Cage,* see William Veeder, "Toxic Mothers, Cultural Criticism: *In the Cage* and Elsewhere," *The Henry James Review,* forthcoming.

42 Eve Kosofsky Sedgwick, *Epistemology of the Closet* (Berkeley: University of California Press, 1990), p. 210.

43 Ibid., p. 211.

44 Morton Dauwen Zabel, introduction to *In the Cage and Other Tales* (New York: W. W. Norton, 1958), p. 9; the anecdote was first told in Forrest Reid's *Private Road* (London: Faber and Faber, 1940), then quoted in Simon Nowell-Smith's *The Legend of the Master* (New York: Charles Scribner's Sons, 1948).

45 David Hilliard, as quoted in Richard Dellamora, *Masculine Desire,* pp. 148–49.

46 Kaplan, *Imagination of Genius,* p. 455.

Conclusion: Henry James and the Art of Teaching

1 Rowe, "The New Pedagogy," *South Atlantic Quarterly* 91 (summer 1992): pp. 765–84.

2 My observations here are based in part on my work with high school, community college, and four-year college teachers in a summer institute I developed and administered at the University of California–Irvine in the summers of 1995 and 1996, "Bridging the Gaps: Critical Theory, American Literature, and American Cultures," funded by the National Endowment for the Humanities. One of our goals was to help teachers catch up with developments in literary theory and practical criticism since they had completed their undergraduate literature majors and obtained their certification as teachers. Although there are fortunately many different outreach and development programs available in most states for public school teachers, relatively few acknowledge the crucial changes in literary study and other humanities caused by postformalist critical theories.

3 The single biggest change in our English 28 series was to drop "Epic" from English 28A after teaching assistants argued successfully that there was insufficient time in the course to teach both epic and lyric genres. That change alone took a year and involved virtually no reflection on the basic pedagogical principle of "introducing" students to literary study by introducing them to genres, forms, and techniques.

4 High school teachers with whom I have worked in "Bridging the Gaps" and in the Summer Masters Program sponsored by the Department of English and Comparative Literature at Irvine repeatedly mention this problem. It is compounded by the lack of resources to obtain new books, so that books already

owned by the school frequently determine the curriculum. Many progressive teachers will purchase their own set of books for their students just to overcome such problems, but this option becomes impossible when teachers are trying to overhaul an entire literature curriculum involving many texts for hundreds of students. A partial solution to this problem is for teachers to change the focus from exclusively aesthetic and formal issues in the texts they already use to consider other social, historical, psychological, and moral questions in these same texts. There are, however, limitations to this approach that I consider in the concluding paragraph of this chapter; simply teaching the same canonical texts "differently" is often insufficient to address the demands of literary study for this generation of students.

5 Percy Lubbock, *The Craft of Fiction* (New York: Viking, 1957), p. v.

6 Ibid., pp. v–vi.

7 Ibid., p. 17.

8 This apparently liberating appeal is central not only to formalist aesthetics but also to phenomenological, structuralist, and poststructuralist approaches to literature, to mention only the most obvious. Poulet's phenomenological appeal to the reader in "The Phenomenology of Reading" (1969), in *Critical Theory since Plato,* ed. Hazard Adams, rev. ed. (New York: Harcourt Brace Jovanovich, 1992), p. 1149, is familiar: "This *I* who thinks in me when I read the book, is the *I* of the one who writes the book. . . . Thus a book is not only a book, it is the means by which an author actually preserves his ideas, his feelings, his modes of dreaming and living. It is his means of saving his identity from death." Poulet's idea of how the author *possesses* the reader has always struck me as perverse and ghoulish; it is quite amazing that faithful readers and dedicated students would accept such an idea! Barthes's conception of the "readerly text" in *The Pleasure of the Text,* trans. Richard Miller (New York: Farrar, Straus and Giroux, 1975), p. 27, has also become a structuralist convention borrowed by many other schools: "As institution, the author is dead: his civil status, his biographical person have disappeared; dispossessed, they no longer exercise over his work the formidable paternity whose account literary history, teaching, and public opinion had the responsibility of establishing and renewing; but in the text, in a way, *I desire* the author: I need his figure (which is neither his representation nor his projection), as he needs mine." And Derrida's notion of "free-play," much misunderstood as an invitation of the interlocutor to construct his or her own meaning out of the speaker's intended message (*vouloir-dire*), has frequently been invoked as evidence supporting this function of literature to liberate the reader, in contrast with the ways that referential language depends on a passive receiver.

9 Mark Schorer, foreword to *Craft of Fiction,* p. i.

10 See Fredric Jameson, *The Political Unconscious: Narrative as a Socially Symbolic Act,* pp. 221–22.

11 Not all formalists have denied this connection between literary technique and ontology. See, for example, Murray Krieger, "The Existential Basis of Contextual

Criticism," in *Critical Theory since Plato,* ed. Hazard Adams (New York: Harcourt Brace Jovanovich, 1971).

12 My understanding of "postmodern education" follows the theories of Stanley Aronowitz and Henry Giroux, *Postmodern Education: Politics, Culture, and Social Criticism* (Minneapolis: University of Minnesota Press, 1991), and Henry Giroux, *Border Crossings: Cultural Workers and the Politics of Education* (London: Routledge, 1992). My own theory of postmodern education is elaborated in "The Writing Class," and "The New Pedagogy."

13 Shlomith Rimmon, *The Concept of Ambiguity: The Example of James* (Chicago: University of Chicago Press, 1977); Tzvetan Todorov, *The Fantastic: A Structural Approach to a Literary Genre,* trans. Richard Howard (Ithaca, N.Y.: Cornell University Press, 1975), first published in French in 1970; Ruth Bernard Yeazell, *Language and Knowledge in the Late Novels of Henry James* (Chicago: University of Chicago Press, 1976). My *Henry Adams and Henry James: The Emergence of a Modern Consciousness* (Ithaca, N.Y.: Cornell University Press, 1976) also contributed to this textualist theory of literature as a contribution to linguistics.

14 Such use of James to "exemplify" different theoretical approaches was my primary aim in *The Theoretical Dimensions of Henry James,* following the general assumption that the important writer's sustained reflection on the problem of representation is itself a version of what we today call "critical theory."

15 This is effectively the argument of Mark Seltzer in *Henry James and the Art of Power.*

16 Hélène Cixous, "The Laugh of the Medusa" (1975), in *Critical Theory since 1965,* ed. Hazard Adams and Leroy Searle (Tallahassee: Florida State University Press, 1986), pp. 309, 320.

17 Of course, I am thinking of Eve Sedgwick's pioneering work in this regard in such important books as *Between Men: English Literature and Male Homosocial Desire* and *Epistemology of the Closet,* as well as the remarkable work by a wide range of scholars such as Richard Dellamora, Wendy Graham, Eric Haralson, Michael Moon, Scott Derrick, and others who have shaped the argument of this book.

18 Edward Said, "Jane Austen and Empire," in *Culture and Imperialism* (New York: Random House, 1993), pp. 80–97.

19 Veronica Gregg, *Jean Rhys's Historical Imagination: Reading and Writing the Creole* (Chapel Hill: University of North Carolina Press, 1995), p. 91. Gregg, pp. 114–15, also points out the racist assumptions of Rhys's white Creole perspective in her representation of Afro-Caribbeans in *Wide Sargasso Sea.*

20 Blair, *Race and Nation,* pp. 15–59, offers a fine analysis of the ethnography involved in James's travel writings and book reviews.

21 See Posnock, *Trial of Curiosity,* and Haviland, *Henry James's Last Romance.*

22 Robert Sklar, "A Novel Approach to Movie Making: Reinventing 'The Portrait of a Lady,'" *Chronicle of Higher Education* 43, no. 23 (14 February 1997): p. B7. Sklar quotes Campion in a *Vanity Fair* profile as criticizing the recent cinematic adaptations of Jane Austen's *Persuasion* and *Sense and Sensibility* as "too soft," presumably

because they aspire to strict historical reconstruction rather than postmodern interpretation. I assume she would judge the Merchant-Ivory productions of *The Europeans* and *The Bostonians* in a similar fashion.

23 Catherine's skill with embroidery links her with Hester Prynne and thus with vaguely feminist sentiments in James's narrative. But Agnieszka Holland's addition of the day care center, however anachronistic, offers a more progressive interpretation to the meaning of Catherine Sloper's destiny to be the "maiden-aunt to the younger portion of society" and also distinguishes her from her matchmaking Aunt Lavinia Penniman.

24 Dominick Argento's opera *The Aspern Papers* was first produced by the Dallas Opera in November 1988, in commemoration of the 100th anniversary of Henry James's novella.

25 See, for example, Anthony J. Mazella's work on cinematic and televisual adaptations of Henry James in such essays as "The String That Would Raise the Curtain: The B.B.C. Video Adaptation of *The Spoils of Poynton,*" *The Henry James Review* 15, no. 1 (winter 1994): pp. 31–37.

Index

Achebe, Chinua, 198
Adams, Henry: *The Education,* 8
Andersen, Hendrik, xii, 179
Ansieaux, Napoléon, 138–40
Argento, Dominick: opera of *The Aspern Papers,* 196
Aristotle, 90
Arnold, Matthew, 10
Atwood, Margaret, 198
Auerbach, Nina, 43
Austen, Jane, 11: works: *Mansfield Park,* 149, 194; *Sense and Sensibility,* 87

Barthes, Roland, 230 n.8
Bauer, Dale, 166
Bernini, Giovanni Lorenzo: *Abduction of Proserpine,* 51, 54
Black Elk, Nick, 198
Blair, Sara, 77–80, 82–83, 89, 98, 143, 194
Boott, Elizabeth, 42
Boott, Francis, 42
Borges, Jorge Luis, 198
Bosanquet, Theodora, 157–58, 163. *See also* James, Henry: life: dictation of works
"Brada," Henrette Consuelo (Samson), contessa di Pugala: *Notes sur Londres,* 122–23, 134, 217 n.3
Briggs, Asa, 150
Bristow, Joseph, 28, 118
Brontë, Charlotte: *Jane Eyre,* 149, 194
Browning, Robert, 42
Burney, Fanny, 185
Butler, Judith, 171, 173
Butterfield, R. W., 66

Campion, Jane: film of *The Portrait of a Lady,* 195–96, 231–32 n.22

Castelfidardo, Battle of, 61
Castle, Terry, 215 n.10
Catherine, Saint, 71
Cavour, (Conte) Camillo Benso di, 50
Cenci, Beatrice, 42–49
Cenci, (Conte) Francesco, 43–44
Channing, William Ellery, 42
Chopin, Kate, 198
Cixous, Hélène, 192
Clarke, J. F., 42
Coburn, Alvin Langdon: photographs for the New York Edition, xii
Cody, William ("Buffalo Bill"), 150
Columbus, Christopher, 67, 74
Cooper, Michael, 117
Criminal Law Amendment Act (1885), 103
Cryptography, 161–65, 228 n.21
Crystal Palace Exhibition (1851), 150
Cultural Studies, 183–84

Deconstruction, 155–56, 183–84, 187–90, 214 n.3, 230 n.8
Defoe, Daniel, 185
Dellamora, Richard, 102–3
Derrida, Jacques, 189, 214 n.3, 230 n.8
Descartes, René, 17, 36
Don Juanism, 60–65, 73–74. *See also* Mozart, Wolfgang Amadeus: *Don Giovanni*
Donoso, José, 198
Dos Passos, John, 198
Du Bois, W. E. B., 198

East India Company, 147
Eliot, T[homas] S[tearns], 7–8, 35, 42, 197; *The Waste Land,* 54
Ellmann, Richard, 93

Emerson, Ralph Waldo, 38–42, 73; "Woman," 39

Erdrich, Louise, 198

Faderman, Lillian, 215 n.9

Faulkner, William, 197; *Absalom, Absalom!,* 149, 225 n.66

Felman, Shoshana, 14

Feminism, 10–11, 39–42, 54–55, 68–74, 102, 122–23, 169–71, 192–94, 203 n.41. *See also* Gay and lesbian approaches to literature and culture; James, Henry: subjects in his works: women's rights movement

Foucault, Michel, 103, 160, 189–90

Franco-Prussian War, 73; Ems Dispatch, 160

Frankfurt school, 1, 7, 9, 14–15, 31, 191

Freud, Sigmund, 108; works: *Beyond the Pleasure Principle,* 208 n.7; "The Uncanny," 66

Freudian Literary Criticism, 14, 28–30, 175

Fuller, Margaret, 12, 38–48, 50, 55; works: *Memoirs of Margaret Fuller Ossoli,* 42; *Woman in the Nineteenth Century,* 38–39, 49

Fullerton, Morton, 179

Gay and lesbian approaches to literature and culture, 19–20, 102–4, 193–95, 213–14 n.47, 216 nn. 19, 20. *See also* James, Henry: subjects in his works: gay identity and culture; lesbian identity and culture

Geismar, Maxwell: *Henry James and the Jacobites,* xiii–xiv, 75–77, 89, 143–44

Gilbert, Sandra, 11

Gilbert, W. S.: *Pygmalion and Galatea,* 51

Gilman, Charlotte Perkins, 198

Gordon, Charles George ("Chinese"), 147

Gosse, Edmund, 118

Greenblatt, Stephen, 13, 202 n.26

Gubar, Susan, 11

Guercino, Giovanni Francesco Barbieri: *Aurora* (fresco), 51

Guerrazzi, Francesco Domenico: *Beatrice Cenci,* 44, 206 n.19

Habegger, Alfred, 2, 12, 38, 128, 137, 217 n.3, 224 n.61

Haralson, Eric, 93–94

Haviland, Beverly, 143

Hawthorne, Nathaniel, 39–42, 49, 96; works: *The American Notebooks,* 40; *The Blithedale Romance,* 40, 46; *French and Italian Notebooks,* 44–48, 50–51, 54; *The Marble Faun,* 42, 45; *The Scarlet Letter,* 24

Hay, John, 15

Hocks, Richard, 1, 16

Holland, Agnieszka: film of *Washington Square,* 195–96, 232 n.23

Holland, Laurence, 197

Holly, Carol, 137

Homer, 53

Homosexuality, 101, 193–94, 213–14 n.47, 214–15 n.6, 216 n.20, 223 n.49

Homosociality, 101, 103, 193–94

Horkheimer, Max: "Traditional and Critical Theory," 1, 14–18, 26, 30–32

Hurston, Zora Neale, 198

Imperialism, British, 84–87, 90, 98, 100, 146–48, 150–51

Imperialism, U.S., 15–16, 148, 150–51

Indian Mutiny (1857), 146–47

Irigaray, Luce, 214–15 n.6

Ishiguro, Kazuo, 198

Italian risorgimento, 41, 47–48, 61

James, Garth Wilkinson ("Wilky") (brother), 137
James, Henry, Sr. (father), 38–39, 136–37
James, Henry: life: in Boulogne, 136–41, 146–47; critical approaches to, 1–37, 182–98 (*see also* separate entries for specific schools and approaches); dictation of works, 157–59, 163; as gay writer, 104–6, 117, 193–94; subjects in his works: children, 19–23, 34, 123–54; ethnicity and race, 30–32, 142–54, 181–82, 194–95; gay identity and culture, 19–20, 26–30, 34, 55, 92–100, 104–6, 110, 128–30, 141, 174–80, 191–94, 198; homoeroticism, 51–52, 95–96, 106, 108, 110, 116–17, 127, 141, 176–80; homosociality, 27, 29, 94, 98, 117, 129, 141, 174–75, 193; Jewish identity and culture, 32, 78–83, 98–100, 142, 144–45, 153, 209–10 n.4; lesbian identity and culture, 19–20, 26–30, 34, 55, 99, 104–6, 108, 111–12, 116–18, 125–28, 191–94, 198, 201 n.20; nationalism, 35, 81–83, 84–87, 144–46, 182, 194–95, 198; prostitution, 24, 150–52; technology, 155–56, 158–66, 170–72; women's rights movement, 38–55, 68–74, 79, 104–5, 122–23, 129–30, 198; works: nonfiction: *The American Scene*, 7, 68–69, 100, 144, 195, 226 n.71; *The Complete Notebooks*, 107, 112, 122–23; *Hawthorne*, 39–41, 46, 207 n.22; introduction to Shakespeare's *The Tempest*, 210 n.8; *Italian Hours*, 50–51; *The Middle Years*, 107; *Notes on Novelists*, 181; *Parisian Sketches*, 8; *Partial Portraits*, 40; "The Question of Our Speech," 31–36, 204–5 n.63; *A Small Boy and Others*, xiv, 4, 134–41, 146–48; *William Wetmore Story and His Friends*, xiv, 8, 39, 42–48, 50–51; novels: *The Ambassadors*, 15, 23, 25, 41,

161; *The American*, xiv, 5, 15, 18, 20, 25–27, 30, 41, 49, 56–74, 81, 105, 118, 128, 134, 148, 152, 161–62, 182–83, 187; *The Aspern Papers*, 18, 21–22, 24, 27, 41–42, 66, 77, 121, 134, 207 n.27; *The Awkward Age*, 119; *The Bostonians*, 11, 15, 20, 24, 28, 41–42, 76, 104–5, 118, 125, 167, 173; *Daisy Miller*, 41–42, 89; *The Golden Bowl*, 15, 20, 23, 41, 53, 115, 128, 148, 197; *In the Cage*, xii, xiv, 5, 19, 25–26, 104, 119, 142, 155–80, 187, 197, 227 n.19; *The Other House*, 55, 207 n.30; *The Portrait of a Lady*, 5, 11–12, 17, 18, 20–21, 23, 26–27, 41–42, 76, 104–5, 118, 125, 128, 152, 173, 192; *The Princess Casamassima*, 25, 27, 42, 104–5, 167; *Roderick Hudson*, 15, 27, 42; *The Sacred Fount*, 26, 66, 189; *The Spoils of Poynton*, 77, 119, 125, 127; *The Tragic Muse*, xii, xiv, 4, 18, 20, 27, 28, 30, 33, 34, 55, 75–100, 115, 145, 148, 210 n.10; *The Turn of the Screw*, xii, 5, 19, 20, 22, 24–25, 66, 119, 121, 128, 134–35, 142, 155, 158, 161–62, 165–66, 174, 177, 189, 192, 194, 197; *Washington Square*, 53; *What Maisie Knew*, xii, xiv, 4–5, 11, 18–22, 25, 30, 100, 115, 119, 120–58, 164, 174, 176–77, 187, 218 n.8; *The Wings of the Dove*, 23–26, 34, 41; short fiction: "The Author of Beltraffio," 22; "The Beast in the Jungle," xii, 4, 20, 114, 174, 197; "The Death of the Lion," xii, xiv, 26–27, 77, 101, 104, 107, 108, 112–21, 177; "The Figure in the Carpet," 116; "The Jolly Corner," xii, 53–54; "The Last of the Valerii," xiv, 5, 39, 47–55, 91, 128, 148, 187, 207 n.27; "The Middle Years," xii, xiv, 26–27, 104, 107–15, 118, 120–21, 177; *A Passionate Pilgrim*, 47; "The Pupil," 22–23; *Terminations*, 107
James, Robertson ("Bob") (brother), 137

James, William (brother), 136–37
Jameson, Fredric, 9–10
Joyce, James: *Ulysses*, 155

Kaplan, Fred: *Henry James: The Imagination of Genius*, xii, 93, 106, 157, 179
Kappeler, Susanne, 11
Kingston, Maxine Hong, 198
Kipling, Rudyard, 146
Krafft-Ebing, Richard von: *Psychopathia sexualis*, 111–12
Krook, Dorothea, 75

Laclos, Pierre [Ambroise François] Choderlos: *Les Liaisons dangereuses*, 64
Lakritz, Andrew, 166
Lane, Christopher, 98
Legitimists, Catholic, 67
Lloyd, David, 9–10
Lowell, James Russell, 46
Lubbock, Percy: *The Craft of Fiction*, 184–89

MacAlpine, William, 157–58, 163. *See also* James, Henry: life: dictation of works
Magdala, Battle of, 147
Marconi, Guglielmo: Wireless Telegraph and Signal Co., 165
Marcuse, Herbert, 14
Marxism, 8–9, 16–20, 30–32, 35–36, 167, 190–92
Maves, Carl, 42
Médicis, Marie de, 71
Melville, Herman: *Moby-Dick*, 47
Merimée, Prosper: "La Venus d'Ille," 47
Merrill, Stuart: petition for clemency for Wilde, 93
Michaels, Walter Benn, 143–44, 153, 194
Miller, J. Hillis, 36
Mitchell, Juliet, 11, 134–35

Morrison, Toni: *Playing in the Dark,* 143–44, 194
Morse, Samuel F[inley] B[reese], 156, 162–64, 166; and the Morse code, 160–61, 228 n.20; paintings: *Allegorical Landscape of New York University,* 163; *The Muse,* 163. *See also* James, Henry: subjects in his works: technology; Telegraph
Mozart, Wolfgang Amadeus: *Don Giovanni,* 59–65, 73–74, 187

Napier, Robert Cornelius, 1st Baron of Magdala, 147, 224 n.62, 224–25 n.63
Nashe, Thomas, 96
New Criticism, 7, 14–15, 122, 182–88, 194, 197, 214 n.3
New Historicism, 8, 12–13
Norrman, Ralf, 160–61, 164–65

Olsen, Tillie, 198
Ossoli, (Conte) Angelo, 41, 47–48. *See also* Fuller, Margaret
Ovid, 52

Plessy vs. Ferguson, 144
Poe, Edgar Allan: "The Gold Bug," 161, 228 n.20
Porter, Carolyn, 70–71, 208 n.9
Posnock, Ross, 81, 204 n.61, 211 n.19, 212 n.26
Poststructuralism. *See* Deconstruction
Poulet, Georges, 230 n.8
Pound, Ezra, 42; *Hugh Selwyn Mauberley,* 120, 197

Queer theory. *See* Gay and lesbian approaches to literature and culture

Rachel [Élisa Félix], 81, 211 nn. 15, 20, 211–12 n.22, 212 n.25, 212–13 n.36
Raffalovich, Marc André, 179

Reader-response criticism, 185, 230 n.8
Reni, Guido, 42–45; works: *Aurora,* 42, 45; *Beatrice Cenci,* 42–51
Rhys, Jean, 198; *Wide Sargasso Sea,* 194
Rivkin, Julie, 134–35
Rosenheim, Shawn, 163, 171
Rowe, John Carlos, 181; *The Theoretical Dimensions of Henry James,* 1–2, 13
Rushdie, Salman, 198

Said, Edward, 194
Sainte-Beuve, Charles Augustin, 140
Salmon, Richard, 78, 86
Sand, George, 12
Sargent, John Singer: portrait of Henry James, xi, xiv
Saussure, Ferdinand de, 189
Schorer, Mark, 185
Sedgwick, Eve Kosofsky, 26–27, 140–41, 203 n.53; *Epistemology of the Closet,* 2–3, 101–4
Seltzer, Mark, 12, 157
Sesquicentennial Conferences [on Henry James], xi
Sexuality, 101–2
Shakespeare, William, 6, 33, 79, 90, 101; works: *King John,* 77, 83–84, 91; *Romeo and Juliet,* 77, 83–84
Shaw, George Bernard: *Pygmalion,* 52
Shelley, Percy Bysshe: *The Cenci,* 43, 49
Silverman, Kaja, 28–30, 92, 107–8, 204 nn. 58, 60
Smith-Rosenberg, Caroll, 111, 216 n.19
Softley, Iain: film of *The Wings of the Dove,* 196
Staiti, Paul, 162–64
Steinbeck, John, 198
Stevens, Wallace, 197
Story, William Wetmore, 42
Structuralism, 188–89
Sturgis, Howard, xii, 179
Swedenborg, Immanuel, 38

Symbolists, French, 110
Symonds, John Addington, 217 n.30; "A Problem in Modern Ethics," 118

Taylorism, 166, 171
Telegraph, 156–62, 165, 170–71. *See also* James, Henry: subjects in his work: technology; Morse, Samuel F. B.
Terry, Ellen, 78
Thackeray, William Makepeace, 137–38, 140, 221–22 n.39, 224 n.61; works: *The History of Arthur Pendennis,* 137; *The Newcomes,* 137
Theodore, Emperor of Abyssinia, 147
Tompkins, Jane, 11
Trollope, Anthony, 89; anti-Semitism in his fiction, 79–83, 142; works: *He Knew He Was Right,* 171; *The Land-leaguers,* 80, 211 n.15; *Nina Balatka,* 80, 210–11 n.14; *Orley Farm,* 79; *Phineas Finn,* 172–73; *Phineas Redux,* 172–73; *The Small House at Allington,* 172–73; *The Way We Live Now,* 79
Twain, Mark, 23

Veeder, William, 12
Vercellana, Rosina, 50
Vicinus, Martha, 111–12
Victor Emmanuel II, King (Italy), 50
Victoria, Queen (England), 212 n.23; Diamond Jubilee (1897), 150; Golden Jubilee (1887), 150, 225 n.68

Walker, Alice: *The Color Purple,* 168
Walker, Pierre A., 138–39, 222 nn. 41, 46
Walton, Priscilla, 55
Warner, Susan, 11
Warren, Kenneth, 143, 194
Warren, Robert Penn: *All the King's Men,* 74
Weld, Mary, 157, 163. *See also* James, Henry: life: dictation of works

Whitman, Walt, 16
Wicke, Jennifer, 166
Wilde, Oscar, 13, 93, 102, 194; works:
   "The Decay of Lying," 12; *An Ideal
   Husband,* 75; *The Picture of Dorian
   Grey,* 4, 93

Wolk, Merla, 134–36
Woolson, Constance Fenimore, 38

Yale school, 10, 200 n.12

Zouaves, 61

John Carlos Rowe is Professor of English and Comparative Literature at the University of California–Irvine. He is the author of *Henry Adams and Henry James: The Emergence of a Modern Consciousness, Through the Custom-House: Nineteenth-Century American Fiction and Modern Theory, The Theoretical Dimensions of Henry James, At Emerson's Tomb: The Politics of Classic American Literature,* and *The Other Henry James,* and the editor of *New Essays on "The Education of Henry Adams," "Culture" and the Problem of the Disciplines,* and (with Rick Berg) *The Vietnam War and American Culture.*

Library of Congress Cataloging-in-Publication Data
Rowe, John Carlos.
The other Henry James / John Carlos Rowe.
    p.   cm. — (New Americanists)
Includes index.
ISBN 0-8223-2128-9 (alk. paper). — ISBN 0-8223-2147-5 (pbk. : alk. paper)
1. James, Henry, 1843–1916—Political and social views.
2. Literature and society—United States—History.
3. Literature and society—Great Britain—History.
4. Social classes in literature. 5. Homosexuality and literature. 6. Social ethics in literature. 7. Children in literature. 8. Sex role in literature. 9. Women in literature.
10. Gays in literature. I. Title. II. Series.
PS2127.P6R69   1998
813'.4—DC21   98-18977